Transfer Pricing Developments Around the World 2023

Transfer Pricing Developments Around the World 2023

Edited by

Michael Lang
Raffaele Petruzzi

Wolters Kluwer

Published by:
Kluwer Law International B.V.
PO Box 316
2400 AH Alphen aan den Rijn
The Netherlands
E-mail: lrs-sales@wolterskluwer.com
Website: www.wolterskluwer.com/en/solutions/kluwerlawinternational

Sold and distributed by:
Wolters Kluwer Legal & Regulatory U.S.
920 Links Avenue
Landisville, PA 17538
United States of America
E-mail: customer.service@wolterskluwer.com

ISBN 978-94-035-0167-3

e-Book: ISBN 978-94-035-0177-2
web-PDF: ISBN 978-94-035-0187-1

Editors

Prof. Dr DDr h.c. Michael Lang is the head of the Institute for Austrian and International Tax Law of WU (Vienna University of Economics and Business) and academic director of both the LLM Program in International Tax Law and the Doctoral Program in International Business Taxation (DIBT) of this university. He is the president of the Austrian branch of the International Fiscal Association (IFA) and has been a visiting professor at Georgetown University, New York University, Sorbonne, Bocconi, Peking University (PKU), University of New South Wales (Sydney), and others.

Dr Raffaele Petruzzi, LLM is an independent advisor on international tax and transfer pricing matters, the CEO and Founder of PETRUZZI Advisory, and the Managing Director of the WU Transfer Pricing Center at the Institute for Austrian and International Tax Law at WU (Vienna University of Economics and Business).

Raffaele gained extensive experience by working for many years with Big Four firms, international law firms, and in-house positions. He regularly advises clients across numerous industries on international tax and transfer pricing issues related to services, financing, intangibles, business restructuring, permanent establishments, indirect taxes, and digital business transformation. Moreover, he provides assistance on risk management and compliance, international tax planning and strategy, policy design and implementation, valuation of companies and intangible assets, tax audit defence, implementation of mechanisms of dispute avoidance (e.g., rulings and APAs) and dispute resolution (e.g., MAPs and arbitration), and training programmes. He also provides assistance on tax policy issues and capacity building for tax administrations, and he advises governments on projects related to fight against tax evasion.

Raffaele is a frequent speaker at international conferences and lecturer of numerous courses all over the world, as well as author of many publications. He regularly cooperates with professionals in advisory, the business community, governments and international organizations such as the OECD, the United Nations, the World Bank Group, the International Monetary Fund, and the European Commission. Amongst others, he is a member of the United Nations Subcommittee on Transfer Pricing, of the

International Fiscal Association (IFA), and of Transfer Pricing Economists for Development (TPED).

Raffaele holds a PhD in International Business Taxation from WU, an LLM in International Tax Law from WU, and an MSc in Business Administration and Law from Bocconi University.

Assistant Editors

Marcelo H.B. Moura, LLM received his law degree from the University of São Paulo in Brazil and an LLM from the Ludwig-Maximilians-Universität München in Germany. He is a teaching and research associate at the Institute for Austrian and International Tax Law at WU (Vienna University of Economics and Business). He is pursuing a doctoral degree in business law from WU. Previously, he was employed as an international tax consultant in Brazil and Germany. *Marcelo has contributed to Chapter 1 of this book.*

Thomas Frenkenberger holds a degree in business law from the Vienna University of Economics and Business (WU). He is a teaching and research associate at the Institute for Austrian and International Tax Law and is pursuing a doctorate in business law. He has also gained some practical experience in various (tax) law firms. *Thomas has contributed to Chapter 1 of this book.*

Contributors

Andrea Tolley, LLB BCom., is the KPMG Global Tax lead for the Lifesciences industry and currently leads the Corporate Transfer Pricing team at KPMG in the UK. Andrea joined KPMG from GSK where she was the Head of Tax for the Consumer business, and prior to that, she was the Global Head of Transfer Pricing and Tax Strategy.

Originating from New Zealand, Andrea began her transfer pricing career with KPMG, in New Zealand, the US and the UK. In addition, Andrea has worked in-house in both the UK and Australia for a global Mining firm and in Singapore for a global Industrial Manufacturing company, working with the diverse approaches of different tax authorities across the world. *Andrea has contributed to Chapter 3 of this book.*

Annabel Buschkämper is a former Law Clerk of the Practice Group Tax and is currently a Law Clerk in the Practice Group Corporate at Baker McKenzie (Düsseldorf). Annabel is studying law at the Westfälische-Wilhelms-University Münster. During her studies, she successfully completed specialization in the area of international criminal law and participated in the Jessup Moot Court Competition. She joined Baker McKenzie's Practice Group Tax in August 2022. In April 2023, she joined Baker McKenzie's Practice Group Corporate under the direction of Dr Richard Stefanink. *Annabel has contributed to Chapter 5 of this book.*

Benedict Behmenburg is a Law Clerk in the Practice Group Tax at Baker McKenzie (Düsseldorf). Benedict is studying law at the Heinrich-Heine-University Düsseldorf since 2019. During his studies, he specialized in taxation. After completing an internship with Baker McKenzie's Tax Practice Group in February and March 2022, he joined the firm as a Law Clerk in April 2022. He focuses on international taxation and transfer pricing. *Benedict has contributed to Chapter 5 of this book.*

Brendan Van Kets is an associate in the transfer pricing team of PwC Belgium since 1 June 2022, where he focuses on value chain transformation and economic value creation. He holds a Master's Degree in Laws from KU Leuven University (2018-2020) and graduated with an LLM in Asian Economic Integration and Law from Waseda University in Tokyo in March 2022. Next to transfer pricing, Brendan's research is primarily dedicated to comparative law research of estate planning with a specific focus on trusts and foundations. *Brendan has contributed to Chapter 2 of this book.*

Charles Havisham CTA is an experienced Senior Manager in KPMG's Global Transfer Pricing Services practice. He brings this experience to bear as a highly regarded technical adviser to all of KPMG UK's transfer pricing professionals for wide-ranging or client-specific advice.

Charles has worked in UK and handled global TP documentation production, analysis of transactions including funding, intangibles, centre-led and localized business models, services costs, commercial risk analysis, APA and MAP negotiations, and others. He has also provided BEPS 2.0 advice and training for clients and colleagues. Charles is a UK Chartered Tax Adviser with education including an LLB (Hons) in taxation and international law, BSc in mathematics and physics (both from the University of Melbourne) and postgraduate accounting and finance (University of New South Wales). *Charles has contributed to Chapter 3 of this book.*

Hendrik Menzel is a Law Clerk in the Practice Group Tax at Baker McKenzie (Düsseldorf). Hendrik is studying law at the Heinrich-Heine-University, Düsseldorf. During his studies, he successfully completed specialization in the area of taxation. He joined Baker McKenzie's Practice Group Tax in February 2020. He focuses on international taxation and transfer pricing. *Hendrik has contributed to Chapter 5 of this book.*

Ilka Ritter is a Tax Policy Advisor for the United Nations in New York, USA where she supports the United Nations Tax Committee in developing guidance with a special focus on developing countries and emerging economies. Prior to joining the UN, Ilka worked as a Transfer Pricing Senior Manager at EY's Berlin office where she advised multinational enterprises in the area of transfer pricing, ranging from compliance to structuring and tax audit defence including competent authority procedures. She holds a degree in Business Economics (BSc) and a degree in European Studies (BA) from University Maastricht as well as a Master's degree in Public Policy. *Ilka has contributed to Chapter 7 of this book.*

Isabel Verlinden is a Corporate Strategy Partner helping the world's most successful and admired companies navigate through the current plethora of (draft) rules destined to transform the International Tax Architecture. As a strategic priority, building and maintaining resilient value chains encompasses a fiscal dimension which is rooted in a deep technical approach to Transfer Pricing which Isabel has at her fingertips thanks to over thirty years of mileage within PwC (in Brussels and Washington DC). It is of paramount importance to ensure that tax policy initiatives that are often inspired by political and (social) media sentiments are turned into actionable priorities to marry value chain and corporate tax sustainability. Pivotal in Isabel's work is clients' unfettered access to a global market without being overly hampered by an avalanche of derogating domestic interpretations and codifications.

Isabel is an arbitrator under the EU Arbitration Convention.

She holds Master's Degrees in Applied Economics: Financial Economics and Commercial and Financial Sciences. Isabel is an active writer for international tax and business periodicals. She has (co-)authored over 125 articles and books to date. She teaches at various academic institutions and is an active IFA Member. She is a regular speaker at conferences and seminars. She is listed in Euromoney's 'Best of the Best Transfer Pricing Advisors'. *Isabel has contributed to Chapter 2 of this book.*

Kevin Perry, LLB, CA is a Senior Manager at KPMG Acor Tax in Denmark. Kevin trained in the UK, initially working in corporate tax before moving to transfer pricing. Kevin has gained experience through working in a wide range of transfer pricing advisory projects, across many industries. Kevin holds a bachelor's in law from the University of Bristol and is a Charted Accountant. *Kevin has contributed to Chapter 3 of this book.*

Kriti Chawla is a Chartered Accountant and a Company Secretary. She has completed LLM. in International Tax Law from King's College London. She has a decade of experience working in International Tax and Transfer Pricing. Presently, Kriti is an Associate Professor for Law of Taxation at Jindal Global Law School (JGLS), O.P. Jindal Global University. In addition, she also holds the position of Director at the Centre for Comparative and International Taxation, the tax research centre under the aegis of JGLSD. She is the course instructor for Advanced Diploma in International Taxation (ADIT) and Association of Taxation Technicians, UK. She is also an Expert Member of the Direct Taxes Committee, The Institute of Chartered Accountants of India. Kriti regularly contributes to various tax publications. She is also an active speaker at tax events. *Kriti has contributed to Chapter 4 of this book.*

Mukesh Butani is the Founder and Managing Partner of BMR Legal Advocates, a Tier 1 law firm. He served as Co-founder and Chairman of BMR Advisors, amongst India's leading professional services firms, in the areas of Tax, Risk and M&A, which was featured in the Harvard Business Review case study, BMR Advisors – 'Competitive on Quality'. Besides, Mukesh held leadership positions in two of the Big 4 firms. With specialization in corporate international tax and transfer pricing, he has experience in advising multinationals and Indian conglomerates on a range of matters concerning business re-organizations, cross-border structuring, and tax controversy. He is an acknowledged expert in the area of international tax policy, controversy and advocacy and has to his credit several landmark judicial pronouncements and depositions before expert committees. He is an expert in issuing opinions, witness statements, examinations and cross-examination before appellate/arbitration forums. He has also deposed as an expert witness on contentious cross-border tax treaties, and TP matters in foreign jurisdictions.

Mukesh served as Vice-Chair of the ICC Paris Tax Commission and a member of the Permanent Scientific Committee of the International Fiscal Association and OECD BIAC. Mukesh engages with Indian Government agencies and Thinktanks, NITI Aayog, Prime Minister's Economic Advisory Council & Invest India on public policy aspects. A Fellow Chartered Accountant, he holds a double bachelor's in Accounting & Financial Management and a degree in Law, practising before Indian Tribunals and Courts. He serves as an Independent Board Member in leading Indian and multinational corporations. He is a visiting faculty at the University of Vienna and the University of

Lausanne. He shall be defending his thesis on 'Allocation of Taxing Rights' from the University of Lausanne Faculty of Law Justice and Public Administration. He has consistently featured in India Business Law Journal 'A-List' amongst India's top 100 lawyers and in the FORBES India Legal Power list. He has to his credit several authorships. *Mukesh has contributed to Chapter 4 of this book.*

Paulina Witomski is a former Law Clerk in the Practice Group Tax at Baker McKenzie (Düsseldorf). Paulina has successfully finished her law studies at the University of Konstanz with her first state examination in 2021. During her studies, she successfully completed specialization in the area of taxation. She joined Baker McKenzie's Practice Group Tax in June 2022, where she focused on international taxation and transfer pricing. *Paulina has contributed to Chapter 5 of this book.*

Rutger P.F.M. Hafkenscheid (1964) is one of the founding partners of Huygens, a Dutch firm that provides quantitative tax advice.

Rutger received his degree in tax law from the Rijksuniversiteit Groningen in 1987. After having served a few years as a counsel to one of the political parties in the Dutch Parliament, he started his career as a tax advisor with one of (then) Big Eight accounting firms. In 1995, he continued his career with Arthur Andersen, where he was made partner in 1998. Between 2002 and 2009, Rutger was a tax partner with Deloitte in Amsterdam, where he was Community Head from 2006 to 2008. From 2013 onwards, he worked as a counsel in the transfer pricing and economics practice of Loyens & Loeff.

Rutger serves a wide range of clients, domestic and international, in real estate, private equity and other industries. He specializes in the quantification of risks and rewards in all aspects of corporate taxation and transfer pricing, from business restructurings to financial transactions, including loan financing, derivatives, and captive insurance. Rutger developed a methodology for the valuation of uncertain tax claims in litigation.

Rutger is the Chair of the Teaching Fellows at the Amsterdam Centre for Transfer Pricing and Income Allocation of the Universiteit van Amsterdam and frequently publishes about tax and transfer pricing in Dutch and international journals. *Rutger has contributed to Chapter 6 of this book.*

Seema Kejriwal is a Partner in BMR Legal, specializing in international corporate tax and transfer pricing with over two decades of experience in advising Fortune 500 multinationals and large Indian business houses. Seema focuses on advisory, policy, transaction due diligence and litigation in international tax and transfer pricing matters.

Seema qualified as a Chartered Accountant from the Institute of Chartered Accountants of India in 1999 and is currently pursuing her Master's in Business Law from Golden Gate University, San Francisco. She also has a Bachelor of Commerce degree from the University of Mumbai. She has worked with Big 4 firms, including in India and the US, and across industries, such as FMCGs, Financial Services, Pharmaceuticals, Shipping, Energy, Chemicals & Utilities.

She has co-authored several contributions in transfer pricing compendiums and books by leading organizations and authors, such as Vienna University's publication on Transfer Pricing Developments Around the World, which is edited by Dr Lang & Raffaele Petruzzi, a Wolters-Kluwer soon-to-be-released publication on Transfer Pricing for Intra-Group Financial Transactions edited by leading international tax professors such as Robert Danon, Guglielmo Maisto, Amanda Pletz and Vikram Chand. She has also authored chapters in books by The Chamber of Tax Consultants, Bombay Chartered Accountants' Society, and in-house publications of BMR Legal such as the 2021 Transfer Pricing Treatise, Taxpayers' Rights in India and Doing Business in India. She also recently published a paper on Ethics and Tax Planning which was presented at a leading European conference of tax controversy experts. Besides her contributions to public policy initiatives of the firm, she regularly speaks at global seminars, such as IFA and Pacific-Rim and contributes to research papers and columns on tax and transfer pricing policy that find mention in leading academic publications such as IBFD, Kluwers, Bloomberg, GTDT and ICLG. She was recently awarded as 'Top 10 Women in Legal Consulting - 2022' by CEO Insights. *Seema has contributed to Chapter 4 of this book.*

Stefaan De Baets is a senior counsel in the transfer pricing team of PwC Belgium since 1 January 2016, where he is responsible for avoiding and settlement of transfer pricing controversy, further development of the transfer pricing market, and promoting the key presence of PwC in that market as well as delivering contributions to the development of transfer pricing policies. From 1 April 2011 to 31 December 2015, he was a transfer pricing advisor at the OECD in Paris, France. Until he joined the OECD, Stefaan worked for the Federal Public Service of Finances in Belgium, mostly on transfer pricing and international tax, for more than twenty years. He was a delegate for Belgium to OECD Working Party 6 (transfer pricing) from March 1996 to March 2011 and to the Joint Transfer Pricing Forum from March 2003 to March 2011.

Stefaan is an arbitrator under the EU Arbitration Convention.

He is a guest lecturer on international taxation at the University of Lausanne, Switzerland, the Ecole des Mines (France) and the Catholic University of Leuven, Belgium. He is a regular guest speaker or panellist at international tax events. *Stefaan has contributed to Chapter 2 of this book.*

Dr Stephan Schnorberger is the founder and head of Baker McKenzie's German transfer pricing group and has represented multinational enterprises for three decades. His practice focuses on the resolution of tax conflicts in international tax law, whether through tax audit defence, mutual agreement procedures, advance pricing agreements or litigation. Stephan Schnorberger has successfully conducted numerous tax court and BFH proceedings. He has also been appointed as an expert witness in tax court proceedings. In addition, he advises on cross-border restructurings and tax planning of international companies. Most recently, Stephan Schnorberger obtained a successful tax court decision ruling out exit taxation on a deemed transfer of function. His lecturing and publishing activities focus on international tax law, transfer pricing and procedural issues. Most recent being editor of '*Verrechnungspreise und Verfahrensrecht*', Beck Verlag, to be published in 2023 and moderator of the discussion panel 'Tschüss Deutschland – Steuerfolgen des operativen Wegzugs', Düsseldorfer Steuergipfel 2023. Stephan Schnorberger is a Certified Tax Advisor, Master of Business Administration and Master of Arts (Economics-USA) and holds a doctorate in business administration. *Stephan has contributed to Chapter 5 of this book.*

Vincent Ooi is a lecturer of Law at the Yong Pung How School of Law, Singapore Management University and Specialist Counsel at Legal Ink LLC. He was previously Deputy Head of Tax at a Singapore law firm and has taught at the Universities of Oxford and Cambridge. Vincent has consulted for the United Nations and World Bank and has held research positions at all three law schools in Singapore (SMU, NUS, and SUSS). His work includes both tax law volumes of Halsbury's Laws of Singapore and a textbook on Singapore Trusts Law. Vincent's research has been cited in leading textbooks, by the judiciary and leading bodies within the United Nations and European Commission. He holds a Master of Arts (Jurisprudence) from Trinity College, Oxford and is a PhD Candidate in Tax Law at Downing College, Cambridge. *Vincent has contributed to Chapter 7 of this book.*

Ward Sandra is an associate in the global tax and transfer pricing team of PwC Belgium since 1 September 2022. His practice focuses on international and European taxes. He graduated from the Catholic University of Leuven where he obtained a Master of Laws (LLM), specializing in Tax Law and International and European Law. Afterwards, he obtained a specialized Master in Tax Law (LL.M.) at the same university. In 2022, he obtained a Master of Laws (LLM) in International Tax Law at the Vienna University of Economics and Business. Overall, his research focuses on international tax policy, EU law and the impact on Belgian domestic tax law. *Ward has contributed to Chapter 2 of this book.*

Summary of Contents

Preface

Transfer pricing is currently one of the most relevant and challenging topics in the international tax environment. It is under constant development around the globe, and the year 2022 was certainly no different in this regard. The intense work of international organizations has provided new guidance on transfer pricing topics with several projects while the world around transfer pricing did not cease to be challenging on many different levels.

The year 2022 in general witnessed uncertainty spreading from several directions. While the COVID-19 pandemic was no longer the predominant topic, the world faced new challenges like a war in the heart of Europe, high inflation, and rising interest rates that might lead to an economic downturn. Furthermore, the ongoing climate change is beginning to foreshadow the impact it will have on society in the upcoming decades.

The global legislative framework on transfer pricing has undergone several, relevant changes during the past year in the wake of international guidelines. The OECD and the Inclusive Framework continued their tireless work on Pillars One and Two in order to address the tax challenges arising from the digitalization of the economy along with the implications to transfer pricing. The United Nations continued the work of the Transfer Pricing Subcommittee in accordance with the innovative agendas for the subcommittees set for the 2021-2025 mandate. A potential milestone in 2022 was the United Nations General Assembly Resolution on the Promotion of inclusive and effective international tax cooperation at the United Nations.

The above guidance and reports aim to complement the guidelines that have come into force as part of the legislative changes in several countries. The work of international organizations and the European Union also provided further clarity and support to tax administrations and multinational enterprises to help them to understand the evolution of transfer pricing provisions at the local and global levels. The proposals of the OECD, the UN, and the EU will significantly affect the future understanding of the international transfer pricing environment. Consequently, in-depth comprehension of the proposed concepts and their implications for multinationals, governments, advisors, and academia is crucial.

The WU Transfer Pricing Center at the Institute for Austrian and International Tax Law is conducting research projects to analyse the transfer pricing topics mentioned above and their global impacts. The current research is based on seven topic-based papers that have been drafted by international experts on transfer pricing. The results of this work were presented and discussed at the yearly 'Global Transfer Pricing Conference: Transfer Pricing Developments around the World' in February 2023 organized by the Transfer Pricing Center at WU Vienna University of Economics and Business. This book is aimed at academics and practitioners including the business community and advisory firms, international organizations, and government officials who are tax and transfer pricing experts as well as CEOs and CFOs who are interested in this topic. The book provides an in-depth analysis of the topics described above and the global impact and suggestions for future solutions to any issues that are raised.

The first chapter on Global Transfer Pricing Developments provides not only a general overview of the Transfer Pricing World in 2022, covering the work of international organizations such as the OECD, the UN, and the EU but also critically analyses developments at a country level. As in previous years, it elucidates the most important cases and legislative changes in the transfer pricing world.

The second and third chapters dive into transfer pricing aspects of Pillars One and Two. Regarding Pillar One, especially Amount B is very welcomed by the transfer pricing community whereby their finalization and implementation are still ongoing. Pillar Two, which is already further developed than Pillar One, gained momentum due to the agreement in the European Council in December 2022. With the recently published Safe Harbour Rules and Administrative Guidance, the reality of a global minimum tax continued to take shape and raise questions about the interplay with the arm's length principle.

The fourth chapter debates the interplay between transfer pricing and big data, the emergence of which is disrupting business processes all over the world and leading to the need for new solutions in transfer pricing. The fifth chapter examines the transfer pricing and remote work that not only survived in the post-pandemic world but has become even commonplace and natural to several types of professionals who are on the move and are now able to work from anywhere. The following chapter analyses transfer pricing in times of high inflation and higher interest rates. The book closes with a focus on the emerging topic of crypto assets and how they comply with transfer pricing rules in an intra-group transaction.

The editors would like to express their sincere thanks to the authors who made it possible to provide this ambitious work. Many thanks are forwarded to Kluwer Law International for supporting and cooperating with this publication project. Last, but not least, the editors would like to thank Marcelo H. B. Moura and Thomas Frenkenberger for their precious support and Jenny Hill for providing linguistic support to the authors during the publishing process.

Prof. Dr DDr hc. Michael Lang
Dr Raffaele Petruzzi, LLM

CHAPTER 1

Global Transfer Pricing Developments

Marcelo H.B. Moura & Thomas Frenkenberger

1 INTRODUCTION

The year 2022 came along with several developments in the transfer pricing world at different levels without deviating from the trend observed in recent years. Unsurprisingly, these are not fully innovated in the international tax arena since they mostly derive from the underlying rationale of the search for substance initiated almost two decades ago.[1] Their materialization is mostly represented by the BEPS Project[2] and behaviours of which the initial stages date back to previous years. Nevertheless, they represent a shift to a new international tax environment to which taxpayers and tax administrations will have to conform and demonstrate compliance.[3] It follows that a few trends can be derived that serve as proxies underpinning the ongoing progress of the transfer pricing world.

First, it should be acknowledged that the application of transfer pricing rules is embedded with complexity, evidencing even more the unintuitive feature that they cannot deliver an exact outcome,[4] such as a price, but rather a range in the case of exclusively focusing on the fourth step of the transfer pricing analysis. The current business models accompanied by their commercial arrangements only increase this intricacy whereby a brick-and-mortar logic no longer fits in and needs to be set aside.[5] For instance, the interplay of the detailed and comprehensive proposed revenue sourcing rules within the ambit of Amount A of the Pillar One[6] project along with

1. An example of that is the a round table held by the OECD Centre for Tax Policy and Administration on 26-27 January 2005 focusing on the tax implications of cross-border business restructuring; *see* OECD, *2nd Annual Centre for Tax Policy and Administration Roundtable: Business Restructuring*, https://www.oecd.org/tax/transfer-pricing/2ndannualcentrefortaxpolicyandadministrationroundtablebusinessrestructuring.htm.
2. Regarding transfer pricing, *see* OECD, *Aligning Transfer Pricing Outcomes with Value Creation, Actions 8-10 – 2015 Final Reports* 8 (October 2015).
3. A potential excessive – and mainly from a German perspective – simplification of the transfer pricing developments in the last decade could be summarized in three main subjects, specifically, treatment of intangible assets, tightening of documentation requirements, and analysis of financial transaction; *see* Stephan Rasch, *10 Jahre Globale Verrechnungspreisentwicklungen – Oder die übliche Frage: Fremdvergleich – Quo Vadis?*, ISR 316-320 (2022) DOI: 10.9785/isr-2022-110907.
4. As observed in the well-known sentence from the OECD TPG: '[...] transfer pricing is not an exact science but does require the exercise of judgment on the part of both the tax administration and taxpayer', *see* OECD, OECD *Transfer Pricing Guidelines for Multinational Enterprises and Tax Administrations 2022* 33 (2022), para. 1.13.
5. An example of that is the effort by the OECD in the Two-Pillar Project within the aftermath of BEPS concerning the embryonic idea of tax challenges arising from the digitalization of the economy; *see Addressing the Tax Challenges of the Digital Economy: Action 1: 2015 Final Report* (2015).
6. Article 4 Model Rules, *see* OECD, *Progress Report on Amount A of Pillar One, Two-Pillar Solution to the Tax Challenges of the Digitalisation of the Economy* 13 et seq. (2022).

Model Rules of the proposed Pillar Two project[7] and the necessary coordination with the arm's length principle (ALP) constitute an indisputably complex task. That leads to the second trend, specifically, a clear call for simplifying the application of these rules so that the overwhelming increase in complexity may be partially minimized and counteracted. For example, the long-awaited design framework for Amount B within Pillar One[8] and the newly launched BEFIT[9] project of the European Commission aims at a simplified approach to addressing transfer pricing issues.[10] Third and corollary from simplification, the search for tax certainty within transfer pricing rules remains a common denominator between taxpayers and tax administrations. As such, tax certainty can contribute to enhancing efficiency within transactions between related parties thus avoiding costly and lengthy audits and, in some cases, undesirable unfinished judicial and Mutual Agreement Procedures (MAP) procedures prolonging the amount of time for completion. A tool that can prevent such a scenario is the bilateral advance pricing arrangement (BAPA). It has been the focus of a practical and handy manual recently issued by the OECD that serves as a capacity-building resource for tax administrations.[11] However, achieving tax certainty also implies concerns since it should not occur by overwhelmingly burdening the taxpayer with compliance requirements or allowing opportunities for tax avoidance scenarios. Thus, it is paramount to reach a stable and subtle balance between this goal and the concerns of taxpayers and tax administrations.

In this context, the transfer pricing case law also reflected such trends. Concerning the types of transactions, most of the observed[12] cases had financial transactions as the in-scope controlled transaction (37%), followed by intangibles (26%), intra-group goods and services (24%), and business restructuring (13%).[13] Shifting the focus to the issues of the transfer pricing analysis discussed in these cases, the selection and application of the most appropriate method (MAM) was the most observed issue in 38% of the cases. It was followed by the burden of proof (23%), documentation (13%), General Anti-Avoidance Rules (GAAR) (10%), losses (8%), permanent establishments (PEs) (5%), and recharacterization of the transaction (5%).[14]

At the country level, jurisdictions maintained their focus on updating their transfer pricing legislations, dealing not only with documentation requirements, as with country-by-country reporting (CbCR), but also delving into material issues and aligning their legal framework to the new developments such as the formal incorporation of Chapter X in the OECD TPG. In general, the following topics were identified as the

7. OECD, *Tax Challenges Arising from the Digitalisation of the Economy – Global Anti-Base Erosion Model Rules (Pillar Two): Inclusive Framework on BEPS* (2021).
8. OECD, *Public Consultation Document: Pillar One – Amount B* (2022).
9. Business in Europe: Framework for Income Taxation.
10. European Commission, *Call for Evidence for an Impact Assessment: Business in Europe – Framework for Income Taxation (BEFIT)* 5 (2022).
11. OECD, *Bilateral Advance Pricing Arrangement Manual* (2022).
12. According to a survey carried out by the WU Transfer Pricing Center; *see* Marcelo H.B. Moura et al., *The Transfer Pricing World in 2022: A Review,* Transfer Pricing International 193 et seq. (2022).
13. *See ibid.*, at 194.
14. *See ibid.*, at 195.

focus of attention of countries in 2022, specifically, the application of transfer pricing methods, taxation of the digital economy, environmental aspects related to transfer pricing, consideration of intangibles, financing functions, documentation, and dispute resolution.

Within this context, this chapter highlights the observed developments in the transfer pricing area in 2022 along with a critical analysis and the way forward. Section 1 is this introduction. Section 2 addresses policy and developments within international organizations. Section 3 provides an overview of the transfer pricing developments in jurisdictions, including legislative changes and relevant case law according to the most relevant issues identified. Section 4 concludes.

2 RECENT DEVELOPMENTS IN THE WORK OF INTERNATIONAL ORGANIZATIONS

This section details the outcomes of the work carried out at the level of international and supranational organizations including the OECD, UN, and EU.

2.1 At the OECD

2.1.1 Pillar One

One of the most discussed developments within the OECD consisted of the gradual release on a piece-by-piece basis of the building blocks concerning the model rules of Amount A of the Pillar One project. In this context, substantive rules dealing with nexus and revenue sourcing,[15] tax base determination,[16] scope,[17] extractives and financial services, tax certainty[18] and administration[19] have been released. After the comments provided by the international tax community, the current design rules for Amount A were consolidated in two progress reports,[20] although they still do not cover

15. For specific and detailed comments, see Raffaele Petruzzi & Marcelo H.B. Moura, *Comments to the Public Consultation Document 'Pillar One – Amount A: Draft Model Rules for Nexus and Revenue Sourcing' – WU Transfer Pricing Center* (2022).
16. For specific and detailed comments, *see* Raffaele Petruzzi & Marcelo H.B. Moura, *Comments to the Public Consultation Document 'Pillar One – Amount A: Draft Model Rules for Tax Base Determinations' – WU Transfer Pricing Center* (2022).
17. For specific and detailed comments, *see* Raffaele Petruzzi & Abhishek Padwalkar, *Comments to the Public Consultation Document 'Pillar One – Amount A: Draft Model Rules for Domestic Legislation on Scope' – WU Transfer Pricing Center* (2022).
18. For specific and detailed comments concerning the general issues related to tax certainty and the tax certainty framework of Amount A, *see* Raffaele Petruzzi et al., *Comments to the Public Consultation Document 'Pillar One – Tax Certainty for Issues Related to Amount A' – WU Transfer Pricing Center* (2022); Raffaele Petruzzi et al., *Comments to the Public Consultation Document 'Pillar One – Tax Certainty Framework for Amount A' – WU Transfer Pricing Center* (2022).
19. For specific and detailed comments, *see* OECD, *Progress Report on the Administration and Tax Certainty Aspects of Amount A of Pillar One* (2022).
20. For specific and detailed comments, *see* Raffaele Petruzzi et al., *Comments to the Public Consultation Document 'Pillar One – Progress Report on Amount A of Pillar One' – WU Transfer*

all of the building blocks of Amount A dealing extensively with the marketing and distribution safe harbour, withholding taxes, and unilateral measures. Furthermore, the highly expected outcomes of Amount B were recently released on 8 December 2022 in the format of a consultation document. The focus of Amount B is dissociated from Amount A in the sense that the former seeks to simplify the application of the ALP in a broader scope when dealing with baseline marketing and distribution activities. Ultimately, it is expected that the final design of Amount B will be incorporated in the OECD TPG, although its elective or mandatory nature is still being discussed.[21]

2.1.1.1 Amount A

Focusing on the reaction and interpretation of the Amount A rules by stakeholders throughout 2022, it seems that this section of the Pillar One project is complex and offers implementational challenges, albeit it should function only as an additional layer of tax to redistribute tax revenues between market jurisdictions. From a format perspective, the OECD builds on its previous historical experiences with the OECD Model and the Base Erosion and Profit Shifting's (BEPS) concretization. This is because Amount A's model rules would be materialized within the ambit of a multilateral convention accompanied by a lengthy and comprehensive commentary. In fact, Amount A intends to establish a new system of taxing rights that will coexist with the current system of international taxation in the sense that the former applies as an overlay to the latter. This leads to the question of which, if any, principles govern its design since – thus far – no apparent principled approaches can be identified. For instance, the rules determining a tax base refer to 'Policy Disallowed Expenses'[22] that should be excluded from the determination of the financial accounting profit considered for Amount A. These are defined as expenses incurred by the taxpayer for illegal payments, including bribes and kickbacks, however, the consultation documents do not refer to the underlying rationale that could guide the application of this specific rule. Thus, it leaves room for subjectivity of jurisdictions as to how to define illegal payments which could lead to diverging scenarios in different jurisdictions so that a certain behaviour would be considered as an illegal payment while the other would not.

Another example is the application of the highly debatable[23] 'reasonable steps' by taxpayers in order for them to be allowed to use allocation keys instead of reliable indicators when sourcing revenues.[24] Additionally, within the framework for the elimination of double taxation, the model rules refer to the application of a return on

---

Pricing Center (2022); Raffaele Petruzzi & Marcelo H.B. Moura, *Comments to the Public Consultation Document 'Progress Report on the Administration and Tax Certainty Aspects of Pillar One' – WU Transfer Pricing Center* (2022).

21. OECD, *Public Consultation Document: Pillar One – Amount B* (2022) at 4.
22. *See* Article 5(2)(d) of the Model Rules; Petruzzi et al., *supra* n. 20, at 15.
23. Since, without a proper definition, the subjectivity for interpreting reasonableness cannot be neglected.
24. Schedule E(2)(6)(b), *see* OECD, *Progress Report on Amount A of Pillar One, Two-Pillar Solution to the Tax Challenges of the Digitalisation of the Economy, supra* n. 6, at 65.

depreciation and payroll[25] as well as to 10%[26] as a figure for routine returns. Nevertheless, such references raise questions about which business models are envisaged by the focus on assets and people and to which extent a 10% return can be feasibly considered routine for business in general. Finally, the ambitious tax certainty architecture envisaged in Amount A, even including a binding dispute resolution mechanism, mirrors the material rules mentioned and does not seem to convincingly demonstrate that the aimed goals can be achieved.[27]

In view of that, the proposed Amount A framework worryingly allows uncoordinated situations between countries, and its complexity leads to challenges within its potential implementation. Although the final version of these model rules has not yet been finalized, it is assumed that major U-turns will most unlikely occur.

From a transfer pricing perspective, the concrete interplay of Amount A with the current ALP logically depends on the implementation carried out by countries, notwithstanding that Amount A will work as an overlay to the transfer pricing rules as known today and thus coexist with them. That is to say, the allocation of taxing rights by the ALP as embedded in Article 9 OECD Model will not be prevented by Amount A. Based on that, it can be ascertained that Amount A reinforces the role of the ALP within transfer pricing since the allocation of new taxing rights between the jurisdictions depends on the thorough and correct application of the ALP at first instance. It is thus unclear whether and, if so, to what extent countries will adhere to this set of rules.

2.1.1.2 Amount B

Despite remaining out of attention for almost the entire year,[28] Amount B came back into the spotlight with the publication of a consultation document by the OECD on 8 December 2022[29] and is thus responsible for dominating the discussions in early 2023. Broadly speaking, this section of the Pillar One project unintuitively does not depend on the outcomes of Amount A but rather works independently within a different and dissociated focus, including the outcomes. While Amount A establishes a new taxing right along with the mentioned intricacies and will be implemented throughout an multilateral instrument (MLI), Amount B exclusively focuses on simplifying the application of the ALP. It follows that the envisaged outcome would represent a simplified approach for certain activities that would be included as a section of the OECD TPG. From a timeline perspective, the OECD ambitiously aims to complete this technical work by mid-2023.[30]

25. Schedule J of the model rules, *see ibid.*, at 93.
26. Article 6(2) of the model rules, *see ibid.*, at 16.
27. With further details in relation to the specific procedures herein envisaged, *see* Raffaele Petruzzi & Marcelo H.B. Moura, *Comments to the Public Consultation Document 'Progress Report on the Administration and Tax Certainty Aspects of Pillar One' – WU Transfer Pricing Center, supra* n. 20.
28. Even being referred to as 'forgotten'; *see* Alistair Pepper et al., *Amount B: The Forgotten Piece of the Pillar 1 Jigsaw*, 107 Tax Notes International 143-147 (Tax Analysts 2022).
29. OECD, *Public Consultation Document: Pillar One – Amount B, supra* n. 8.
30. OECD, *OECD Secretary-General Tax Report to G20 Finance Ministers and Central Bank Governors, India, February 2023* 4 (2023).

Regarding scope, Amount B considers the 'baseline marketing and distribution activities' as the controlled transactions to be addressed in theory. In this context, the OECD would set out the quantitative and qualitative in-scope criteria as well as the applicable pricing methodology. As for the former, Amount B's outcomes would determine the amount of remuneration for such activities that would be based on benchmarking studies carried out within the technical work. Finally, the implementation of this architecture would aim at leading jurisdictions to uniformly apply this simplified approach whereby tax administrations from low-income[31] jurisdictions would significantly benefit from circumventing the well-known absence of resources for conducting a transfer pricing analysis for these transactions. Theoretically, the entire concept seems to be logical and appraised, nevertheless, the unfinished[32] design thoughts that have been made available thus far raise several questions.

First, the consultation document seems to focus on the functional profile of the tested party rather than the controlled transaction when dealing with the scoping criteria. It does that by listing twelve general criteria such as a written contract, observance of certain ratios,[33] disqualifying criteria, and indicators of financial statements related to a core distribution function, among others. It follows that, by applying such specific and detailed scoping criteria, the in-scope tested party would indeed be one with a limited-risk profile. Additionally, the consultation document asserts that the general guidance relating to the accurate delineation of the transaction in Chapter I OECD TPG remains applicable.[34] Therefore, the perhaps misleading inputs are not restricted to focusing on the tested party instead of the controlled transaction but also identified when extensively listing scoping criteria dealing with what is known as an accurate delineation while still referring to the general guidance of Chapter I OECD TPG.[35] It thus remains unclear whether the technical work envisages also simplifying the first step of the transfer pricing analysis, i.e., the accurate delineation of the transaction. Consequently, the question addressed by the document referring to the possibility of considering sales agency and commissionaire agreements as within

31. The OECD speaks about 'low-capacity jurisdictions'; *see* OECD, *supra* n. 8, at 6.
32. Apart from general comments being sought, the public consultation document poses 23 direct questions to be answered by commentators; *see ibid.*, at 26-28, 39-40, 45, 47.
33. For instance, sales to foreign jurisdictions/annual sales, net sales retail/annual net sales; operating expenses/annual sales, among others; see *ibid.*, at 9 et seq., paras 18(b), 18(h)(i)-(iv), 18(i). The underlying rationale is that compliance with these maximum ratios ensures that the tested party indeed fits in a limited-risk profile, e.g., by not incurring excessive operating expenses that would denote a potential higher functional profile with more risk assumption.
34. OECD, *OECD Transfer Pricing Guidelines for Multinational Enterprises and Tax Administrations 2022*, *supra* n. 4, Ch. I para. D.1.1.
35. Chapter I reinforces the controlled transaction as the object of analysis since accurate delineation refers to 'identify the commercial or financial relations between the associated enterprises and the conditions and economically relevant circumstances attaching to those relations in order that the *controlled transaction* is accurately delineated; [whereby] the second aspect is to compare the conditions and the economically relevant circumstances of the *controlled transaction* as accurately delineated with the conditions and the economically relevant circumstances of comparable transactions between independent enterprises'. (emphasis added); *see ibid.*, at 39, para. 1.33, third sentence.

scope[36] would be inexistent if the focus of analysis would be the controlled transaction and not the tested party.

Second, the consultation document does not seem to sit well with a potential minimization of the ALP when referring to the MAM and the products-related exemptions.[37] The reasoning for those would rely on the fact that an ALP result can be reached outside of the simplification framework so that such exemptions would prevail. Nonetheless, such an approach tends to be excessively difficult for which the original objective is indeed simplification. Additionally, these cases seem to be resolved by a different framing of Amount B in the sense that it could be designed in the form of a safe harbour in which the taxpayer might opt-in but without a mandatory application. Hence, if the taxpayer does not adhere to it, it will still be subject to comply with a full arm's length analysis that will naturally be subject to the scrutiny of the tax administration. Finally, the OECD seems so far undecided that Amount B should underpin a significant simplification since any simplification would inherently not lead to the precise same outcome derived from a full-fledged arm's length analysis.

Third, the potential mandatory implementation offers challenges. This is because, even if the Amount B framework is incorporated in the OECD TPG (in an optimistic scenario),[38] a mandatory character cannot be derived therefrom. Even if this formal aspect is disregarded, it cannot be assumed that all countries would apply all of the criteria uniformly thus leading to situations of double taxation by the taxpayer and potential disputes with all of them against the general concept of simplification behind this project.

Notwithstanding that, it must be recognized that the current design framework is still an incipient one and is subject to current technical work by the OECD. Based on that, the north star of the upcoming developments of Amount B should rely on simplifying the ALP in line with the successful experience with the low-value-adding services (LVAS)[39] thus avoiding additional complications either on the scoping or pricing methodology criteria.[40] It remains to be seen how the final result of Amount B will comply with its mandate.[41]

2.1.2 Pillar Two

On 14 March 2022, the OECD published the Commentary[42] and illustrative examples[43] for the Global Anti-Base Erosion (GloBE) Model Rules, also known as Pillar Two. The

36. OECD, *supra* n. 8, at 17 et seq., para. 3.4.1.
37. *Ibid.*, at 18 et seq., para. 3.4.2.
38. Which seems to be the goal of the consultation document; *see ibid.*, at 4, 47.
39. *See* OECD, *supra* n. 4, at 326 et seq., paras 7.43 et seq.
40. An example of an unwelcoming complication would be the proposed use of a price matrix for arm's length pricing that could lead to subjectivity and disputes between countries when implementing and interpreting such an approach; *see* OECD, *supra* n. 8, at 33 et seq., paras 61 et seq.
41. For further details, *see* Raffaele Petruzzi et al., *Comments to the Public Consultation Document 'Pillar One – Amount B' – WU Transfer Pricing Center* (2023).
42. OECD, *Tax Challenges Arising from the Digitalisation of the Economy – Commentary to the Global Anti-Base Erosion Model Rules (Pillar 2)* (2022).

GloBE Model Rules,[44] which were published on 20 December 2021, are designed to ensure that every multinational enterprise (MNE) with an annual revenue of at least EUR 750 million shall be subject to a corporate income tax of not less than 15% in each jurisdiction. The difference between the effective tax rate (ETR) under the GloBE Model Rules and the minimum tax rate of 15% in each jurisdiction shall be attributed as a top-up tax to the parent entities through the income inclusion rule (IIR). The residual top-up tax, e.g., if the parent entity has not implemented the GloBE Model Rules, shall be allocated to other constituent entities via the undertaxed payment rule (UTPR).[45] While the GloBE Model Rules published by the OECD are not legally binding as such, they shall ensure a uniform implementation of global minimum taxation within the inclusive framework of BEPS.

The Commentary explains the outcomes striven for under the GloBE Model Rules and clarifies the meaning of certain terms. In the context of transfer pricing, especially the commentary on Article 3.2.3. of the GloBE Model Rules is of utter importance. It stipulates the arm's length requirement for cross-border transactions for the computation of GloBE Income or Loss but does not impose any requirements beyond an arm's length price.[46]

According to Article 3.2.3., second sentence, the ALP is also applicable for the calculation of a loss from a transfer of assets within a jurisdiction and thus not a cross-border transaction. This rule is intended to prevent MNE groups from creating losses in a jurisdiction through artificial transfers of assets.[47] The arm's length requirement for purely domestic intra-group transactions shall not be applied if the losses are excluded from the computation, such as in the case of the MNE group applying consolidated accounting in the jurisdiction.

The Commentary also clarifies that transactions between minority-owned constituent entities and other constituent entities must always be at arm's length because the former is not included in the ETR of a jurisdiction.[48] The OECD additionally explicated that – regardless of whether the ALP is applicable – transactions must always be recorded in the same amount for both constituent entities.[49]

After the completion of the technical work on the GloBE Model Rules and Commentary, the OECD held a public consultation on the Implementation Framework of Pillar Two in April 2022.[50] As a result, the Inclusive Framework agreed on a transitional safe harbour framework and a transitional penalty relief regime as well as a permanent safe

43. OECD, *Tax Challenges Arising from the Digitalisation of the Economy – Global Anti-Base Erosion Model Rules (Pillar 2) Examples* (2022).
44. OECD, *Tax Challenges Arising from the Digitalisation of the Economy – Global Anti-Base Erosion Model Rules (Pillar 2)* (2021).
45. In the Pillar II Directive (Council Directive (EU) 2022/2523 of 14 December 2022 on ensuring a global minimum level of taxation for multinational enterprise groups and large-scale domestic groups in the Union, OJEU L 2022/328, 1) the UTPR is referred to as the undertaxed profit rule.
46. See OECD *supra* n. 42 at para. 104.
47. *Ibid.*, at para. 107.
48. *Ibid.*, at para. 108.
49. *Ibid.*, at para. 109.
50. *See* https://www.oecd.org/tax/beps/oecd-invites-public-input-on-the-implementation-framework-of-the-global-minimum-tax.htm, accessed 11 January 2022.

harbour on simplified calculations.[51] In the transitional CbCR safe harbour, the top-up tax in a jurisdiction shall be deemed to be zero until 2028 if an MNE group has total revenue under a certain threshold, a simplified ETR above a certain rate, or profit that is below the substance-based income exclusion amount.[52] According to the transitional penalty relief regime, no penalties or sanctions should apply if a 'tax administration considers that an MNE has taken 'reasonable measures' to ensure the correct application of the GloBE Rules'.[53] The term 'reasonable measures' is very vague and might therefore allow a substantial amount of discretion in various jurisdictions with a potentially inconsistent practice of imposing sanctions. Finally, this chapter also foresees a regulatory framework for a potential permanent safe harbour regime that involves calculations that are more complicated than those in the transitional safe harbour but less complex than those in the GloBE Model Rules.[54] Overall, those simplifications for Pillar Two are welcoming. It remains unclear, however, to which extent Pillar Two Member States will implement those mechanisms.

At the beginning of 2023, the OECD published administrative guidance on GloBE[55] that will be incorporated into a revised version of the Commentary that will be released in 2023.[56] The administrative guidance covers, *inter alia,* clarifications regarding the scope, income calculations, and the application of qualified domestic top-up taxes (QDMTT). From a transfer pricing perspective, it can be noted that another paragraph will be added to the Commentary on corporate restructurings and holding structures. The envisaged new paragraph 73.1 confirms that the ALP applies to transactions between the constituent entities described in Article 6.3.1.[57] Regarding possible simplifications and the avoidance of possible double taxation, administrative guidance refers to further guidance that will be developed by the Inclusive Framework in the future.[58]

Contrary to the EU,[59] the United States has not yet issued legislation implementing the GloBE Model Rules. According to the New York State Bar Association, the Global Intangible Low-Taxed Income (GILTI) regime - that is currently in place - should be seen as a controlled foreign company (CFC) regime and not as a top-up tax regime.[60] The GILTI, which was introduced by the Trump administration, requires US shareholders to include an amount equivalent to the pro rata portion of a CFC's revenue into their US tax liability regardless of whether it belongs to sources outside the United States and whether the revenue is distributed in the form of dividends.[61] The

51. OECD, *Safe Harbours and Penalty Relief: Global Anti-Base Erosion Rules (Pillar Two)* (2022).
52. *Ibid.*, Chapter 1.
53. *Ibid.*, Chapter 3.
54. *Ibid.*, Chapter 2.
55. OECD, *Tax Challenges Arising from the Digitalisation of the Economy – Administrative Guidance on the Global Anti-Base Erosion Model Rules (Pillar Two)* (2023).
56. *Ibid.*, at 7.
57. *Ibid.*, at 30.
58. *Ibid.*
59. *See* section 2.2.
60. *See* Larissa Neumann & Julia Ushakova-Stein, *U.S. Tax Review: IRA, Medtronic and Exxon, and Pillar 2,* 107 Tax Notes Int'l 1111-1123, at 1119 (TaxAnalyst 2022).
61. Carlos Pérez Gautrin, *United States – US Tax Cuts and Jobs Act: Part 1 – Global Intangible Low-Taxed Income (GILTI),* 73 Bulletin for International Taxation 1 (2019).

administrative guidance issued by the OECD reiterates the GILTI's status as a blended CFC regime in the sense of GloBE and clarifies the interaction between the GILTI and Pillar Two ensuring a level playing field.[62]

2.2 At the European Union

2.2.1 Legislation

2.2.1.1 Pillar Two Directive: A Dearly Bought Agreement

After almost a year of negotiations and alternating vetoes by Poland, Hungary, and other Member States, the finance ministers of the European Union finally agreed upon the Pillar Two Directive.[63] It not only implements the GloBE Model Rules but also follows its structure. In order to comply with the principle of freedom of establishment, the application of the minimum tax is not limited to MNEs and thus covers large-scale domestic groups.[64] Besides the two methods already mentioned in the GloBE Model Rules (IIR and UTPR, the latter being renamed undertaxed *profit* rule),[65] the Pillar Two Directive also foresees a domestic top-up tax that prevents low-taxed jurisdictions within the European Union from ceding their taxing rights to the Member State where the ultimate parent entity resides. The safe harbour regimes proposed by the OECD[66] and the recently published administrative guidelines have not been implemented into the Pillar Two Directive as they were released after it.[67]

As far as transfer pricing is concerned, the wording in Article 16, number 4 Pillar Two Directive follows the wording of Article 3.2.3 GloBE Model Rules. However, the explicit mention of an arm's length requirement for Pillar Two purposes could be seen as the introduction of the ALP into Union law.[68] Therefore, the role of the ALP at stake under the Pillar Two project vis-à-vis the ALP of Article 9 OECD MC and countries' national legislations must still be clarified.

The Member States shall transpose the Pillar Two Directive into national law by 31 December 2023 and apply the rules in respect of the fiscal years beginning from 31 December 2023.[69] Given the complexity of the rules, a transposition within this short period of time seems quite ambitious.

---

62. *Ibid.*, at 67 et seq.
63. Council Directive (EU) 2022/2523 of 14 December 2022 on ensuring a global minimum level of taxation for multinational enterprise groups and large-scale domestic groups in the Union, OJEU L 2022/328, 1 [hereinafter Pillar Two Directive].
64. *Ibid.*, Recital 6, Article 1.
65. *Ibid.*, Recital 5, Article 1 letter b.
66. *See* section 2.1.2.
67. However, Article 32 and Recital 24 of the Pillar Two Directive generally refer to safe harbour rules as the lawmakers in the European Union already expected the publication of those.
68. Contrary to the current situation in which the CJEU neglected an explicit ALP in the European Union in the *Fiat* case (*see infra* section 2.2.1.2).
69. Article 56 Pillar Two Directive.

2.2.1.2 Unshell Directive: No Accordance in Sight

On 22 December 2021, the European Commission launched a proposal for a directive targeting the abusive use of shell companies in the European Union (Unshell Directive).[70] Contrary to the proposal on the Pillar Two Directive, which was published on the same day, the Member States have not yet agreed upon it but the commission is still confident that the proposal will be adopted by the Council. The proposal aims to ensure that entities in the European Union with no or minimal economic activity will not be able to benefit from any tax advantage by forbidding states to issue a certificate of residence.[71] While containing some elements of OECD Transfer Pricing Guidelines (e.g., significant functions),[72] the interplay with transfer pricing rules might occur at the level of accurately delineating a transaction. As long as this proposal seeks substance, it remains unclear whether the denial of tax benefits could also imply the denial of the whole business structure carried out by the taxpayer from a transfer pricing perspective. It is thus important to recall that transfer pricing rules are not strictly oriented to other external rules. This is because transfer pricing seeks for the allocation of taxing rights between jurisdictions according to the ALP and not to ensure a minimal economic activity as is the case with this proposal. Besides leading to an administrative burden, the rules laid down in the Unshell proposal might result in unintended consequences such as ending the outsourcing of some management and administration services, blocking remote work, and even being in conflict with other EU rules.[73] Critics state that it might be better to distinguish between issues of shell entities, tax residence of non-shell entities, and transfer pricing matters separately instead of trying to solve them with a single solution.[74]

2.2.1.3 DEBRA

The debt-equity bias reduction allowance (DEBRA)[75] proposal launched on 11 May 2022 is intended to counteract the debt-equity bias[76] which means that debt financing

70. Proposal for a Council Directive laying down rules to prevent the misuse of shell entities for tax purposes and amending Directive 2011/16/EU, COM(2021) 565 final.
71. For more details on Unshell, *see, e.g.*, René Offermanns, *The Proposed Unshell Directive – The Luxembourg and Netherlands Approach*, European Taxation 231 (2022); Isabel Verlinden, Jean-Philippe Van West & Stefaan De Baets, *Chapter 2: TP Developments in the European Union*, in *Transfer Pricing Developments Around the World 2022* 39 et seq. (Michael Lang & Raffaele Petruzzi eds, 2022).
72. Pasquale Pistone et al., *Abuse, Shell Entities and Right of Establishment: A Plea for Refocusing Current Proposals and Achieving Deeper Coordination Within the Internal Market*, 14 World Tax Journal 187, 209 (2022).
73. Stephanie Kleefstra, *European Union: The (Un)intended Consequences of the Proposed Unshell Directive*, Talking Points 19 (2022).
74. Pasquale Pistone et al., *Abuse, Shell Entities and Right of Establishment: A Plea for Refocusing Current Proposals and Achieving Deeper Coordination within the Internal Market*, 14 World Tax Journal 187, 236 (2022).
75. Proposal for a Council Directive on laying down rules on a debt-equity bias reduction allowance and on limiting the deductibility of interest for corporate income tax purposes, (COM(2022) 216) (2022).
76. *See*, from a tax perspective, 97b *The Debt-Equity Conundrum* (IFA ed., 2012).

of an MNE could contribute to maximizing its profits due to the tax deductibility of interest payments vis-à-vis the mostly non-deductible payment of dividends in the case of equity financing.[77] The goal of reducing the debt-equity bias is achieved with two mechanisms: the allowance on equity[78] and the limitation of interest deduction.[79] The former would result from the product of the variation of equity with the application of a notional interest rate (NIR).[80] The NIR would be comprised of a risk-free and a risk-premium element whereas the latter would equal 1% or 1.5% in the case of small and medium enterprises (SMEs). Additionally, this allowance would embed anti-avoidance provisions, such as a cap of 85% on borrowing costs,[81] and coexist with the general interest limitation rules of the Anti-Tax Avoidance Directive (ATAD).[82] Regarding intra-group transactions, the proposal denies that the equity injection occurring at a higher level of a company (i.e., ACo) could be further computed in the equity variation of an indirectly controlled party (i.e., CCo) if CCo's equity has been increased with an intra-group loan between ACo and an intermediary related party (i.e., BCo) so that BCo was able to inject capital in CCo.[83] Nonetheless, the proposal concedes that the taxpayer provides evidence of the commercial rationality of the relevant transaction and that no double deduction of the allowance on equity has been granted.[84] In this context, it is welcoming that the European Commission intends to provide harmonization for addressing this topic since each Member State can treat this issue differently which could ultimately lead to a cross-border scenario in which the taxpayer faces double non-deduction of interest payments. Finally, it is uncertain to what extent the adoption of this proposal could interfere with the pattern of intra-group financing of MNEs that should be reflected in its transfer pricing policy.

2.2.1.4 BEFIT

The long-term goals of the European Commission laid down in its communication on business taxation for the 21st century on 18 May 2021[85] became more concrete following the call for comments concerning a single corporate tax rulebook for the European Union within 'Business in Europe: Framework for Income Taxation'

77. Abhishek Padwalkar, Marcelo H.B. Moura & Ruth Mirembe, *The Transfer Pricing World in 2022*, 6 TPI 189, 190 (2022).
78. Article 4 of the DEBRA Proposal.
79. Article 6 of the DEBRA Proposal.
80. Allowance on equity = Allowance Base X NIR, *see* Proposal for a Council Directive on laying down rules on a debt-equity bias reduction allowance and on limiting the deductibility of interest for corporate income tax purposes (COM(2022) 216), at 7 (2022).
81. Understood as the difference between the amount of interest paid and received, *see ibid.*, at 10.
82. Council Directive (EU) 2016/1164 laying down rules against tax avoidance practices that directly affect the functioning of the internal market (July 2016).
83. Proposal for a Council Directive on laying down rules on a debt-equity bias reduction allowance and on limiting the deductibility of interest for corporate income tax purposes, *supra* n. 75, Article 5(1)(a).
84. *Ibid.*, Article 5(1) last sentence.
85. Communication from the Commission to the European Parliament and the Council - Business Taxation for the 21st Century, COM(2021) 251) (2021).

(BEFIT).[86] In this context, this proposal dates back to an issue already discussed in recent years, specifically, the adoption of a common corporate tax base (CCTB)[87] whereby an apportionment formulary approach would become relevant. The BEFIT framework, however, is still an incipient proposal with several questions and details to be defined such as the scope to be considered; the design of the formula, e.g., whether intangibles should be included and, if so, to what extent; tax base calculation, administration, and even a potential dispute resolution mechanism.

From a transfer pricing point of view, the consultation document does not completely abolish transfer pricing rules but rather foresees that they will still apply for transactions with related entities outside the consolidated group for BEFIT purposes in either the EU or outside it.[88] Therefore, it refers to a simplified approach concerning the administration of transfer pricing rules based on macroeconomic industry benchmarks.[89] Consequently, this would not prevent the taxpayer from carrying out its transfer pricing analysis as usual but rather function as guidance and support for tax authorities when assessing the risk of the transactions as low, medium, or high risk, for instance.[90] Indeed, it seems that these initial transfer pricing considerations of the BEFIT project create some inabilities for it to achieve its full potential for addressing simplification in transfer pricing which is different from the scope of Amount B mentioned above. While risk assessment tools for tax authorities serve as an important methodology for tax audits and optimization in the use of resources, the taxpayer would not experience a significant advantage therefrom. Thus, in order to allow a benefit also for taxpayers, the use of the mentioned industry benchmarks could be designed as a safe harbour rule so that, if the taxpayer falls within a certain pre-established arm's length compliant range, the tax authorities should[91] accept it. This rule assumes that the parameters applied for the industry benchmarks are compliant with the arm's length without preventing the accurate delineation of the transaction to align with these ranges.[92] Hence, the BEFIT proposal could also benefit from and consider the outcomes and perspectives of the work carried out in the Amount B design.

86. Call for Evidence for an Impact Assessment – Business in Europe: Framework for Income Taxation (BEFIT) (Ares(2022)7086603) (2022).
87. Proposal for a Council Directive on a Common Corporate Tax Base (COM(2016) 685) (2016).
88. Call for Evidence for an Impact Assessment – Business in Europe: Framework for Income Taxation (BEFIT), *supra* n. 86 at 5.
89. *Ibid.*
90. *Ibid.*
91. Instead of 'must' since tax authorities could always audit the previous steps of the transfer pricing analysis, i.e., accurate delineation and recognition of the controlled transaction. For further details, *see* Raffaele Petruzzi & Marcelo H.B. Moura, *Safe Harbor Regimes, in Transfer Pricing in Brazil* (OECD/RFB/IFA Brazil 2023, pp. 543-593). Full reference: *Petruzzi/Moura,* Safe Harbour Regimes, in *Monguilod/Gomes de Oliveira/Camargo Ferrari/Pimentel/Cavalcanti/Balco* (Hrsg), Transfer Pricing in Brazil - Towards Alignment with the OECD Standard (2023) 543.
92. Also, the recognition step of the transfer pricing analysis would not be set aside by such a safe harbour. For further details, *see ibid.*

2.2.2 *Case Law*

2.2.2.1 *Fiat: ALP and State Aid*

One of the most awaited decisions of 2022 dealt with the analysis of the European Court of Justice (ECJ) in relation to the notion and extent of the ALP in the *Fiat* case on 8 November 2022.[93] Basically speaking, the case concerned an advance pricing arrangement (APA) granted[94] by the tax administration of Luxembourg after the taxpayer (Fiat group)[95] established a finance entity, i.e., Fiat Finance and Trade Ltd. (FFT), in this country to carry on treasury and financing activities therefrom to European Fiat companies. Such a set up followed a business strategy of decentralization regarding financing activities so that the entity Fiat Finance S.p.A. (FF) remained as an Italian-based treasury company focused mainly on the financing operation of the Fiat entities based in Italy. FFT had FF (60%) and the parent entity of the group, Fiat S.p.A. (40%), as its shareholders and mainly conducted two types of transactions, specifically with other treasury companies located in Brazil, Canada, and the United States as well as with other group companies. Under the former, intra group loans would be granted by FF and by the US treasury company that were responsible for raising capital in the market to FFT. As for the latter, FFT would grant loans and manage a cash pool structure with the group companies. The mentioned APA was subject to a formal investigation by the European Commission (EC) that ended up with a final decision that considered the tax ruling granted by the Luxembourg tax authority as state aid according to Article 107(1) TFEU.[96] Such a decision was contested by the taxpayer before the ECJ whose general court (GC) rendered a judgment on 24 September 2019 upholding the EC's decision (Figure 1.1).[97]

93. Case C-885/19 P, *Fiat Chrysler Finance Europe v. European Commission.*
94. And applicable to the period 2012-2016.
95. Whereby the ultimate parent, Fiat S.p.A., incorporated in Italy was succeeded by Fiat Chrysler Automobiles NV after a merger operation with the Chrysler group on 12 October 2014. Currently, the ultimate parent of the group is Stellantis NV which followed the merger of the Fiat Chrysler group with the French PSA group on 16 January 2021.
96. European Commission, *Commission Decision (EU) 2016/2326 of 21 October 2015 on State aid SA. 38375 (2014/C ex 2014/NN) which Luxembourg granted to Fiat*, section 7.4.
97. *Fiat Chrysler Finance Europe v. European Commission*, No. T-759/15 (24 September 2019).

Figure 1.1 Structure of the Fiat Group

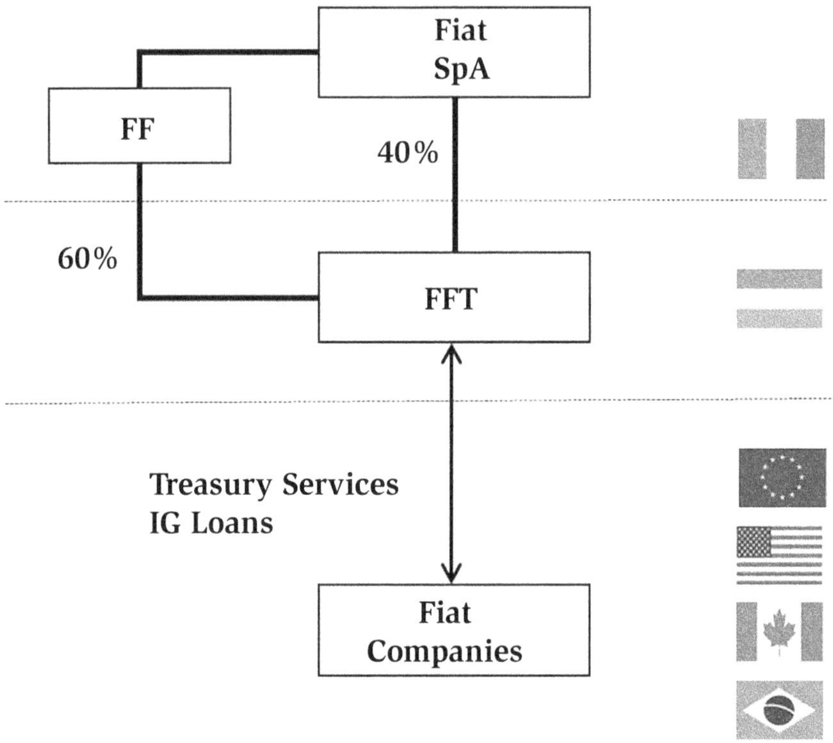

From a transfer pricing lens,[98] the core of the EC's decision refers to the disagreement with the APA's methodology to remunerate FFT's activities. Accordingly, the APA accepted the transactional net margin method (TNMM) methodology presented by the taxpayer in which the application of the capital asset pricing model (CAPM) was mainly based on the regulatory framework applicable for financial institutions, i.e., the Basel II framework.[99] In particular, the assumptions used by the taxpayer to arrive at a final return figure have been mainly challenged by the EC's decision that did not accept the calculation of the amount of capital remunerated nor the level of remuneration applied.[100] Concerning the former, the EC questioned the exclusion of the amount related to equity injected by FFT in related companies that 'lead to a too low taxable basis' as well as the weight factor applied to counterparty risk.[101] Regarding the latter, the EC decision challenged the comparables brought by the taxpayer to justify the beta

98. Since the scope of this section is not to delve into the state aid analysis.
99. Basel Committee on Banking Supervision, *International Convergence of Capital Measurement and Capital Standards: A Revised Framework* (Bank for International Settlements June 2004); *supra* n. 96, para. 59.
100. *Supra* n. 96, para. 133.
101. *Ibid.*, para. 134.

figure in the CAPM model, questioning also the resort to the 25th percentile of the values identified instead of using the median.[102] The taxpayer along with Luxembourg counterargued in the sense that the exclusion of equity equivalent to the investment in its subsidiaries reflects the nature of non-portfolio investments that are remunerated through dividends, thus remaining outside of the scope of transfer pricing rules and in accordance with the underlying regulatory framework.[103] Additionally, FFT argued that even the exclusion of certain comparables would not significantly affect the final outcome and that the best comparables for this methodology would consist of financing companies and not banks.[104] Finally, it argued that the use of the lower quartile remains within the arm's length range according to the OECD TPG.[105]

Faced with this situation, the GC restrained itself from considering the EC's transfer pricing analysis since the 'the analysis of the pleas in law raised in such an action has neither the object nor the effect of replacing a full investigation of the case in the context of an administrative procedure'.[106] Nevertheless, the GC opined on the calculation of the capital at risk and upheld the EC's decision since the segmentation of capital carried out by the taxpayer would be artificial[107] and, in the case of insolvency, the entire amount of capital would be relevant.[108] Consequently, it considered that the APA endorsed a methodology inconsistent with an arm's length outcome.[109] By the judgment of the appeal before the ECJ, the Court overturned the GC's decision and held that the GC erred in law by validating the EC's decisions without taking into account the national Luxembourg law.[110] Thus, the EC's approach led to the application of an ALP different from the one defined in Luxembourg law that is vitiated and therefore necessarily invalidates the entirety of the reasoning of EC's decision relating to selective advantage.[111]

The outcome of the ECJ's decision is welcoming by establishing legal certainty[112] since, otherwise, the EC's application of the ALP would remain rather undefined. Without sticking to the national legislation of countries, there would be a significant leeway open to the EC's inquiries that, based on Article 107(1) TFEU, could reject the transfer pricing analysis of a controlled transaction. However, taxpayers would not be able to figure out the precise scope of the EC's ALP since it would be different from

102. *Ibid.*, para. 135.
103. *Ibid.*, para. 165. It is interesting to note that the application of the Basel II framework is not direct and one-by-one but rather on an analogy basis that 'corresponds to FFT's understanding of the Basel II framework transposed to non-bank financial institutions in certain EU jurisdictions'; *see supra* n. 96, para. 167.
104. *Supra* n. 96, para. 168.
105. *Ibid.*, para. 168.
106. *Fiat Chrysler Finance Europe v. European Commission*, No. T-759/15 (24 September 2019), para. 205.
107. *Ibid.*, para. 242.
108. *Ibid.*, para. 244.
109. *Ibid.*, para. 286.
110. Case C-885/19 P, *Fiat Chrysler Finance Europe v. European Commission*, para. 90.
111. *Ibid.*, para. 118.
112. *See also* Ruth Mason, *Ding-Dong! The EU Arm's-Length Standard Is Dead*, 108 Tax Notes International 1249-1256, 1253 (Tax Analysts 2022).

national legislation and from the OECD TPG.[113] Apart from the inconsistencies in interpreting the ALP using the state aid doctrine, this case evidences the fact that a transfer pricing analysis cannot be treated as an exact science. Indeed, when dealing with the calculations of the CAPM, economic assumptions have to be made that essentially define the outcome. For instance, the selection of comparables to determine the mentioned beta figure or the amount of capital exposed to risk can be differently modelled according to the economic rationale that is used. This is the essence and, at the same time, difficulty of the ALP since the principle can accommodate different views – and results – for which correctness depends on the adopted coherent economic rationale. Perhaps this was acquiesced by the EC when not using the national Luxembourg legislation as the starting point of the analysis because it would be broad enough to accept the taxpayer's calculations.[114] Additionally, the EC's transfer pricing analysis of the case falls short of addressing the functional profile of the entities involved in order to question the methodology and final rate of return advanced by the taxpayer in the accepted tax ruling. Finally, even with the recent advent of Chapter X OECD TPG, it does not seem that reasonings of the EC would be successful.

2.2.2.2 Finanzamt Bremen: Documentation and Penalty Fee

In this case,[115] X GmbH & Co KG (X KG) was a German limited partnership with an unlimited partner resident in Germany and a limited partner resident in the Netherlands. The latter was owned by Y, another Dutch company, that indirectly held 100% of the interests in X KG. Y provided advisory services to X KG and charged around EUR 6 million for the services. Due to a lack of proper transfer pricing documentation for those fees, the German tax administration levied a tax surcharge amounting to 5% of the additional profit. X KG appealed against this surcharge and argued, among other things, that transfer pricing documentation requirements only for cross-border transactions in combination with high penalties are a breach of the European fundamental freedoms. The German Bremen Tax Court stayed the proceedings and referred to the ECJ for a preliminary ruling to determine if the German rules are in accordance with EU primary law, specifically the freedom of establishment and the freedom to provide services.[116]

The ECJ declared that the national legislation had to be examined exclusively in light of the freedom of establishment without considering the freedom to provide services that had been introduced as an alternative standard of review by the fiscal court.[117] The obligation to provide additional fiscal documentation only for cross-border activities is

113. The EC's decision does not explicitly and specifically refer to the OECD TPG to assert what would be an arm's length outcome in the controlled transaction at stake.
114. Luxembourg direct tax authorities, *Circulaire du directeur des contributions L.I.R. n° 164/2 du 28 janvier 2011* (2011).
115. Case C-431/21, *X GmbH & Co KG v. Finanzamt Bremen*, 13 October 2022.
116. FG Bremen, *Finanzamt Bremen*, 2 K187/17, 7 July 2021.
117. Case C-431/21, *X GmbH & Co KG v. Finanzamt Bremen*, paras 23 et seq. with reference to Case C-382/16, *Hornbach-Baumarkt*, 31 May 2018, ECLI:EU:C:2018:366.

seen as a restriction on the freedom of establishment[118] but can be justified under the overriding reason in the public interest of preserving the allocation of the power of taxation between Member States.[119] The tax surcharge of 5% has not been considered disproportionate by the ECJ.[120] The fact that the consequences of an infringement to submit a tax declaration are less severe than non-compliance with transfer pricing documentation requirements does not affect the outcome because the rules are different in nature. A tax surcharge is 'not intended to penalise failure to comply [...] but rather to correct the taxpayer's taxable income'.[121] The ECJ, therefore, concluded that Article 49 TFEU does not preclude national legislation under which Member States foresee a tax surcharge of at least 5% and, at most, 10% of the excess income.

This outcome was unexpected for part of the literature that had argued that the tax surcharge could have been regarded as disproportionate.[122] It confirms that even high penalties for non-compliance with transfer pricing standards are in line with EU law and that MNEs must not neglect the importance of transfer pricing documentation in order to avoid amendments and penalties by the tax authorities. However, it should not be ignored that the ECJ did not examine the compatibility of the whole section 162, paragraph 4 of the German Fiscal Code with EU law. According to the ECJ, it did not appear necessary for the dispute in the main proceedings to answer the questions relating to the tax surcharge in the event of a late submission[123] which could therefore still be seen as potentially disproportionate. Furthermore, the compatibility of the administrative ordinance on documentation of profit allocations[124] still has to be assessed by the Bremen Tax Court.[125]

2.2.3 ETACA

As part of the Communication on its 'Action Plan for Fair and Simple Taxation in Support of the Recovery Strategy',[126] the EU Commission announced the preparation of a European Cooperative Compliance Framework in the form of two non-legislative pilot projects for MNEs and SMEs on 15 July 2020.[127] Launched in October 2021, the

118. Case C-431/21, *X GmbH & Co KG v. Finanzamt Bremen*, paras 30 et seq.
119. *Ibid.*, at paras 35 et seq. with reference to Case C-558/19, *Impresa Pizzaroti*, 8 October 2020, ECLI:EU:C:2020:806.
120. *Ibid.*, at paras 49 et seq.
121. *Ibid.*, at para. 59.
122. Rust, *Germany: Finanzamt Bremen, C-431/21*, in *ECJ – Recent Developments in Direct Taxation 2021* 47 (Kofler et al. eds, 2022).
123. Case C-431/21, *X GmbH & Co KG v. Finanzamt Bremen*, at para. 22.
124. Gewinnabgrenzungsaufzeichnungs-Verordnung (GAufzV) 12 July 2017, BGBL I 47/2017, 2367.
125. Florian Rosenberger, Die Entscheidung des EuGH in der Rechtssache Finanzamt Bremen, 6 TPI, 200, 205 (2022).
126. Communication from the Commission to the European Parliament and the Council: An Action Plan for Fair and Simple Taxation Supporting the Recovery Strategy, Brussels 15 July 2022, COM(2020) 312 final.
127. European Commission, European Trust and Cooperation Approach – ETACA Pilot Project for MNEs, available at https://taxation-customs.ec.europa.eu/eu-cooperative-compliance-programme/european-trust-and-cooperation-approach-etaca-pilot-project-mnes_en, accessed on 11 January 2023.

initiative of a European Cooperative Compliance Framework for MNEs (The European Trust and Cooperation Approach (ETACA))[128] is designed to focus on cross-border tax issues in the area of corporate income tax and to help avoid disputes and double taxation as well as reduce tax compliance costs. At the heart of the ETACA is a two-step risk assessment aimed at achieving a common understanding among the tax administrations involved in the transfer pricing transactions under consideration. The ETACA is designed to ensure a degree of certainty through an efficient and rapid analysis of low-risk transfer pricing transactions. The process is to be conducted over a short, pre-determined period of time. [129]

The ETACA pilot implementing phase started in March 2022. All MNEs with a consolidated revenue of at least EUR 750 million and their headquarters in the European Union are allowed to participate. This programme is neither seen as a financial auditing nor an APA but rather as a risk screening. Although, so far,[130] no results from this promising project have been published, this initiative evidences the shift towards improving the relationship between tax administrations and taxpayers, particularly in the transfer pricing field where several disputes arise. In this regard, focus can be rendered to enhance taxpayers' transfer pricing compliance activities and the communication channel between taxpayers and tax authorities. This is of extreme relevance in the current uncertain economic scenario that started with the COVID-19 pandemic and was affected by rising inflation and disruptions caused by the Ukraine war.[131] Therefore, the current trend drifts apart from an almost exclusive litigation mindset to enhancing mutual cooperation as a dispute prevention tool.

2.3 At the United Nations

The transfer pricing subcommittee (TP SC) within the United Nations Tax Committee (UNTC) kept with the ambitious agenda approved for its mandate during 2022. Therefore, so far, the TP SC has presented the provisory outcomes of its seven work streams in a progress report.[132] In the first focus concerning guidance for primary products, an unpublished outline has been developed that covers the global value chain analysis of such types of products. This is illustrated by case studies dealing with the soybean and coffee industry that seek to describe the typically controlled transactions at stake in this industry along with the likelihood of transfer pricing disputes arising. Similarly, regarding the guidance work on the pharmaceutical industry, an unpublished outline details the transfer pricing analysis of this sector along with an overview of applicable particularities such as governmental regulations, price controls, and parallel imports. In this context, the role of intangibles in this industry is currently

128. *Ibid.*
129. Philipp Gmoser, Der European Trust and Cooperation Approach (ETACA), IWB 4, (NWB Verlag 2022).
130. 17 March 2023.
131. For further details on high inflation, *see* Chapter 6.
132. Transfer Pricing Subcommittee, *Transfer Pricing Co-Coordinator's Report – Committee of Experts on International Cooperation in Tax Matters Twenty-Fifth Session* (E/C.18/2022/CRP.16 (October 2022)).

being considered. The third workstream advanced in the development of a toolkit for tax administrations to better enhance their risk assessment framework from a tax auditing perspective. However, the TP SC put a temporary hold on the activities related to the workstream addressing transfer pricing domestic anti-abuse rules in order to prioritize the others.

The fifth focus of work on the transfer pricing aspects of CO_2 certificates significantly progressed following cooperation with the subcommittee on environmental taxation to deepen the description of the relevant regulatory framework, the notion of carbon credits, and the involved supply chain. Based on that, draft guidance should be presented in the next meeting of the UNTC in early 2023. Likewise, the workstream on COVID-19 and the economic downturn advanced considerably such that an unpublished draft guidance has been circulated internally. This focuses on the economic downturn caused by the COVID-19 pandemic and its unique challenges for taxpayers and tax administrations to deal with uncertainties within the application of transfer pricing rules. In this regard, all of the steps of the transfer pricing analysis when dealing with such an adverse economic context were considered, including addressing potential approaches to improve standardization and simplification during the relevant years that were analysed. Finally, the work concerning dispute avoidance and resolution experienced developments in cooperation with the dedicated subcommittee on dispute avoidance and resolution.

The topics covered by the TP SC reflect current practical concerns of the transfer pricing rules, and the final results will deliver valuable guidance to be applicable in the upcoming years in line with the resolution recently adopted by the UN General Assembly on 22 November 2022 reinforcing the role of the entity on developing the international tax cooperation framework.[133]

3 RECENT DEVELOPMENTS AT COUNTRY LEVEL

3.1 Arm's Length Principle

During 2022, countries pushed forward to enhance adherence to the ALP. Montenegro is an example of that by approving amendments to its tax legislation on 31 December 2021 according to which a new set of transfer pricing regulations were introduced that included the redefinition of related parties, a list of applicable transfer pricing methods, and provisions for documentation to be submitted by the taxpayer.[134] The same trend has also been adopted by Malta whose Ministry of Finance, based on Article 51A of the Maltese Income Tax Act, enacted transfer pricing regulations with explicit reference to the ALP.[135] Following this legislative trend, Cyprus also introduced transfer pricing

133. General Assembly United Nations, *Promotion of inclusive and effective international tax cooperation at the United Nations*, No. A/C.2/77/L.11/Rev.1 (November 2022).
134. *Law on Amendments to the Law on Profit Tax of Legal Entities*, No. 146/2021/1949.
135. *Transfer Pricing Rules, 2022*, 20,961 No. 284 of 2022, B2179-90.

rules and documentation requirements in accordance with the OECD TPG on 30 June 2022.[136]

In a different context focusing not on the introduction but rather on the refinement of the ALP, the Netherlands has issued new decrees dealing with transfer pricing[137] and allocation of profits to PE.[138] The new transfer pricing decree aims to align the Dutch legal basis to the recent developments of the OECD TPG particularly since its formal update in 2022.[139] Accordingly, the main areas experiencing changes are intra-group financing and services, government measures derived from the COVID pandemic, and textual adjustments. Concerning the PE decree, an object exemption for foreign PEs has been included along with the confirmation for applying the updates derived from the 2017 OECD Model update in addition to clarifying the case when double non-taxation occurs. In the same refinement context, Italian tax authorities published a new circular clarifying the ALP application and the definition of an arm's length range.[140] According to it, the latter is derived from the application of the OECD TPG, and the selected value does not limit itself to the interquartile range but is comprised within the full arm's length range. Moreover, the burden of proof has been reinforced so that an arbitrary use of the median by tax authorities should be disregarded but only if expressly justified by the tax administration.

Finally, a long-awaited measure came as a last-minute act of the Bolsonaro administration in 2022 in the form of provisional measure No. 1,152.[141] It confirms the long-term developments that occurred at the Brazilian level regarding the consensus of Brazilian tax authorities (RFB) to align the Brazilian transfer pricing rules to the ALP as laid down by the OECD TPG. This position follows the RFB's cooperation work with the OECD reflected in the report produced and published jointly[142] that concluded that the full alignment of Brazilian transfer pricing legislation to the ALP was required. Accordingly, in a joint presentation that occurred on 13 April 2022, both entities mentioned all of the areas that will be subject to an alignment in the context that the envisaged Brazilian transfer pricing framework will mostly reflect the current OECD

136. Income Tax Law of 2002, Article 33(6), *see* Kyriacos Scordis et al., *Cyprus: Transfer Pricing, in Country Tax Guides* (20222), section 2.
137. Directoraat-generaal Fiscale Zaken, Directie Verbruiksbelastingen, Douane en Internationale Aangelegenheden, *Internationaal Belastingrecht. Verrekenprijzen, toepassing van het arm's-lengthbeginsel en de Transfer Pricing Guidelines for Multinational Enterprises and Tax Administrations (OESO-richtlijnen)*, nr. 2022-0000139020, Staatscourant 2022, nr. 16685 (June 2022), Staatscourant 2022, 16685.
138. *Internationaal Belastingrecht. Winstallocatie vaste inrichtingen* (June 2022), Staatscourant 2022, nr. 16683.
139. OECD, *OECD Transfer Pricing Guidelines for Multinational Enterprises and Tax Administrations 2022, supra* n. 4.
140. Agenzia Entrate, *Circolare N. 16/E – Istruzioni operative in materia di prezzi di trasferimento (articolo 110, comma 7 del Testo Unico delle Imposte sui Redditi): Intervallo di libera concorrenza* (May 2022).
141. *Provisional Measure No 1,152 of 28 December 2022 – Introduces Changes to the Legislation on Corporate Income Tax (IRPJ) and Social Contribution Tax on Profit (CSLL), Providing for New Transfer Pricing Rules*, No. 1,152/2022 (December 2022).
142. OECD & Receita Federal do Brasil, *Transfer Pricing in Brazil: Towards Convergence with the OECD Standard – A Joint Assessment of the Similarities and Differences Between the Brazilian and OECD Frameworks* (2019).

TPG, however, with an intention on simplification and safe harbour measures that can assure tax certainty, ease of administration, and less burden for the taxpayers. This seems to be partially reflected in the mentioned provisional measure, however, on several points, it refers to regulations that will be enacted by the RFB to deal with important topics. Accordingly, examples of this upcoming regulation can be seen:

- in the potential combination of transfer pricing methods;[143]
- in databases for transactions involving commodities;[144]
- when determining other arm's length ranges not described in the provisional measure;[145]
- in conditions for carrying out compensating adjustments;[146] or
- in simplification measures for the comparability analysis.[147]

From a legislative perspective, this draft must still be approved within 120 days by the partially recently elected Brazilian congress in order for it to become a final and valid piece of legislation. Since it has been submitted as a provisional measure, its procedure is oriented by urgency according to the procedural legal basis. Considering the change of administration in the Brazilian Government as of 1 January 2023, it remains uncertain whether and how this welcoming movement towards alignment with the ALP will be implemented.[148] Finally, due to the importance and comprehensiveness of the topic as well as the questionable broadness and potential improvements that could be included in the proposed legislation, it is highly doubtful that the new Brazilian congress will pass this legislation in such a short period.

3.2 Application of the Transfer Pricing Methods under *Medtronic II*

One of the most discussed cases of 2022 was the *Medtronic II* case[149] which is another act in a years-long legal debate between Medtronic and the US tax authorities.[150] Medtronic is an MNE that manufactures and sells implantable medical devices and the leads that connect those devices to the human body. The judgment concerns a licence agreement between two entities within the group: Medtronic US, a corporation resident in the United States, that is responsible, among others, for research and development activities and MPROC (Medtronic Puerto Rico Operations Co.), a Puerto Rican subsidiary that manufactured and sold certain finished medical devices and leads. Medtronic US licensed its intellectual property (IP) to MPROC for a royalty rate of 29% of US net

143. *Provisional Measure No 1,152 of 28 December 2022 – Introduces Changes to the Legislation on Corporate Income Tax (IRPJ) and Social Contribution Tax on Profit (CSLL), Providing for New Transfer Pricing Rules*, *supra* n. 141, Article 11(4).
144. *Ibid.*, Article 12(4)-(5).
145. *Ibid.*, Article 16(5).
146. *Ibid.*, Article 17(2).
147. *Ibid.*, Article 38 I.
148. This chapter was finalized on 20 February 2023. Until this date, the approval of the provisional measure was uncertain.
149. *Medtronic Inc. v. Commissioner*, T.C. Memo. 2022-84 (Medtronic II).
150. For a detailed analysis, *see* Harold McClure, *Medtronic II: A Bizarre Application of the Unspecified Methods*, 107 Tax Notes Int'l 1125-1130 (TaxAnalysts 2022).

intercompany sales for devices and 15% for leads. The US Internal Revenue Service (IRS) objected to this royalty rate and argued that MPROC was merely engaged in manufacturing and that a bigger share of the profits belonged to the parent company in the United States where the IP was generated. The taxpayer countered that MPROC had a crucial role in ensuring quality control. In its first decision, the tax court originally accepted the transfer pricing analysis used by the taxpayer that was based on the comparable uncontrolled transaction (CUT, the US version for the comparable uncontrolled price (CUP)) method, This was grounded on a litigation settlement between Medtronic US and Siemens Pacesetter, Inc. who had produced other electronic devices presumably using IP originally created by Medtronic.[151] The IRS appealed and the Eight Circuit set aside the decision by the tax court, ruling that the Siemens Pacesetter agreement was not comparable.[152] As the IRS had not provided an appropriate transfer pricing alternative, the case was remanded to the tax court.

The decision now issued by the tax court is therefore referred to as *Medtronic II* and can be seen as a sort of Solomon's judgment as the royalty rate decided by it (48%) fell roughly in between the ones suggested by the taxpayer (22%) and the IRS (67%). The judge attempted to use the CUT method again, taking into account that the royalty rate agreed with Siemens Pacesetter was negotiated under totally different conditions. As no adequate comparables were available, the tax court was forced on remand 'to essentially invent a royalty rate out of nothing'.[153]

What remains is a decision that deviates from all known transfer pricing methods. Instead of striving for a stringent embedding in an overall system, the court aimed for the solution of a single legal dispute that looks more like a compromise than a well-founded legal approach. The outcome therefore contrasts with the *Coca-Cola*[154] case which had a general disfavour of unsound transfer pricing methods.[155]

3.3 Taxation of the Digital Economy

Even though COVID-19 is still a serious disease, 2022 was the first year in which the pandemic was no longer the predominant topic in most people's lives anymore. While people were able to meet in physical presence again, the digital economy did not forfeit any of its importance and, therefore, the unsolved question of how to tax the digital economy will stay on the agenda of many governments and international organizations in 2023.

A topic that had not been illuminated enough in the past was the role of big data in the taxation of the digital economy. Data are defined as 'characteristics or information, which are collected by observation', and big data sums up a high amount of data and

151. *See Medtronic Inc. v. Commissioner*, T.C. Memo. 2016-112.
152. *See Medtronic Inc. v. Commissioner*, 900 F.3d 610 (8th Cir. 2018).
153. Reuven S. Avi-Yonah, *Medtronic II and the Profit-Shifting Problem*, 107 Tax Notes Int'l 1147-1150 (TaxAnalysts 2022).
154. *The Coca-Cola Co. v. Commissioner*, 155 T.C. No. 10 (2020).
155. Ryan Finley, *Medtronic II and the U.S. Tax Court's Mixed Signals Regarding the CPM*, 108 Tax Notes Int'l 7-11 (TaxAnalysts 2022).

'requires sophisticated algorithms to convert them into useful information'.[156] While the potential of the use of the latter itself as a business model in the digital economy is not new, the transfer pricing analysis and valuation of big data remain a challenge for tax administrations. Chapter 4 of this book delves into the transfer pricing aspects of big data, including the potential for tax administrations to use it, e.g., for determining whether a significant economic presence of foreign companies has been established.

3.4 Sustainability

Commonly understood under the trinomial concept involving environmental, social, and governance (ESG), the transversal topic of sustainability gained importance in the last years following the action not only of private actors but also of public bodies internationally. This trend was substantially reinforced in 2015 by the adoption of UN Member States of the Agenda 2030 which stipulates seventeen sustainable development goals.[157] Within Europe, the implementation framework of such an agenda from an environmental perspective was presented by the EC on 11 December 2015 through the 'European Green Deal'.[158] Accordingly, it laid down a roadmap with key policies and envisaged measures to be implemented by 2050 thus including the ambitious goals of reducing greenhouse gas (GHG) emissions by at least 50% along with 'climate neutrality' by 2050.[159] As a starting point to achieve them, the EC focuses on developing a strategy for sustainable investment,[160] including therein the adoption of a taxonomy legislation for the classification of environmentally sustainable activities along with the revision of the non-financial reporting directive (NFRD)[161] and the establishment of an EU green bond standard.[162] Whereas the taxonomy regulation was enacted already in 2020,[163] the revision of the NFRD ended in the approval of a directive establishing a new standard of reporting, i.e., the Corporate Sustainability Reporting Directive (CSRD),[164] and the discussion of an EU green bond standard is still

156. Victor Calijuri, *Is Big Data That Simple? An Analysis of the Transfer Pricing Aspects of Value Creation of Data in the Digitalized Economy*, 5 International Tax Studies 8 (2022).
157. General Assembly United Nations, *Resolution adopted by the General Assembly on 25 September 2015 – 70/1 Transforming our world: the 2030 Agenda for Sustainable Development*, No. A/RES/70/1 (September 2015).
158. European Commission, *Communication from the Commission to the European Parliament, the European Council, the Council, the European Economic and Social Committee and the Committee of the Regions – The European Green Deal*, No. COM(2019) 640 (December 2019).
159. *Ibid.*, at 4.
160. *Ibid.*, at 17.
161. *Directive 2014/95/EU of the European Parliament and of the Council of 22 October 2014 amending Directive 2013/34/EU as regards disclosure of non-financial and diversity information by certain large undertakings and groups* (October 2014).
162. *Supra* n. 158, at 2.2.1.
163. *Regulation (EU) 2020/852 of the European Parliament and of the Council of 18 June 2020 on the establishment of a framework to facilitate sustainable investment, and amending Regulation (EU) 2019/2088* (June 2020).
164. *Directive (EU) 2022/2464 of the European Parliament and of the Council of 14 December 2022 amending Regulation (EU) No 537/2014, Directive 2004/109/EC, Directive 2006/43/EC and Directive 2013/34/EU, as regards corporate sustainability reporting* (December 2022).

ongoing.[165] Finally, the members of the European Council and European Parliament reached a provisional agreement on the design of a Carbon Border Adjustment Mechanism (CBAM) in December 2022.[166] Such a focus on sustainability was also observed in national legislation such as in the massive investments in carbon mitigating measures laid down in the American Inflation Reduction Act of 2022,[167] in the application on 1 January 2023 of the German Act on Corporate Due Diligence Obligations in Supply Chains,[168] and in the introduction of a CO_2 pricing in Austria within its national emission certificates trading framework.[169]

All of these measures impact the behaviour of MNEs when conducting their business, thus affecting the format in which value is created. This may embrace the supply chain structure of a company to conform to new legal standards, i.e., relocation of production assets to sites that are more strongly committed to human rights conventions or minimization of the supply chain's carbon footprint. Beyond that, the impact could also be of a strategic nature[170] in which an MNE, for instance, may opt for a strongly ESG-oriented vision, e.g., a net zero emission target by 2030, that enhances its value creation from the business perspective. The consequences of that could be an increase in revenues due to new ESG-friendly customers, a reduction of costs by minimizing the use of natural resources, minimization of risk exposure to regulatory intervention, or an increase of returns due to investment in sustainable activities instead of in environmentally harmful activities.[171] Hence, the activities performed by each involved entity and an MNE's entrepreneur could be subject to a different transfer pricing assessment.

Based on that, several functions of an MNE remain affected by the transversal nature of the ESG theme with potential impacts for a transfer pricing analysis regardless of their routine status prior to a sustainable-oriented adjustment or implementation. This includes purchasing and procurement activities that generally would not lead to a remuneration beyond a routine figure. However, with the new developments, the acquisition of goods could assume a particular effort of the entity when reviewing all of its suppliers and their compliance with social and working conditions standards, for

165. Despite the publication of a proposal by the EC, this topic is still being discussed; *see* European Commission, *Proposal for a Regulation of the European Parliament and of the Council on European Green Bonds COM/2021/391*, No. COM/2021/391 (July 2021); European Parliament, *Report A9-0156/2022 on the Proposal for a Regulation of the European Parliament and of the Council on European Green Bonds*, No. A9-0156/2022 (May 2022).
166. European Council, Press Release: EU Climate Action: Provisional Agreement Reached on Carbon Border Adjustment Mechanism (CBAM) (13 December 2022) (December 2022).
167. *Inflation Reduction Act of 2022*, Nos 117-169 (August 2022).
168. *Gesetz über die unternehmerischen Sorgfaltspflichten zur Vermeidung von Menschenrechtsverletzungen in Lieferketten (Lieferkettensorgfaltspflichtengesetz – LkSG)*, No. BGBl I 2959-2969 (July 2021).
169. *Bundesgesetz über einen nationalen Zertifikatehandel für Treibhausgasemissionen (Nationales Emissionszertifikatehandelsgesetz 2022 – NEHG 2022)*, No. BGBl I 10/2022, 16-31.
170. Stefan Greil et al., *Verrechnungspreise und Nachhaltigkeit – ein weiterer Vergleichbarkeitsfaktor bei der Verrechnungspreisbestimmung?*, Der Betrieb 2641-2645, 2641 (Otto Schmidt 2021).
171. Witold Henisz et al., *Five Ways that ESG Created Value*, McKinsey Quarterly (McKinsey & Company November 2019).

example.[172] Additionally, the development of intangible assets, allocation of costs, or even the financial activities of the group could assume a different character underpinned by a sustainable bias.[173] An example of this issue can be seen in the voluntary intra-group trading of emission certificates whereby the question arises as to which valuation would be applicable to such carbon credits. Although there is a potential comparison of market prices in the European market, other entities of the group besides the one carrying out the carbon mitigating activity, i.e., seller of the certificate, may incur costs for validating the certificate within the regulatory body of a country. Accordingly, this performed function should be also taken into account within the transfer pricing analysis to determine whether and to what extent such activities could be, for instance, factored in the price of the transaction or if different specific transactions should be conceived.

3.5 Financing

The transfer pricing analysis of intra-group financial transactions was kept high on the agenda throughout 2022. An example of that is seen in the British case *BlackRock* for which an appeal was decided by the Upper Tribunal Tax and Chancery Chamber (UTT) on 19 July 2022.[174] The transactions at stake concerned the acquisition by the BlackRock group of a North American investment management business of Barclays Global Investors (BGI US) from Barclays Bank plc in December 2009.[175] The financing of such a purchase included a debt-down comprising BlackRock Financial Management, Inc. (BFM); BlackRock Holdco 4, LLC (LLC4); BlackRock Holdco 5, LLC (LLC5); and BlackRock Holdco 6, LLC (LLC6). BFM is incorporated in Delaware, is a US tax resident, and accounts for an indirectly held subsidiary of the ultimate parent entity, BlackRock, Inc (BRI). LLC4, LLC5, and LLC6 are incorporated and registered in the state of Delaware whereby LLC4 is the sole shareholder of LLC5, and LLC6 has LLC5 and LLC4 as shareholders with preference and ordinary shares. LLC4 is solely controlled by BFM. The LLCs[176] elected to be disregarded for US tax purposes so that all transactions carried out by them were considered as being carried out by BFM directly. In this context, the focus of the case lies in LLC5 which was resident for tax purposes in the United Kingdom and registered for corporation tax.[177] After a series of contribution agreements between LLC4 and LLC5, LLC4 and LLC6, and LLC5 and LLC6, LLC5 issued loan notes in four tranches amounting to USD 4 billion to be paid back to LLC4. Finally, because of the contribution agreements with LLC6, this entity had the funding

172. Susann Karnath, *Der Einfluss von ESG-Maßnahmen auf die Verrechnungspreise*, IStR 920-926, 922 (2022).
173. *Ibid.*, at 923 et seq.
174. *The Commissioners for Her Majesty's Revenue and Customs v. Blackrock Holdco 5 LLC [2022] UKUT 00199 (TCC)*, (Upper Tribunal Tax and Chancery Chamber, 19 July 2022).
175. *Ibid.*, 2, para. 1.
176. LLC4, LLC5 and LLC6.
177. *The Commissioners for Her Majesty's Revenue and Customs v. Blackrock Holdco 5 LLC [2022] UKUT 00199 (TCC)*, (Upper Tribunal Tax and Chancery Chamber, 19 July 2022) at 4, para. 16(1), last sentence.

available for completing the acquisition of BGI US. The following figure depicts the factual scenario (Figure 1.2).

Figure 1.2 Description of the BlackRock Case

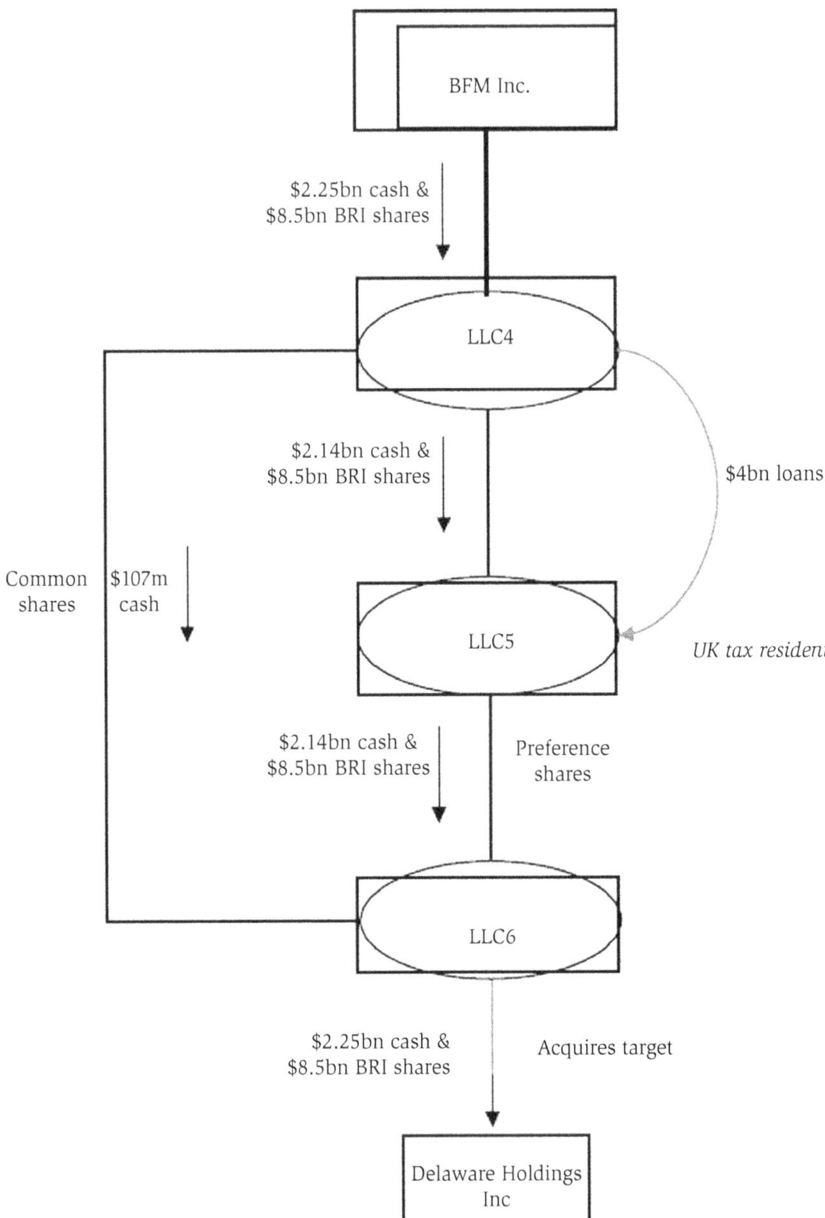

Apart from the discussion over an unallowable purpose regarding the interest deductions, the main issue from a transfer pricing perspective was whether the loans were issued on an arm's length basis. Stated differently, would an arm's length independent lender have provided a loan in the amount of USD 4 billion to LLC5 in the same terms as LLC4? The First-Tier Tax Tribunal (FTT) decided,[178] based on the evidence brought by one of the two[179] experts, that unrelated parties would have entered into such an agreement provided that additional financial covenants from other entities of the group could be provided.[180] Following a rather formalistic approach, the UTT overturned the FTT's decision since the provision of additional covenants would involve the participation of third parties absent in the original controlled transaction.[181] Additionally, the UTT sought support in the national legal provision[182] according to which the controlled transaction is of a bilateral nature. Hence, the court concluded that the controlled transaction would not have occurred between independent enterprises.[183] Consequently, all of the interest deductions have been disallowed as originally made by the His Majesty's Revenue & Customs (HMRC) since there would not be any comparable arm's length transaction.[184]

From a transfer pricing perspective, it seems that the framing of the case does not achieve theoretical coherence. Regardless of any national disposition similar to a GAAR, the way in which a potential comparable scenario has been pursued seems odd. This is because the court completely disregards the effect of implicit support when orienting itself exclusively on one of the evidence experts who asserted that a similar transaction would not have occurred between independent enterprises. Logically, if LLC5 is individually considered, it remains clear that the entity lacks financial capacity or even substance to pay the accrued interest of a USD 4 billion loan. Stated differently, it seems indeed unlikely that, for instance, a bank would grant such a loan to LLC5 without any other forms of securing this debt. Nonetheless, the scenario is quite different if this bank considers LLC5 as part of an international MNE whose parent company offers enough creditworthiness to enter into such debt. That is the reason

178. *Blackrock Holdco 5 LLC v. The Commissioners for Her Majesty's Revenue and Customs*, ([2020] UKFTT 443 (TC), 3 November 2020).
179. Since one of the experts concluded that a similar transaction would not have taken place between unrelated parties; *see ibid.*, 37, para. 92.
180. *Ibid.*, 37 et seq., paras 90 et seq. Although it is quite debatable whether with the provision of additional covenants the transaction is entered into the 'same terms', as the FTT asserted in para. 103: 'Therefore, for the reasons above I find that although an independent enterprise would not have entered into the Loan on the same terms as the actual transaction it would, subject to the covenants described above, have entered into the Loans on the same terms as the parties in the actual transaction.'
181. *The Commissioners for Her Majesty's Revenue and Customs v. Blackrock Holdco 5 LLC [2022] UKUT 00199 (TCC)* (Upper Tribunal Tax and Chancery Chamber, 19 July 2022), at 17, para. 76.
182. Section 152(5) TIOPA.
183. *The Commissioners for Her Majesty's Revenue and Customs v. Blackrock Holdco 5 LLC [2022] UKUT 00199 (TCC)* (Upper Tribunal Tax and Chancery Chamber, 19 July 2022) at 17, para. 76.
184. *Ibid.*, 32, para. 100. Albeit unnecessary, the court also discussed the unallowable purpose issue of Ch. 15 Part 5 sections 441-442 CTA 2009, concluding that the loans would have no commercial purpose but rather only a tax advantage purpose so that they should be disregarded; *see ibid.*, 45, para. 200.

why one of the experts referred to the need for financial covenants that would allow the transaction to be conducted between unrelated parties.

This is specifically addressed by the recently included Chapter X OECD TPG that recognized the need for accounting for the incidental benefit derived from group affiliation, that is to say, implicit support.[185] This has a direct impact on the credit rating of the entity that ultimately reflects not only the capacity to take such debt but also the amount of interest payable.[186] This analysis reflects the first step of the transfer pricing analysis, i.e., accurate delineation of the transaction,[187] which has not been addressed by both courts. Nevertheless, what both courts did was conduct a certain miscarried second step of the transfer pricing analysis dealing with the recognition of the transaction. Indeed, this step aims at determining whether the controlled transaction is embedded with commercial rationality.[188] As such, the OECD TPG recognizes that non-recognition should be carefully applied so that 'every effort should be made to determine the actual nature of the transaction and apply arm's length pricing'.[189] Additionally, the guidance recognizes that the mere fact that a transaction may not be seen between independent enterprises does not mean that it should not be recognized since, given the nature of associated enterprises, they have more ability to enter into more different arrangements when compared to unrelated parties.[190]

In the case at stake, it does not seem that the controlled transactions lack commercial rationality which has even been recognized by the FTT when dealing with the unallowable purpose issue.[191] Most importantly, however, would be to have placed the focus on the role developed by the group affiliation in order to factor it into the transfer pricing analysis. It remains to be seen how the UK court will react to other similar intra-group financing cases vis-à-vis the non-recognition of the controlled transactions.

Finally, a few developments could be observed in the Australian practice. The Federal Court of Australia (FCA) ruled in the *Singapore Telecom* case on a loan granted to an Australian subsidiary and upheld the assessment carried out by the commissioner in order to reduce the amount of interest payable by accurately delineating the transaction.[192] Still, in Australia, the Australian Taxation Office (ATO) provided direct and practical guidance[193] dealing with the reform of the interbank offered rate (IBOR)

185. OECD, *OECD Transfer Pricing Guidelines for Multinational Enterprises and Tax Administrations 2022*, *supra* n. 4, at 418, para. 10.77.
186. *Ibid.*, at 419, para. 10.78. In this case, most probably, the amount of interest payable under this analysis would have been reduced since it seems clear that LLC5 benefited from the parent's creditworthiness.
187. *Ibid.*, at 404, para. 10.6.
188. *Ibid.*, at 75, para. 1.142.
189. *Ibid.*, para. 1.142.
190. *Ibid.*
191. *Blackrock Holdco 5 LLC v. The Commissioners for Her Majesty's Revenue and Customs*, ([2020] UKFTT 443 (TC), 3 November 2020) 47, para. 123.
192. *See* with further details, Michael Butler et al., *Federal Court Disagrees with SingTel Australia that Interest Paid to British Virgin Islands Company Was Arm's Length*, 29 International Transfer Pricing Journal (2022); Anton Joseph, *Singapore Telecom Case – Reconstruction Powers in Transfer Pricing*, 29 International Transfer Pricing Journal (2022).
193. ATO, *Inter-Bank Offered Rate (IBOR) Reform – Last Modified: 11 Mar 2022 – QC 68045*, https://www.ato.gov.au/Business/Inter-bank-Offered-Rate-reform/.

and its transition to risk-free rates (RFRs). The IBOR includes, for instance, the London Inter-Bank Offered Rate (LIBOR), Euro Inter-bank Offered Rate (EURIBOR), and the US Effective Federal Funds Rate. Such guidance contains two examples dealing with the transition from LIBOR to Sterling Overnight Index Average (SONIA) and EURIBOR to euro short-term rate (€STR), respectively. Discussion about intra-group financial transactions and their transfer pricing implications will continue to be a highly debatable topic in the next years.

3.6 Intangibles

Following the observed trend of the case law mentioned in the introduction, cases dealing with intangibles remained in the limelight during 2022. One example of that is the *Ferragamo* case for which a decision was rendered by the administrative court from Paris (CAA)[194] on 30 June 2022.[195] The central point of analysis, in this case, referred to the nature of the distribution activities performed by Ferragamo France and to what extent they should be further remunerated due to a more complex functional profile that might have contributed to creating intangibles. Accordingly, the facts of the case concern the Italian Ferragamo group specialized in the fashion and luxury industry[196] of which its ultimate parent company, Salvatore Ferragamo S.p.A. (SpA), is based in Florence, Italy. It designs and produces the brand's articles and performs all related functions.[197] Additionally, it owns the brand and bears the marketing and promotional expenses. It owns the Dutch company Ferragamo International BV that, in turn, wholly owns Ferragamo France (FF). The latter was set up in 1992 to explore the French market by conducting the business of retailing shoes, leather goods, and luxury accessories as the distributor in shops in France of products from the Salvatore Ferragamo brand.[198] As a result of an audit, French tax authorities considered that the transfer pricing policy applied by the group led to a distribution of profits from FF to SpA so that the corporate income tax assessment for the financial year 2010 charged additional values[199] to the latter.

From a time perspective, FF had been incurring losses since 1996 with the exception of the year of the tax assessment of 2010. As for the transfer pricing policy of the group,

194. Court administrative d'appel.
195. In this case, the CAA had already decided in favour of the tax administration in 2018, however, the Conseil d'État overruled this decision in 2020 and sent the case back again to the CAA to determine the quantification of profits and method of calculation. *See* Conseil d'État (France), 23 November 2020, no. 425577; C.A.A. Paris (France), 17 September 2018, no. 17PA02617.
196. Salvatore Ferragamo Italia S.p.A., *Salvatore Ferragamo Consolidated Annual Report as at 31 December 2009 and 2008 – Board of Director's Report on Operations, Financial Statements and Notes* 123 (April 2010).
197. Cour administrative d'appel (France), 30 June 2022, no. 20PA03601, para. 6.
198. *Ibid.*, para. 1.
199. Including additional tax, interest, and penalties whereby accrued losses have been used to partially compensate the tax due, however, withholding taxes were also charged by the tax administration due to the alleged transfer of profits to the SpA; *see ibid.*, para. 1.

it submitted that it acquired goods from SpA applying the resale price method (RPM) for which the Italian company granted a 25% discount compared to the price charged to independent distributors that further allowed the return of unsold goods at their purchase price without any quantity limitation. This policy would better take into account the functions performed by FF that are different from the ones of a simple distributor in light of the high-quality standards required in the business, according to the argumentation of FF. Based on that, the French company provided a list of comparables and calculations of the ratio between operating costs, excluding the purchase of goods, and the turnover of those undertakings. Accordingly, an average expense ratio of 61.76% for an average gross margin of 55.23% has been reached in relation to the years 2005-2010.[200] Nevertheless, the auditor ascertained that, in general,[201] external expenses accounted for absorbing more than half of the trading margin granted to FF. Additionally, the auditor took a different perspective by adjusting the list of comparables[202] provided by FF and looking into the ratio of external and wage costs from the turnover of these. As a result, the auditor concluded that the external and wage cost ratios of FF were significantly higher in relation to the comparables. This discrepancy would also apply to the ratio of operating profit to turnover of these companies, which was positive, whereas the one of FF was constantly negative. Therefore, such findings would lead to the conclusion that the margin granted by SpA to FF was insufficient to absorb the operating costs of the French commercial operation, particularly when considering the FF's brand development function. This is because FF would incur high costs due to its positioning in prestigious locations and the qualified staff required to meet its customers' requirements. Faced with that, the tax administration proceeded to make adjustments based on the margins reached by using the comparables mentioned by the auditor, focusing on the gross margin, wages, and external expenses.[203]

FF disputed the methodology proposed by the tax administration, thus including the extension and selection of the list of comparables since these would operate in the provinces while FF's business activity was concentrated in international tourist areas such as Paris.[204] Moreover, it argued that the difference between the ratios concerning salaries was not materially relevant since it was below 10%.[205] Additionally, FF argued that a capital gain realization in the approximate amount of EUR 10.5 million should have been considered within the calculations of the tax authority.[206] Finally, it advanced that the TNMM proposed by the tax assessment falls outside the arm's length range and should thus be disregarded.[207]

200. *Ibid.*, para. 4.
201. Since 2008 was an exception.
202. The auditor selected nineteen companies, differently from the sixteen originally selected by the FF; *see* Cour administrative d'appel no. 20PA03601, para. 4.
203. For a detailed description, *see ibid.*, para. 11.
204. *Ibid.*, para. 15.
205. *Ibid.*, para. 17.
206. *Ibid.*, para. 18.
207. *Ibid.*, para. 19.

Faced with that, the court ruled in favour of the tax administration. First, the CAA asserted that the majority of comparables selected by the tax administration were proposed already by FF which also did not propose any adjustments to deal with the clear discrepancy regarding the wages and external costs.[208] Second, the court dismissed the absence of material relevance brought by FF since the national legislation does not provide any minimum threshold to allow adjustments.[209] Third, the CAA did not allow the inclusion of EUR 10.5 million in the calculation as requested by FF since this amount referred to a capital gain derived from the sale of real estate that therefore falls outside the scope of ratios dealing with the turnover of the company.[210] Fourth, the court held that FF did not provide any reliable calculations to reach an arm's length outcome due to the inclusion of the EUR 10.5 million value so the numbers advanced by FF could not substitute the adjustments brought by the tax administration.[211]

Although the decision is not final and does not deliver all of the relevant figures and calculations, a few takeaways can be mentioned. Initially, the case was judged without following a full transfer pricing analysis, perhaps mostly because of the way in which the tax assessment was conducted. This is because the approach seems to be inverted since the selection and application of the transfer method remain in focus, i.e., by referring initially to the losses incurred by the entity and thereafter exclusively to the ratios and their divergence to the comparables. Nevertheless, the first question that could be raised would be a detailed functional profile of the involved entities within the accurate delineation of the transaction. This would contribute to understanding whether FF is a mere distributor with a few other functions associated with a limited risk profile or if FF indeed performs more activities that lead to a more complex assumption of risks or may even create intangibles by, for instance, contributing to the trademark. Additionally, it seems that the whole case does not refer to the potential payment of royalties to FF to use the brand owned by SpA or whether such activity is already correctly remunerated by the RPM applied in the sale of goods by SpA to FF. Finally, the CAA's reasonings sit unconvincingly with the perspective of an arm's length outcome by stating that FF was not able to provide any other more reliable calculation. It indeed seems that the court considered that the losses of FF should be anyhow counteracted due to the functions performed regardless of a solid transfer pricing calculation. It is yet uncertain whether the French Conseil d'État will again render a decision in this case.

With an eye on a potential transfer of intangibles as well, Germany updated its ordinance dealing with the application of the ALP in the transfer package of a cross-border situation.[212] This was a result of the need to align the ordinance with the changes of section 1 of the German Foreign Income Tax Act (FTA) carried out in

208. *Ibid.*, para. 18.
209. *Ibid.*, para. 17.
210. *Ibid.*, para. 18.
211. *Ibid.*, para. 19.
212. *Verordnung zur Anwendung des Fremdvergleichsgrundsatzes nach § 1 Absatz 1 des Außensteuergesetzes in Fällen grenzüberschreitender Funktionsverlagerungen (Funktionsverlagerungsverordnung – FVerlV)*, BGBl. I 38/2022 at 1803 (October 2022).

2021[213] according to which definitions on the transfer of functions were inserted in section 1(3b) FTA.[214]

Finally, the uncertainty arising from the valuation of intangibles has recently been addressed by the Tel Aviv-Yafo District Court in the *CA Software Israel* case.[215] This case revolved around the assessment made by the tax administration increasing the deemed value of IP[216] sold by the taxpayer based on adjustments over the economic assumptions of the valuation analysis.[217] This included the expected economic life of the intangible and applicable growth rates and was upheld by the court. According to it, the taxpayer failed to provide sufficient and consistent documentation, although acknowledging the difficulties in discount cash flow modelling.[218] It is expected that the case law dealing with intangibles transactions will increase in the upcoming years for addressing contentious and complex situations.

3.7 Documentation/CbCR

The fifth annual peer review of the Action 13 Minimum Standard of the CbC report was published on 4 October 2022.[219] It proceeded in stages with four other annual reviews from 2018 to 2021. The process focused on four elements of the minimum standard:

(1) the domestic legal and administrative framework;
(2) the exchange of information (EOI) framework;
(3) confidentiality; and
(4) the appropriate use of CbC reports.

One hundred and thirty-four jurisdictions were examined throughout this annual peer review. According to it, their CbC reporting is well advanced with over 100 jurisdictions having now introduced obligations for relevant MNE Groups to file a CbC report in their domestic legal framework.[220] In this context, 28 jurisdictions received a general recommendation to put in place or finalize their legal or administrative

213. *Gesetz zur Modernisierung der Entlastung von Abzugsteuern und der Bescheinigung der Kapitalertragsteuer (Abzugsteuerentlastungsmodernisierungsgesetz – AbzStEntModG)* (June 2021).
214. For a comprehensive analysis highlighting the tighten of the rules in relation to the previous versions, *see* Siegfried Grotherr, *Neufassung Der Funktionsverlagerungsverordnung – Teil 1*, IWB 625-633 (26.8.2022); Siegfried Grotherr, *Neufassung Der Funktionsverlagerungsverordnung – Teil 2*, IWB 672-681 (16.9.2022).
215. *CA Software Israel Ltd. v. Tel Aviv 3 Assessing Office*, Nos 61226-06-17, 64191-06-18, 58418-06-19 (25 October 2022).
216. Among it, programmes for data protection; *see ibid.*, para. 2.
217. *Ibid.*, paras 35 et seq.
218. *Ibid.*, paras 62 et seq.
219. OECD, Country-by-Country Reporting – Compilation of 2022 Peer Review Reports, 4 October 2022, https://www.oecd.org/tax/beps/country-by-country-reporting-compilation-of-2022-peer-review-reports-5ea2ba65-en.htm.
220. *Ibid.*, at p. 9.

framework while 27 received recommendations for specific areas of them.[221] Additionally, 82 jurisdictions have competent authority agreements in place, and 88 have undergone an assessment concerning confidentiality and data safeguards.[222] Finally, 64 jurisdictions have provided detailed information to ensure the appropriate use of CbC reports.[223] As of 2021, delays in reporting due to the impact of the COVID-19 pandemic had not been included in the annual peer review.[224]

One of the countries that recently introduced CbC reporting was Barbados.[225] MNE Groups with a total consolidated group revenue of at least USD 850 million are now obligated to submit CbC reports according to this new legislation.

Against this background, a growing number of countries are going one step further to increase transparency by starting to require public CbCR in the sense that the information contained in it shall be disclosed to the general public. In the European Union, the Public CbCR Directive,[226] which was agreed upon on 24 November 2021, shall be implemented until 22 June 2023 and will be applicable, at the latest, for financial years starting on or after 22 June 2024.[227] Some Member States such as Germany[228], Slovakia[229] or Romania[230] have already implemented public CbCR into their national law.[231]

While the public is looking forward to seeing CbCRs from MNEs, the question arises whether total transparency could infringe on the fundamental rights of the people involved. The ECJ ruled in November 2022 that the provision to disclose the beneficial owner to any member of the general public in Article 1(15)(c) of the Money Laundering Directive[232] violated primary EU law.[233] While the disclosure of the beneficial owner and other business information might not be comparable as such, it might at least be

221. *Ibid.*, at p. 10.
222. *Ibid.*
223. *Ibid.*
224. *Ibid.*
225. *See* https://bra.gov.bb/Download.ashx?file=Attachments%2fIncome+tax+(Country+by+Country+reporting)+Act+2021-27.pdf&name=Income+Tax+(Country-by-Country+Reporting)+Act+2021-27; https://home.kpmg/us/en/home/insights/2022/02/tnf-barbados-rules-requiring-country-by-country-reporting-enacted.html.
226. Directive (EU) 2021/2101 of the European Parliament and of the Council of 24 November 2021 amending Directive 2013/34/EU as regards disclosure of income tax information by certain undertakings and branches, OJEU L 2021/429, 1.
227. *Ibid.*, Article 48g.
228. *Gesetz zur Umsetzung der Richtlinie (EU) 2021/2101 im Hinblick auf die Offenlegung von Ertragsteuerinformationen durch bestimmte Unternehmen und Zweigniederlassungen sowie zur Änderung des Verbraucherstreitbeilegungsgesetzes und des Pflichtversicherungsgesetzes* BGBl 2023 I Nr 154 (June 2023).
229. https://home.kpmg/us/en/home/insights/2022/12/tnf-slovakia-public-cbc-reporting-implemented.html.
230. https://home.kpmg/us/en/home/insights/2022/12/tnf-romania-public-country-by-country-reporting-implemented.html.
231. For more information, *see* https://home.kpmg/xx/en/home/insights/2022/11/etf-493-eu-public-country-by-country-reporting-implementation.html.
232. Directive (EU) 2018/843 of the European Parliament and of the Council of 30 May 2018 amending Directive (EU) 2015/849 on the prevention of the use of the financial system for the purposes of money laundering or terrorist financing, and amending Directives 2009/138/EC and 2013/36/EU (Text with EEA relevance), OJEU L 2018/156, 43.
233. Case C-37/20 & C-601/20, *Luxembourg Business Registers*, 22 November 2022.

questioned if some conclusions of the ECJ can be transferred to the transparency requirements laid down in the Public CbCR Directive.

While EU Member States are obligated to implement public CbCRs, other countries are taking these actions on a voluntary basis. Australia, for example, proposed a public CbCR during its federal budget released on 25 October 2022.[234] Even the US Securities and Exchange Commission (SEC) signalled its general support for higher tax transparency through public CbCRs.[235] Based on that, the tightening of documentation requirements and the increase of compliance burden is a trend observed in the last years that will most likely not diminish in the next years.

3.8 Dispute Resolution

Regarding the dispute resolution prism, the 2021 MAP statistics were recently published by the OECD on 2 November 2022.[236] On a broad perspective, significant shifts to the trends observed in the last years cannot be identified, although marginal positive moves can be ascertained. This is because the average length for transfer pricing cases decreased from 35 to 32.3 months,[237] the overall inventory of MAP cases slightly decreased by 176 cases, and the percentage of one of the major outcomes[238] of avoiding double taxation increased by 2%, thus 53% of the cases closed. Building on the MAP numbers, the OECD released the 2021 MAP awards[239] in which certain jurisdictions fall under evidence due to their handling of MAPs according to considered proxies. In this context, the following eight categories were considered:

- average monthly time to close transfer pricing MAP cases: Spain (19.6), United Kingdom (20.9), Germany (23.1), Canada (25.4), and Denmark (26.8);
- average monthly time to close other MAP cases: Ireland (5), Australia (7.5), Spain (9), Luxemburg (11.6), and Portugal (12.3);
- lowest pre-2016 cases inventory: Canada (2.05%), Ireland (4.03%), Spain (4.1%), Sweden (4.18%), and the Netherlands (4.18%);
- closing ratio large[240] inventory: Ireland (73%), Luxemburg (63%), United Kingdom (49%), United States (46%), and Belgium (43%);
- closing ratio medium[241] inventory: New Zealand (65%), Norway (38%), South Africa (37%), Australia (36%), and Turkey (31%);

234. https://home.kpmg/us/en/home/insights/2022/10/tnf-australia-public-cbc-reporting-proposed-federal-budget.html.
235. https://home.kpmg/us/en/home/insights/2022/09/tnf-us-sec-signals-support-for-country-by-country-reporting.html.
236. OECD, *2021 Mutual Agreement Procedure Statistics* (2 November 2022), https://www.oecd.org/tax/dispute/mutual-agreement-procedure-statistics.htm.
237. Although the average length for the 'other cases' increased from 18.5 to 20.7 months.
238. The major outcomes in a 75% breakdown in avoidance of double taxation (53%), unilateral relief (12%), and domestic remedies (10%).
239. OECD, *2021 Mutual Agreement Procedure Awards* (2 November 2022), https://www.oecd.org/tax/dispute/mutual-agreement-procedure-awards.htm.
240. More than 100 cases left in 2021 end inventory.
241. More than 20 cases but fewer than 100 cases left in 2021 end inventory.

- transfer pricing cases fully solved by agreement: France/United States (63), Germany/United States (54), and Germany/Denmark (53);
- other cases fully solved by agreement: Ireland/United Kingdom (103), Belgium/Luxemburg (40), and Belgium/Italy (33); and
- most improved jurisdiction in relation to an increase in cases:[242] Germany (144).

In summary, countries are investing efforts and resources to increase the effectiveness of MAP procedures, resuming the trend of past years.

3.9 Significant Domestic Case Law

The year 2022 was again a time in which several significant transfer pricing cases throughout the world were issued. According to the analysis of certain landmark cases conducted by the WU Transfer Pricing Center, no major deviations from the trends in previous years could be identified. Financing and intangibles remained the predominant transactions decided upon by the courts with the most frequent legal questions being transfer pricing methods and burden of proof. There was no discernible tendency for the courts to rule in favour of the taxpayer or the tax administration; the outcome was almost as often for one side as for the other. Similar to the years before, however, most of the cases were settled in a prelitigation stage perhaps as a result of both taxpayers and tax administrations attempting to avoid lengthy litigation procedures.[243]

In addition to the cases mentioned above,[244] the following countries issued decisions that are significant for domestic practice and also of interest from an international perspective:

Australia

- Burden of Proof: *Australia v. PwC*, 25 March 2022, Federal Court of Australia, Case No. FCA 278.

Austria

- Delineation - Substance over Form, Financial Transactions: *Austria v. C-Group*, 8 March 2022, BFG, Case No. RV/7102553/2021.
- Financial Transactions, Intangibles - Goodwill Know-How Patents: *Austria v. 'ACQ-Group'*, 8 February 2022, BFG, Case No. RV/7104702/2018.

242. Greatest increase in number of cases closed with unilateral relief or full agreement (2021 versus 2020) with an increase for both transfer pricing and other cases.
243. For a detailed analysis, *see* Marcelo H.B. Moura et al., *The Transfer Pricing World in 2022: A Review*, Transfer Pricing International 193 et seq. (2022).
244. *See Medtronic Inc. v. Commissioner*, T.C. Memo. 2022-84; *The Commissioners for Her Majesty's Revenue and Customs v. Blackrock Holdco 5 LLC [2022] UKUT 00199 (TCC)*, (Upper Tribunal Tax and Chancery Chamber, 19 July 2022).; Conseil d'État (France), 23 November 2020, no. 425577; C.A.A. Paris (France), 17 September 2018, no. 17PA02617.

Belgium

- Arm's Length Principle, Legality - Legitimacy - Constitutional: Belgium, 16 December 2021, Constitutional Court, Case No. 184/2021.

Bulgaria

- Benchmark, Range and Median, Comparability Analysis, Transfer Pricing Methods: *Bulgaria v. Rubbertek Bulgaria EOOD*, 12 April 2022, Supreme Administrative Court, Case No. 3453.
- Beneficial Owner, Royalty and License Payments, Tax Treaty Interpretation: *Bulgaria v. CBS*, 3 March 2022, Supreme Administrative Court, Case No. 3012.

Canada

- Legality - Legitimacy - Constitutional: *Canada v. Dow Chemicals*, 26 April 2022, Federal Court of Appeal, Case No. 2022 FCA 70.

Costa Rica

- Services and Fees, VAT and Customs Valuation, Withholding Tax (WHT), *Costa Rica v. British Tobacco Centroamérica S.A.*, 29 March 2022, Supreme Court, Case No. 750-2022.
- Burden of Proof, Comparability Analysis, Transfer Pricing Methods: *Costa Rica v. GlaxoSmithKline Costa Rica S.A.*, 24 February 2022, Supreme Court, Case No. 4-001638-1027-CA.

Czech Republic

- Benchmark, Range and Median, Losses that continue indefinitely, Sales and Marketing Hubs, Services and Fees, VAT and Customs Valuation: *Czech Republic v. Eli Lilly ČR, s.r.o.*, 8 December 2022, Supreme Administrative Court, No. 7 Afs 279/2021-65.
- Services and Fees: *Czech Republic v. ANITA B s.r.o.*, 21 November 2022, Supreme Administrative Court, Case No. 4 Afs 381/2021-40.
- Legality - Legitimacy - Constitutional: *Czech Republic v. DFH Haus CZ s.r.o.*, 11 November 2022, Supreme Administrative Court, Case No. 4 Afs 98/2022-45.
- Burden of Proof, Financial Transactions, Transfer Pricing Methods: *Czech Republic v. HPI – CZ spol. s r.o.*, 10 November 2022, Supreme Administrative Court, Case No. 9 Afs 37/2022-37.
- Burden of Proof, Losses that continue indefinitely, Transfer Pricing Documentation, Transfer Pricing Methods: *Czech Republic v. Aisan Industry Czech, s.r.o.*, 27 April 2022, Supreme Administrative Court, Case No. 7 Afs 398/2019-49.
- Beneficial Owner, Royalty and License Payments, Withholding Tax (WHT): *Czech Republic v. Avon Cosmetics Ltd*, 3 February 2022, Municipal Court, Case No. 6 Af 36/2020-42.

Denmark

- Burden of Proof, Disallowed Deduction, Services and Fees, Transfer Pricing Documentation, *Denmark v. 'C-Advisory Business ApS'*, 7 November 2022, Supreme Court, Case No. BS-22176/2021-HJR.
- Benchmark, Range and Median, Disallowed Deduction, Financial Transactions: *Denmark v. Codan Forsikring A/S*, 17 August 2022, Eastern High Court, Case No. BS-11370/2020.
- Beneficial Owner, General Anti-Avoidance Rules (GAAR), Tax Avoidance Schemes, Tax Treaty Interpretation, Withholding Tax (WHT): *Denmark v. Heavy Transport Holding Denmark ApS*, 31 March 2022, High Court, Case No. B-721-13.
- Financial Transactions, Losses that continue indefinitely, Non-Recognition and Recharacterisation, Royalty and License Payments, Services and Fees: *Denmark v. Maersk Oil and Gas A/S*, 28 March 2022, Regional Court, Case No. BS-41574/2018 and BS-41577/2018.

France

- Business Restructuring, Intangibles - Goodwill Know-How Patents, Permanent Establishments: *France v. Bupa Insurance*, 21 December 2022, Conseil d'État, Case No. 450796.
- Financial Transactions: *France v. Fibusa SAS*, 22 November 2022, CAA, Case No. 21BX00968.
- Financial Transactions: *France v. Electricité de France*, 16 November 2022, Conseil d'État, Case No. 462383.
- Intangibles - Goodwill Know-How Patents, Valuation - DCF and CUT/CUPs: *France v. SA SACLA*, 27 October 2022, Conseil d'État, Case No. 457695.
- Disallowed Deduction: *France v. Yazaki Systems Technologies France*, 18 October 2022, CAA de Versailles, Case No. 20VE02286.
- Financial Transactions: *France v. HCL Maître Pierre*, 20 September 2022, Conseil d'État, Case No. 455651.
- Business Restructuring, Permanent Establishments: *France v. SA Tropicana Europe Hermes*, 25 August 2022, CAA of DOUAI, Case No. 20DA01106.
- Royalty and License Payments, Shares and Dividends, Tax Treaty Interpretation, Withholding Tax (WHT): *France v. Accor (Hotels)*, 21 June 2022, CAA de Versailles, Case No. 20VE02607.
- Beneficial Owner, Royalty and License Payments, Tax Treaty Interpretation, Withholding Tax (WHT): *France v. Société Planet*, 20 May 2022, Conseil d'État, Case No. 444451.
- Burden of Proof, Business Restructuring, Disallowed Deduction, Intangibles - Goodwill Know-How Patents: *France v. SAS Oakley Holding*, 18 May 2022, CAA of Lyon, No. 19LY03100.
- Burden of Proof, Losses that continue indefinitely, Transfer Pricing Methods: *France v. ST Dupont*, 13 April 2022, CAA of Paris, No. 19PA01644.

- Royalty and License Payments, Services and Fees: *France v. Rayonnages de France*, 10 February 2022, CAA of Douai, No. 19DA01682.
- Beneficial Owner, Intangibles - Goodwill Know-How Patents, Royalty and License Payments, Tax Avoidance Schemes, Tax Planning, Withholding Tax: *France v. IKEA*, 8 February 2022, CAA of Versailles, No. 19VE03571.
- Financial Transactions: *France v. Electricité de France*, 25 January 2022, CAA de Versailles, Case No. 20VE00792.

Germany

- Arm's Length Principle, VAT and Customs Valuation: *Germany v. 'H-Customs GmbH'*, 17 May 2022, BFH, Case No. VII R 2/19.
- Financial Transactions, Non-Recognition and Recharacterisation: *Germany v. 'HQ Lender GmbH'*, 13 January 2022, BFH, Case No. IR 15/21.

Greece

- Comparability Analysis, Disallowed Deduction, Transfer Pricing Methods: *Greece v. 'Tin Cup Ltd'*, 23 November 2022, Tax Court, Case No. 3743/2022.
- Benchmark, Range and Median, Comparability Analysis, Losses that continue indefinitely, Transfer Pricing Methods: *Greece v. 'Clothing Distributor Ltd.'*, 27 June 2022, Tax Court, Case No. 2400/2022.
- Disallowed Deduction, Services and Fees, VAT and Customs Valuation: *Greece v. 'VAT Ltd.'*, 30 May 2022, Tax Court, Case No. 2074/2022.

Hong Kong

- Legality - Legitimacy - Constitutional, *Hong Kong v. Directors of Nam Tai Trading Company Limited*, 5 August 2022, Court of Appeal, Case FACV No. 1 of 2022.

India

- Advertising, Allowable business expenditure, Disallowed deduction, Documentation request, Promotion expenses, *India v. Mylan Pharmaceuticals Private*, 26 December 2022, Income Tax Appellate Tribunal, ITA No. 122/Hyd/2022.
- Digital Economy, Royalty and License Payments, Tax Avoidance Schemes, Withholding Tax: *India v. Google India Private Limited*, 19 October 2022, ITAT, 1513/Bang/2013, 1514/Bang/2013, 1515/Bang/2013, 1516/Bang/2013.
- Disallowed Deduction, Services and Fees: *India v. Akzo Nobel India Pvt Ltd*, 27 September 2022, High Court of Delhi, Case No. ITA 370/2022.
- Benchmark, Range and Median, Royalty and License Payments: *India v. Amway India Enterprises Pvt. Ltd.*, 8 September 2022, High Court of Delhi, Case No. ITA 313/2022.

- Benchmark, Range and Median, Burden of Proof, Services and Fees, Transfer Pricing Methods, *India v. Sulzer Tech India Pvt Ltd*, 25 July 2022, ITAT, Case No. 633-MUM-2021.
- Transfer Pricing Documentation, Transfer Pricing Methods: *India v. Olympus Medical Systems India Pvt. Ltd.*, 20 April 2022, ITAT - New Delhi, Case No. 838/DEL/2021.
- Permanent Establishments, Tax Treaty Interpretation: *India v. UPS Asia Group Pte. Ltd.*, 8 March 2022, ITAT - Mumbai, Case No. 220/Mum./2021.
- Disallowed Deduction, Services and Fees: *India v. Akzo Nobel India Pvt Ltd*, 28 February 2022, ITAT Delhi, ITA No. 6007/Del/2014.
- Sales and Marketing Hubs, Transfer Pricing Methods: *India v. Kellogg India Private Limited*, 24 February 2022, ITAT - Mumbai, Case No. ITA No. 7342/Mum/2018.
- Intangibles - Goodwill Know-How Patents, Royalty and License Payments, Tax Treaty Interpretation, Withholding Tax: *India v. Synamedia Limited*, 14 February 2022, ITAT - Bangalore, Case No. 3350/Bang/2018.

Israel

- Business Restructuring, Intangibles - Goodwill Know-How Patents, Valuation - DCF and CUT/CUPs: *Israel v. CA Software Israel Ltd*, 25 October 2022, Tel Aviv District Court, Case No. 61226-06-17.
- Business Restructuring, Delineation - Substance over Form, Intangibles - Goodwill Know-how Patents, Non-Recognition and Recharacterisation, Series of Related Transactions, Valuation - DCF and CUT/CUPs: *Israel v. Medingo Ltd*, 8 May 2022, District Court, Case No. 53528-01-16.

Italy

- Arm's Length Principle, Intangibles - Goodwill Know-How Patents, Royalty and License Payments: *Italy v. Arditi S.p.A.*, 21 December 2022, Supreme Administrative Court, Case No. 37437/2022.
- Transfer Pricing Methods: *Italy v. Prinoth S.p.A.*, 13 December 2022, Supreme Administrative Court, Case No. 36275/2022.
- Legality - Legitimacy - Constitutional, Transfer Pricing Methods: *Italy v. Quaker Italia Srl*, 25 November 2022, Supreme Administrative Court, Case No. 34728/2022.
- Burden of Proof, Transfer Pricing Methods: *Italy v. Ferrari SpA*, 12 September 2022, Supreme Court, Case No. 26695/2022.
- Financial Transactions, General Anti-Avoidance Rules (GAAR), Tax Avoidance Schemes, Tax Planning (Aggressive): *Italy v. BASF Italia s.p.a.*, 17 June 2022, Supreme Court, Case No. 19728/2022.
- Benchmark, Range and Median, Comparability Analysis, Transfer Pricing Methods, *Italy v. Promgas s.p.a.*, 17 May 2022, Supreme Court, Cases No. 15668/2022.

- Arm's Length Principle, Disallowed Deduction: *Italy v. Vincenzo Zucchi Spa*, 2 May 2022, Supreme Court, Case No. 13718/2022.
- Financial Transactions, Transfer Pricing Methods: *Italy v. Mauser S.p.A.*, 24 February 2022, Supreme Court, Case No. 6283/2022.
- Beneficial Owner, Financial Transactions, General Anti-Avoidance Rules (GAAR), Tax Treaty Interpretation, Withholding Tax (WHT): *Italy v. Arnoldo Mondadori Editore SpA*, 3 February 2022, Supreme Court, Case No. 3380/2022.
- Burden of Proof, Losses that continue indefinitely: *Italy v. SKECHERS USA ITALIA SRL*, 31 January 2022, Supreme Court, Case No. 02908/2022.

Japan

- Disallowed Deduction, Financial Transactions, General Anti-Avoidance Rules (GAAR), Tax Avoidance Schemes: *Japan v. Universal Music Corp*, 21 April 2022, Supreme Court, Case No. 令和2(行ヒ)303.

Korea

- Benchmark, Range and Median, Comparability Analysis, Transfer Pricing Methods: *Korea v. 'Semicon-sales'*, 9 June 2022, Tax Court, Case No. 2020-서-2311.
- Beneficial Owner, Royalty and License Payments, Services and Fees, Tax Treaty Interpretation, Withholding Tax (WHT): *Korea v. Microsoft*, 10 February 2022, Supreme Court, Case No. 2019두50946.

Luxembourg

- Disallowed Deduction, Financial Transactions, Shares and Dividends, Withholding Tax (WHT): *Luxembourg v. 'TR Swap SARL'*, 22 November 2022, Administrative Tribunal, Case No. 43535.
- Financial Transactions, Non-Recognition and Recharacterisation, Tax Avoidance Schemes: *Luxembourg v. 'Lux SARL'*, 23 September 2022, Administrative Tribunal, Case No. 44902.

Malaysia

- Legality - Legitimacy - Constitutional, Transfer Pricing Documentation: *Malaysia v. Executive Offshore Shipping SDN BHD*, 18 December 2022, High Court, Case No. WA-25-388-12/202.
- Burden of Proof, Business Restructuring, Intangibles - Goodwill Know-How Patents, Tax Planning (Aggressive): *Malaysia v. Keysight Technologies Malaysia*, 20 May 2022, High Court, Case No. WA-144-03-2020.

Netherlands

- Burden of Proof, Financial Transactions: *Netherlands v. 'Tobacco B.V.'*, 17 October 2022, Rechtbank Noord-Holland, Case No. ECLI:NL:RB-NHO:2022:8936.
- Business Restructuring, Intangibles - Goodwill Know-how Patents, Valuation - DCF and CUT/CUPs: *Netherlands v. 'Agri B.V.'*, 30 September 2022, Court of Appeal, Case No. AWB-16_5664 (ECLI:NL:RBNHO:2022:9062).
- Financial Transactions, General Anti-Avoidance Rules, Non-Recognition and Recharacterisation, Tax Avoidance Schemes: *Netherlands v. 'Owner B.V.'*, 26 July 2022, District Court, Case No. ECLI:NL:RBNHO:2022:6584.
- Benchmark, Range and Median, Comparability Analysis, Financial Transactions, Permanent Establishments: *Netherlands v. 'Fertilizer BV'*, 13 2022, Court of Appeal, Case No. ECLI:NL:GHSHE:2022:1198.
- Royalty and License Payments, Tax Avoidance Schemes: *Netherlands – Crop Tax Advisers*, 18 January 2022, Court of Appeal, Case No. 200.192.332/01, ECLI:NL:GHARL:2022:343.

New Zealand

- Financial Transactions, General Anti-Avoidance Rules (GAAR), Tax Avoidance Schemes: *New Zealand v. Frucor Suntory*, 30 September 2022, Supreme Court, Case No. [2022] NZSC 113.

Norway

- Commodity Transactions, Transfer Pricing Methods: *Norway v. Equinor Energy AS*, 29 August 2022, Court of Appeal, Case No. LB-2021-126759.
- Financial Transactions, General Anti-Avoidance Rules (GAAR), Transfer Pricing Methods: *Norway v. Petrolia No.co AS*, 31 May 2022, Court of Appeal, Case No. LB-2022-18585.
- Business Restructuring, Disallowed Deduction, Financial Transactions, Services and Fees, Tax Avoidance Schemes, Tax Planning (Aggressive): *Norway v. Fortis Petroleum Norway AS*, 25 March 2022, Court of Appeal, Case No. LB-2021-26379.
- Comparability Analysis, Financial Transactions, Transfer Pricing Methods: *Norway v. Conoco Phillips Skandinavia AS*, 16 March 2022, Court of Appeal, Case No. LG-2021-38180.
- Commodity Transactions, Transfer Pricing Methods: *Norway v. Neptune Energy Norge AS*, 22 February 2022, Court of Appeal, Case No. LG-2021-8008 – UTV-2022-697.

Poland

- Benchmark, Range and Median, Comparability Analysis, Transfer Pricing Methods: *Poland v. C. spółka z o.o.*, 23 November 2022, Supreme Administrative Court, Case No. II FSK 974/22.

- Disallowed Deduction, Services and Fees: *Poland v. 'H. LVAS Sp. z o.o.'*, 8 September 2022, Administrative Court, Case No. I SA / Go 234/22.
- Comparability Analysis, Financial Transactions: *Poland v. 'Shopping Centre Developer sp.k.'*, 29 June 2022, Supreme Administrative Court, Case No. II FSK 3050/19.
- Business Restructuring, Commercially Irrational Transactions, Disallowed Deduction, Financial Transactions, Non-Recognition and Recharacterisation, Services and Fees, Tax Avoidance Schemes: *Poland v. D. Sp. z o.o.*, 26 April 2022, Administrative Court, Case No. I SA/Bd 128/22.
- Delineation - Substance over Form, Royalty and License Payments, Transfer Pricing Methods: *Poland v. 'Fertilizer Licence SA'*, 26 April 2022, Provincial Administrative Court, Case No. I SA/Po 788/21.
- Delineation - Substance over Form, Royalty and License Payments, Transfer Pricing Methods: *Poland v. 'Sport O.B. SA'*, 15 March 2022, Provincial Administrative Court, Case No. I SA/Rz 4/22.
- Commercially Irrational Transactions, General Anti-Avoidance Rules, Intangibles - Goodwill Know-how Patents, Non-Recognition and Recharacterisation, Royalty and License Payments, Valuation - DCF and CUT/CUPs: *Poland v. 'X-TM' sp. z o.o.*, 28 March 2022, Administrative Court, SA/PO 1058/21.
- Arm's Length Principle, Shares and Dividends: *Poland v. M.P. sp. z o.o.*, 22 March 2022, Administrative Court, Case No. I SA/Bd 30/22.
- Arm's Length Principle, Shares and Dividends: *Poland v. K.O.*, 11 February 2022, Supreme Administrative Court, Case No. II FSK 1544/20.
- Arm's Length Principle, Financial Transactions, Transfer Pricing Documentation: *Poland v. A. Sp. z o.o.*, 3 February 2022, Supreme Administrative Court, Case No. II FSK 1475/19.
- Business Restructuring, Disallowed Deduction, MAP - APA: *Poland v. R. Sp. z o.o.*, 11 January 2022, Supreme Administrative Court, Case No. II FSK 990/19.

Portugal

- Burden of Proof, Financial Transactions, Transfer Pricing Methods: *Portugal v. L. Engenharia e Construções, S.A.*, 30 June 2022, Tribunal Central Administrativo Sul, Case No. 1339/13.0BELRA.
- Disallowed Deduction, Financial Transactions, Services and Fees, VAT and Customs Valuation: *Portugal v. 'A S.A.'*, 23 March 2022, CAAD - Administrative Tribunal, Case No. 213/2021-T.
- Disallowed Deduction, Financial Transactions, Legality - Legitimacy - Constitutional, Services and Fees: *Portugal v. 'A SGPS S.A.'*, 9 March 2022, CAAD - Administrative Tribunal, Case No. P590_2020-T.
- General Anti-Avoidance Rules, Tax Avoidance Schemes, Withholding Tax: *Portugal v. 'GAAR S.A.'*, 12 January 2022, Supremo Tribunal Administrativo, Case No. JSTA000P28772.

Spain

- Comparability Analysis, Royalty and License Payments, Transfer Pricing Methods: *Spain v. Universal Pictures International Spain SL*, 7 December 2022, Audiencia Nacional, Case No. SAN 5855/2022 - ECLI:EN:AN:2022:5855.
- Services and Fees: *Spain v. La Rehos, S.L.*, 6 July 2022, Supreme Court, Case No. 7268/2021, ATS 10616/2022 - ECLI:EN:TS:2022:10616A.
- Financial Transactions: *Spain v. 'XZ SA'*, 23 March 2022, TEAC, Case No. Rec. 4377-2018.
- Benchmark, Range and Median, Comparability Analysis, Losses that continue indefinitely, Transfer Pricing Methods: *Spain v. Delsey España S.A*, 11 February 2022, Tribunal Superior de Justicia, Case No. 483/2022 (Roj: STSJ CAT 1467/2022 - ECLI:ES:TSJCAT:2022:1467).
- Legality - Legitimacy - Constitutional: *Spain v. Dasher Spain S.A.*, 26 January 2022, Supreme Court, Case No. ATS 601/2022 - ECLI:EN:TS:2022:601A.
- Services and Fees, Shares and Dividends: *Spain v. Narcea Producciones y Promociones S.L.*, 26 January 2022, Tribunal Superior, Case No. STSJ M 122/2022 - ECLI:ES:TSJM:2022:122.

Sweden

- Disallowed Deduction, Financial Transactions, General Anti-Avoidance Rules (GAAR): *Sweden v. 'A Share Loan AB'*, 1 December 2022, Supreme Administrative Court, Case No. 3660-22
- Business Restructuring, Intangibles - Goodwill Know-How Patents, Tax Avoidance Schemes, Valuation - DCF and CUT/CUPs: *Sweden v. Swedish Match Intellectual Property AB*, 2 May 2022, Supreme Administrative Court, Case No. Mål: 5264-5267-20, 5269-20.
- Delineation of transaction: *Sweden v. Pandox AB*, 28 February 2022, Administrative Court.
- Business Restructuring, Intangibles - Goodwill Know-How Patents, Tax Avoidance Schemes, Valuation - DCF and CUT/CUPs: *Sweden v. Flir Commercial Systems AB*, 26 January 2022, Administrative Court of Appeal, Case No. 2434-2436-20.

Ukraine

- Benchmark, Range and Median, Commodity Transactions, Comparability Analysis, Transfer Pricing Methods: *Ukrain v. PrJSC 'Poltava GZK'*, 27 June 2022, Supreme Court, Case No. 440/1053/19.

United Kingdom

- Disallowed Deduction, Shares and Dividends: *UK v. NCL Investments Ltd*, 23 March 2022, UK Supreme Court, Case No. [2022] UKSC 9.

United States

- MAP – APA, Transfer Pricing Methods: *US v. Eaton Corp.*, 25 August 2022, Sixth Circuit, No. 21-1569/2674.
- Business Restructuring, Intangibles – Goodwill Know-How Patents, Tax Planning, Valuation – DCF and CUT/CUPs: *US v. TBL Licensing LLC*, 31 January 2022, U.S. Tax Court, Case No. 158 T.C. No. 1 (Docket No. 21146-15).

4 CONCLUSIONS AND INSIGHTS

In 2022, there were important developments in transfer pricing that can hardly be summarized in a few paragraphs. The OECD continued its innovative work on the two-pillar solution that started from the initial concern of addressing the tax challenges arising from the digitalization of the economy and has now developed into a complex framework of rules that affect conventional business models along with the digitalized economy. Amount A of Pillar One, which had received much more attention than Amount B in the past, is a convoluted set of rules for which its implementation offers several practical problems for allocating new taxing revenues to market jurisdictions. Amount B, however, is a potential welcoming framework that addresses the general call for simplification in transfer pricing rules. Its upcoming work will reflect the delicate balance between the accuracy of the ALP and the need for tax certainty in the form of simplification.

From a different perspective, Pillar Two intends to introduce a global minimum rate of corporate taxation and will certainly stay one of the hot topics in the global tax community in 2023 due to its worldwide implementation, particularly considering its agreement on a European directive in European Union. Thus, MNE groups or large-scale domestic groups with at least EUR 750 million in revenue and at least one constituent entity in the European Union will have to comply with the rules laid down in this directive.

The TP SC of the UN presented its provisory outcomes in a progress report evidencing under-researched areas that need guidance. It has yet to be determined what 2023 will bring, especially considering the resolution recently adopted by the UN General Assembly towards the development of an international tax framework through the UN.

The legislative bodies of the European Union maintained their active role in direct tax matters. The Pillar-Two Directive as well as public CbCR have to be transposed into national law in 2023 while the Unshell and DEBRA proposals have not yet passed the Council. A promising development is the ETACA project that entered a pilot phase in March 2022. This risk assessment screening programme is designed to increase trust and cooperation between MNEs and tax administrations and avoid resources bound by burdensome conflicts.

The ECJ issued some landmark judgments. In the long-awaited *Fiat* case concerning state aid, it persisted in a formal approach requiring the European Commission to undertake a careful transfer pricing analysis to disclose hidden state aid. As the EC was not able to satisfy the demands of the ECJ, the latter overturned the judgment by the GC that had maintained the Commission's decision regarding illegal state aid. This decision thus provided tax certainty for the application of the ALP, opposed to the reasoning advanced by the European Commission in the *beginning of this* case. In *Finanzamt Bremen*, the ECJ stated that the German tax surcharges for non-compliance with transfer pricing documentation were in accordance with the freedom of establishment.

On a country level, the same hot topics observed in previous years could again be identified. Several new acts of legislation and judgments revolved around the ALP, financing transactions, intangibles, and the application of transfer pricing methods. In the United States, the *Medtronic II* decision by the US Tax Court received a lot of attention because it led to the application of an unspecified method that allows room for criticism due to the lack of methodology. Big data and sustainability are global trends that also impact transfer pricing and will do so even more in the years to come. The inexorable movement of transparency has also impacted the transfer pricing world in the form of public CbCRs that are implemented by a rising number of countries all over the world.

It can be assumed that those trends that often come with significant administrative burdens will continue in 2023, and it is therefore essential for businesses all over the world to continue adapting to the challenges related to transfer pricing. Contrary to some recent commentators,[245] the reports of an upcoming death of transfer pricing are therefore not only highly exaggerated; the trends in 2022 proved that the importance of transfer pricing might even further increase in the upcoming years.

245. *See, e.g.*, Peter Mason, *Who Killed Transfer Pricing*, 109 Tax Notes Int'l, 1343 (Tax Analysts 2023).

CHAPTER 2

Transfer Pricing Aspects of Pillar One

Isabel Verlinden, Stefaan De Baets, Brendan Van Kets & Ward Sandra[*]

* The authors also thank Héline Dolvelde, intern at PwC, for her contribution and research. The views expressed are to be attributed solely to them.

1 INTRODUCTION

For several years now, the taxation of the digital economy – or so it was called at the beginning – has been at the centre of the tax news; well, not quite. After the OECD/G20 BEPS Project (BEPS), there was quite some noise around Pillar One, but it merely ebbed away in favour of Pillar Two that came at the forefront of what became known in common parlance as *global tax reform*. It was only recently that Pillar One was moved from the back burner into the heat of the furnace again. So do we almost come to a close on the revamp of the taxation of the digital economy – digitization of the economy?

Many things have happened particularly since the focus of Pillar One no longer lies with the digital or tech multinational enterprises (MNEs) but instead became of industry-generic relevance as all groups can be in scope as long as the MNE is sizable and profitable enough (Amount A) or entities perform the *right* kind of marketing and distribution activities (Amount B).

Pillar One should not be construed as a revenue-generating measure for countries. Rather, it reshuffles part of the taxable mass from residence countries to market jurisdictions (Amount A) or by a type of guaranteed return for baseline marketing and distribution (Amount B). The OECD impact assessment indicates that about USD 200 billion of taxing rights could be shifted under Amount A (2021), but it is silent, unfortunately, on what would be the effect of Amount B.[1]

Actually, in the opinion of the authors, Pillar One no longer relates to the taxation of the digital economy or the digitization of the economy as such. This chapter provides a general overview of Amount A and Amount B followed by a deep dive into each of them before concluding.

1. OECD – Webinar: Economic impact assessment of the Two-Pillar Solution – 18 January 2023 – available at https://www.oecd.org/tax/beps/economic-impact-assessment-presentation-january-2023.pdf (visited 25 January 2023).

2 A BIRD'S EYE OVERVIEW

It should be understood that Pillar One is actually composed of two different projects so to say. The first is called Amount A and covers the reallocation of a certain amount of profit of the largest and quite successful MNEs to market or user states. The second one aims at simplifying, streamlining, or standardizing transfer pricing (TP) for baseline marketing and distribution in accordance with the arm's length principle (ALP). At first sight, the two projects under Pillar One have little in common and are simply brought together under one banner, i.e., the Pillar One umbrella.

The journey for Pillar One was and still is anything but an easy ride. At the time of writing this chapter, it was not yet finished, mildly said. Building an overlay to an international tax system that spans almost a century might be complex. On top of the inclusive framework (IF) level, there is the need to reconcile countries' interests in order to find common ground regarding its implementation. The IF was created in 2016 in order to 'ensure interested countries and jurisdictions, including developing economies, can participate on an equal footing in the development of standards on BEPS related issues, while reviewing and monitoring the implementation of the OECD/G20 BEPS Project'.[2]

Everything began with the idea of 'the taxation of the digital economy' that may eventually lead to a global reform of the international tax system. Discussions at the OECD level that were mandated by the G20 resulted in the description of certain measures to tax the digital economy under BEPS Action 1 in the autumn of 2015.[3] This part of the fifteen actions under the BEPS Action Plan can be considered the foundation of Pillar One. After the publication in 2018 of an interim report,[4] it became clear that no consensus on a single way forward was reached. This was followed by the adoption of a policy note[5] and a programme of work in 2019[6] which determined the roadmap. The OECD published the 'Tax Challenges Arising from Digitalisation – Report on Pillar One Blueprint'[7] in 2020. This marks the first step in the adoption of a two-pillar system: Pillar One on the reallocation of taxing rights and Pillar Two[8] on introducing a global minimum tax (Global Base Erosion Mechanism – GloBE). In 2020, the OECD published

2. Flyer: OECD/G20 Inclusive Framework on BEPS, p. 1, https://www.oecd.org/tax/beps/flyer-inclusive-framework-on-beps.pdf.
3. OECD (2015), Addressing the Tax Challenges of the Digital Economy, Action 1 – 2015 Final Report, OECD/G20 Base Erosion and Profit Shifting Project, OECD Publishing, Paris 10.1787/9789264241046-en, p. 148.
4. OECD (2018), Tax Challenges Arising from Digitalisation – Interim Report 2018: Inclusive Framework on BEPS, OECD/G20 Base Erosion and Profit Shifting Project, OECD Publishing, Paris 10.1787/9789264293083-en 'It provides a sense of direction that reflects the commitment of the Inclusive Framework to work towards a consensus-based, global solution on these matters', p. 20.
5. Addressing the Tax Challenges of the Digitalisation of the Economy – Policy Note as approved by the Inclusive Framework on BEPS on 23 January 2019.
6. OECD/G20 Inclusive Framework on BEPS, Programme of Work to Develop a Consensus Solution to the Tax Challenges Arising from the Digitalisation of the Economy (OECD 2019).
7. OECD (2020), Tax Challenges Arising from Digitalisation – Report on Pillar One Blueprint: Inclusive Framework on BEPS, OECD/G20 Base Erosion and Profit Shifting Project, OECD Publishing, Paris, https://doi.org/10.1787/beba0634-en.
8. Pillar Two is discussed in Chapter 3.

the 'Statement by the OECD/IF on Base Erosion and Profit Shifting (BEPS) on the Two-Pillar Approach to Address the Tax Challenges Arising from the Digitalisation of the Economy'[9] which confirmed a formulaic allocation mechanism of Amount A. It also stated that Amount B will be based on the ALP. It called upon states to withdraw their unilateral measures taxing the digital economy for the correct functioning of Pillar One.[10]

As already mentioned, Pillar One contains two completely different sets of rules known as Amount A and Amount B. There was previously also an *Amount C* that has been reworded and redesigned as binding dispute resolution mechanism. The final implementation plan for Pillar One was released in October 2021 with the 'Statement on a Two-Pillar Solution to Address the Tax Challenges Arising from the Digitalisation of the Economy'.[11] It provided an overview of the state of play at that time concerning the Two-Pillar approach and what remained to be done.

Before proceeding to the main course served in the following sections of this chapter, here is already an appetiser, i.e., *une amuse bouche,* as they say in French. After all, the OECD is Paris based.

Amount A only concerns multinational companies with total revenues exceeding EUR 20 billion and profitability versus total revenues measuring 10%.[12] Due to this restricted scope, it only involves just over 100 (give or take a few) of the biggest and most profitable MNEs. Quite a few of them (unsurprisingly) have the United States as their home turf. No official list of these Pillar One targets exists. The aim of Amount A is to redistribute/reallocate tax income to market or user states in what is called a fairer way. Undertakings may not necessarily have a physical presence there but instead a (deemed) economic footprint due to remote sales or users' reach. Amount A is not intended to substitute the ALP, but a formulaic approach is used as an overlay for the redistribution or reallocation of part of the profit and taxing rights to market/user states. The rationale is that it allows these states to benefit to a certain extent and under certain conditions from tax revenues generated *on their soil* in the absence of a physical presence in their territory. The mechanism, as such, is not rocket science. In brief, 25% of the differences between the company's profit before tax (PBT) and the minimum profitability of 10% is reallocated to the concerned countries. For example, if a company has a PBT of 30%, 20% forms the basis of the amount for reallocation (30% PBT - 10% threshold). Then, 25% of that 20% may be reallocated under certain

9. OECD (2020), Statement by the OECD/G20 Inclusive Framework on BEPS on the Two-Pillar Approach to Address the Tax Challenges Arising from the Digitalisation of the Economy - January 2020, OECD/G20 Inclusive Framework on BEPS, OECD, Paris. www.oecd.org/tax/beps/statement-by-the-oecd-g20-inclusive-framework-on-beps-january-2020.pdf.
10. OECD (2020), Statement by the OECD/G20 Inclusive Framework on BEPS on the Two-Pillar Approach to Address the Tax Challenges Arising from the Digitalisation of the Economy - January 2020, OECD/G20 Inclusive Framework on BEPS, OECD, Paris. www.oecd.org/tax/beps/statement-by-the-oecd-g20-inclusive-framework-on-beps-january-2020.pdf, p. 8.
11. OECD (2021), Statement on a Two-Pillar Solution to Address the Tax Challenges Arising from the Digitalisation of the Economy, OECD/G20 Base Erosion and Profit Shifting Project, OECD Publishing, Paris - 8 October 2021.
12. OECD (2021), Statement on a Two-Pillar Solution to Address the Tax Challenges Arising from the Digitalisation of the Economy, OECD/G20 Base Erosion and Profit Shifting Project, OECD Publishing, Paris - 8 October 2021, p. 1.

conditions to countries under Amount A. More details will follow further in this chapter. This reallocation mechanism hence ruptures the existing international tax system where a physical presence is needed to create a taxable presence or nexus. This also means that new nexus rules must be designed in order to implement this Amount A.[13] For market and user jurisdictions, it creates a new taxing right based on this new taxable presence or nexus.[14]

For Amount B, unlike Amount A, no scope limitations will be introduced that are said to be in accordance with the ALP. It will likely introduce some form of fixed returns for so-called *baseline marketing and distribution activities*. It seems to refer to what some call mere routine activities that do not require proprietary contributions and hence do not generate (sizeable) economic rents (whatsoever). Some authors question the qualification of Amount B and its interactions with Amount A particularly with regard to its potential qualification as a safe harbour in its own capacity or its role in the marketing and distribution profits safe harbour (MDSH) under Amount A to avoid double counting and double taxation.[15] The aim of Amount B is to standardize, simplify, and streamline TP rules for tax authorities as well as undertakings.[16] On 8 December 2022, the OECD released a public Consultation Document on Amount B (Consultation Document)[17] with a deadline for comments of 25 January 2023. This should not be construed as a consensus document and contained the suggested principal features of Amount B and requested comments from any interested party.

One of the main complexities of Pillar One stems from its political sensitivity. Tax policies and tax politics seem to become intertwined in the quest for a technically robust and socially acceptable outcome. For example, it is the intention that Amount A will be implemented through a multilateral convention (MLC) which, if everything happens according to plan, will be open for signature by mid-2023. This may not exactly be a slam dunk in the current geopolitical context. The Economist pictures today's world through a gloomy lens arguing that unprecedented economic integration has come to a halt and that the system is in peril. It states, 'Countries race to subsidise green industry, lure manufacturing away from friend and foe alike and restrict the flow of goods and capital. Mutual benefit is out, and national gain is in. An era of zero-sum thinking has begun'.[18] Industrial policy is used as an instrument to give a new (protectionist) twist to globalization. The good news for the Organisation for Economic Co-operation and Development Inclusive Framework (OECD/IF) is that countries may

13. I. Verlinden, J.P. Van West & S. De Baets, *Recent Developments on the Two-Pillar Approach, TPI* 241 (2021).
14. OECD (2022), Progress Report on Amount A of Pillar One, Two-Pillar Solution to the Tax Challenges of the Digitalisation of the Economy, OECD/G20 Base Erosion and Profit Shifting Project, OECD, Paris. https://www.oecd.org/tax/beps/progress-report-on-amount-aof-pillar-one-july-2022.pdf, pp. 5-6.
15. I. Verlinden, J.P. Van West & S. De Baets, *supra*, p. 245.
16. OECD, Public Consultation Document Pillar One – Amount B. pp. 3, 6, 7, 20.
17. Tax challenges of digitalisation: OECD invites public input on the design elements of Amount B under Pillar One relating to the simplification of transfer pricing rules – https://www.oecd.org/tax/beps/oecd-invites-public-input-on-the-design-elements-of-amount-b-under-pillar-one-relating-to-the-simplification-of-transfer-pricing-rules.htm.
18. The Economist, 'Zero-Sum: The Destructive Logic That Threatens Globalization', 14 January 2013, p. 9.

continuously seek solutions through fora that promote the virtues of multilateralism and coordination such as the OECD. However, multilateralism may not always lead to the desired outcome for them, definitely when tax sovereignty is at stake. Some scholars claim that 'it would be naïve to imagine that governments limit themselves to efficient policies. From a purely political standpoint, jurisdictions may often confront situations where foreign MNEs are perceived to be entering local markets and earning outsized profits without paying their *fair share*. Efforts to go after the returns to these MNEs may be popular politically without much regard to their long-term economic impact [...]. Governments acting unilaterally pursue their national economic welfare rather than the global economic welfare [...], foreigners generally do not vote'.[19] A focus on national economic welfare implies that tax efficiency comes under pressure. Indeed, a government that extracts economic rents from MNEs to funnel these to their national treasury leads to inefficiencies and externalizes the cost to consumers globally who will need to pay higher prices in the long run. The loss in global welfare may be less of a concern for local governments, and the problem is compounded if they all engage in similar unilateral policies.

The authors believe (and hope) that there is more doom and gloom in this statement than what effectively lies ahead of us. The current trend away from hyper-globalization may not render multilateral cooperation a fiction. Instead, there seems to be a new form of globalization that will not eliminate cross-border cooperation whatsoever. Countries have an interest in leveraging network power to ensure that they have sufficient food, fuel, and consumer demand. From financial networks to production networks to social networks, the companies and countries that own their own or work with allies to own them will do their best. Vertical integration among corporations, for example, is once again gaining momentum as leaders look to buffer supply-chain disruptions, cut transport costs, and reduce geopolitical risk. Regional innovation clusters become the norm thanks to the popularity of decentralized technologies. Blockchain and other decentralized ways of moving and sharing data, although still imperfect, will advance and spread.[20]

What does this side-step to the current geo-political context mean? What if one or more of the world's largest economies does not sign the MLC? This could have the consequence to empty the scope of Pillar One and drastically diminish its application, possibly up to the point that it would even be meaningless to apply Amount A. Without

19. J. Bankman, M. Kane & A. Sykes, Collecting the Rent: Global Battle to Capture MNE Profits, Working Paper Series, Paper No. 527, Stanford Law School, can be downloaded from the Social Science Research Network Electronic Paper Collection, http://ssrn.com/abstract=3273112, p. 11.
20. R. Foroohar, Homecoming: The Path to Prosperity in a Post-Global World, Crown, an imprint of Random House, a division of Penguin Random House LLC, New York, (2022). The author observes that one of the most pernicious parts of globalization is that it has made the planet wealthier as a whole, though it is concentrated largely at the very top. Today's world does not reflect a free-market system that allows productive and fair transactions between buyers and sellers who exist equally but instead a system of concentrated power and oligopoly. The author pleads that businesses and communities reinvent themselves in a new, post-neoliberal world. A different 'globalization' will be the result marked by new regional innovation hubs in order to avoid future shocks, p. 318; *see also* R. Foorohar, *My Guide to a Deglobalizing World*, Financial Times, 28 October 2022, https://www.ft.com/content/f4c17c8c-9097-417e-94d6-36825fe85c24.

the signatures of all *key* countries, Amount A will fail its intended purpose of a reallocation of part of the profits of the biggest and most profitable multinational companies. Even though the signature of the MLC would be an enormous step toward the implementation process, another significant hurdle is its ratification. Assuming that all key countries would sign the MLC, it would still need to pass parliamentary approval of those countries, which can take years (*see*, for example, the BEPS multilateral instrument). At that stage, the Parliament or another constitutional body may also decide not to ratify. Please allow us to say that this raises some serious doubts regarding the feasibility/application of the Pillar One project and particularly Amount A. The way forward for Amount B is still unknown. Some question *what if Amount B is all there is*?[21] Others state that it might work when embedded in the OECD Transfer Pricing Guidelines (OECD TPG).[22]

Actually, in reality, the project is no longer about taxing the digital economy but has proceeded to taxing all major and profitable MNEs that also use digital tools in this modern world. It also regards the tax treatment of sales and marketing enterprises if countries think they do not earn enough as the *intangibles' sweetie trolley* is outside their reach for taxation.

Now, buckle up for the ABCs of Amount A and Amount B.

3 AMOUNT A

In this section, the authors will discuss the recent developments with regard to Amount A and how it is achieved. Then, we will deep dive into the mechanics of Amount A with some critical notes on the side. Further, the TP issues will be addressed followed by a discussion on how digital services taxes (DSTs) are treated and how the European Union views Amount A. Finally, the authors provide some interim conclusions.

3.1 Recent Developments and Formulary Apportionment

In recent years, the perception that MNEs do not pay their *fair* share of tax has been headline news. The accompanying public perception has placed an increasing amount of pressure towards realizing a radical reform to the way the international fiscal system taxes MNEs.[23] The OECD TPG and the ALP have not been spared of this criticism and have even become a focal point. The position that TP rules facilitate tax avoidance that leads to abusive or inappropriate intercompany pricing rather than a way to protect against tax avoidance[24] has led some to adopt the term 'transfer mispricing'.[25] The authors doubt the accuracy and grounds for justification of these allegations as the ALP

21. R. Goulder, *What If Amount B Is All There Is?*, 109 Tax Notes International 281 (9 January 2023).
22. R. Finley, Amount B Proposal Holds Promise, but It Needs Work, 108 Tax Notes International 18-19 (2 January 2023).
23. A. Pepper, J. Coleman & T. Bettge, *Why It's Still Not Time for Global Formulary Apportionment*, 107 Tax Notes International 912 (22 August 2022).
24. P. Sikka, *Shifting Profits Across Borders*, The Guardian, 12 February 2009.
25. A. Pepper, J. Coleman & T. Bettge, *Why It's Still Not Time for Global Formulary Apportionment*, 107 Tax Notes International 912 (22 August 2022).

proves every day to properly accommodate millions of transactions worldwide. Anyway, as the saying goes, *perception is reality,* thus the energy needed to eliminate it will come at a high opportunity cost.[26]

It is in this context that the BEPS Project came into existence with the intent of eliminating these issues by bolstering some of the international tax rules with a specific emphasis perhaps on the TP and/or profit allocation. Just to recap, BEPS Action 7 on avoiding permanent establishment (PE) abuse, BEPS Actions 8-10 on TP outcomes in line with value creation, BEPS Action 13 on TP documentation, and BEPS Action 14 on improving the mutual agreement procedure (MAP), among others, have a specific focus on TP or profit allocation. While the result of the BEPS Project can be seen as a considerable progression in combating tax planning predominantly stemming from shifting risk by contract, its success in terms of political endorsement of its societal goals effectuates mixed views (not to say emotions). When following it, many countries were not satisfied with the way taxing rights were shared between source and residence states.[27] As a result, the same pressures continued to be relevant and have played an important role in motivating governments to move forward with the new two-pillar approach.[28]

In times of difficulty, old ideas are often revisited, and the international tax landscape is no exception to this. Some academics and particularly the European Commission (EC) are once again asking whether now is the time to leave the ALP behind and adopt formulary apportionment.[29] The momentum is mounting given the fact that the OECD has now also proposed a formulaic approach (for part of the taxable basis) in the new two-pillar approach. Specifically, under the income reallocation rules of Pillar One, Amount A is dealt with in a formulaic way. Does this indicate that the OECD has taken a first step in abandoning – or at least softening the link with – the ALP with a view towards a global formulary apportionment system? At least the discussion on formulary apportionment has morphed from a taboo in OECD circles to a state of agnosticism.[30]

26. For a more elaborated view on the merits and demerits of the ALP, *see* M. Lang & R. Petruzzi -(eds) *Transfer Pricing Developments Around the World 2022* 69 (2022).
27. P. Marley, *Is It Time to Admit the Failure of Pillar One?*, 107 Tax Notes International 1531-1533 (26 September 2022).
28. J. Andrus & R. Collier, *Transfer Pricing and the Arm's-Length Principle after the Pillars*, 105 Tax Notes International 544-546 (31 January 2022).
29. Formulary apportionment is an alternate way to allocate taxing rights over multinationals that was first considered and rejected by the League of Nations in the 1930s; A. Pepper, J. Coleman & T. Bettge, *Why It's Still Not Time for Global Formulary Apportionment*, 107 Tax Notes International 911 (22 August 2022). In that respect, reference can also be made to the Business in Europe – Framework in Taxation (BEFIT) Project launched by the European Commission. A discussion on BEFIT is outside the scope of this chapter, but more information can be found on the Website of the European Commission.
30. OECD TPG § 1.32 still rejects formulary apportionment – At the Seoul IFA Congress in 2018, Pascal Saint Amans – as Director of the Centre for Tax Policy and Administration (CTPA) – indicated that the OECD is agnostic on the ALP. *See also* S. Soong Johnston, *OECD Makes Headway on Long-Term Answers to Tax Digital Economy*, Tax Notes International Today (6 September 2018).

3.2 Amount A: What Is It?

3.2.1 Formulaic Approach: It Is All about Data, but the Question Remains: What Data and How Is It to Be Sourced and Used?

The OECD has opted for a formulaic basis for the calculation and allocation of Amount A. As a next logical step, it should be asked what formula is used to allocate profits and on what grounds does this formula find its basis. There are many allocation factors that can be chosen, i.e., employee headcount, payroll, property, sales, etc. Furthermore, there is the question about the weighting that can be applied to these factors based on their importance.[31]

The formulaic approach of Amount A relies on the revenue of the covered group in the market/user jurisdiction and is thus sales-based in principle. The general idea of this type of formulary approach is to shift the taxation of MNEs from where they have employees and operations to where their products are consumed or used.[32]

A sales-based formulary approach entails difficulty in sourcing sales. This is augmented by the very element Pillar One also seeks to target, i.e., the digital economy. The important role of e-commerce makes it incredibly challenging to reliably identify the ultimate destination of goods and services. In short, the globalization and granularization of international supply chains complicate the development of effective sourcing rules for tangible goods and also for digital items, such as streaming services or other 'intangible' products such as online advertising. To achieve this goal, a company might need to identify the ultimate client which may mean they have to ask their direct client (which may be a third party) for the data of the client's client.[33] Along this convoluted process of data sourcing, confidentiality issues will most likely arise.

Implementation of a sales-based formulary approach becomes even more complex when the sourcing of revenue from services or intangibles is thrown into the equation. Take a simple example of one of the industries that Pillar One is targeting. Streaming platform companies spend hundreds of millions of euros licensing content from other media companies. It would not be atypical for all of them to be based in the United States with a single global licence for content agreed between them. Given the situation, should the full amount be sourced to the United States, or should the company be required to source the revenue among countries based on how much their citizens watch or pay to watch the licensed content?[34] If this option is chosen (however unlikely), this could lead to interesting evolutions as the use of a VPN could have an impact on where streaming companies would ultimately pay tax.

31. A. Pepper, J. Coleman & T. Bettge, *Why It's Still Not Time for Global Formulary Apportionment*, 107 Tax Notes International 915-916 (911-922) (22 August 2022).
32. A. Pepper, J. Coleman and T. Bettge, *Why It's Still Not Time for Global Formulary Apportionment*, 107 Tax Notes International 915-916 (911-922) (22 August 2022).
33. A. Pepper, J. Coleman & T. Bettge, *Why It's Still Not Time for Global Formulary Apportionment*, 107 Tax Notes International 915-916 (22 August 2022).
34. A. Pepper, J. Coleman & T. Bettge, *Why It's Still Not Time for Global Formulary Apportionment*, 107 Tax Notes International 917 (22 August 2022).

Thus, questions will be raised as to the practicality of MNEs identifying the location of their customers for every transaction that is made. In drafting the wider Pillar One Amount A framework, the OECD has recognized this challenge and incorporated the possibility within the draft rules to use target proxies or allocation keys based on macroeconomic data on consumption expenditure. These methods can be utilized by companies in the event that identifying the location of the final customer is overly burdensome or impossible. In this way, the OECD is attempting to achieve a balance between the compliance burden and ensuring that Amount A profits are reliably taxed.[35]

3.2.2 *The Six-Step Approach*

As briefly touched upon in the bird's eye overview, the different steps of the formula for allocating profits to the market/user states are as follows (if revenue exceeds EUR 20 billion):

> Step 1: The PBT must be determined.
> Step 2: The PBT must be adjusted for certain items, such as Asset Fair Value or Impairment Adjustments; Acquired Equity Basis Adjustments; Asset Gain (or Loss) Spreading Adjustments; and possibly the treatment of profit attributable to non-controlling interests (there has been no consensus on this last item at the moment of writing this chapter). For ease of compliance, there are links with the Pillar Two PBT determination, but the adjustments are not entirely the same.
> Step 3: If the PBT adjusted under step two is higher than 10%, 25% of the excess (X% minus 10%) is, in principle, reallocated to the market states.
> Step 4: Determine the pro rata part of Amount A for each country entitled to receive Amount A profit taking into consideration the Marketing and Distribution Safe Harbour (MDSH).
> Step 5: Identify the relieving countries in order to avoid double taxation.
> Step 6: Allocate part of the Amount A profit to the relieving countries in order to avoid double taxation.

In its progress report, this formula is reproduced algebraically as:[36]

reallocated profit = (adjusted PBT - 10% of adjusted group revenue) × jurisdictional group revenue/adjusted group revenue

35. OECD Progress Report on Amount A of Pillar One, July 2022, Frequently Asked Questions, Question 5, pp. 2-3.
36. OECD (2022), Progress Report on Amount A of Pillar One, Two-Pillar Solution to the Tax Challenges of the Digitalisation of the Economy, OECD/G20 Base Erosion and Profit Shifting Project, OECD, Paris, p. 16.

A more detailed discussion follows below.

After expanding on the OECD's formulaic approach for Amount A, questions can be asked regarding the objectivity of such an approach. Can the OECD label its chosen allocation factor as not only the most appropriate method for eliminating the nexus problem but also as an objective approach? With regard to the latter, (perceived) objectivity risks being watered down by elements that are more politically driven, such as trade deficits, trade surpluses, level of payroll costs, etc.

Pepper (a former OECD official), Coleman, and Bettge propose the concept that 'the main issue in any international discussion on formulary apportionment would be the formula itself'.[37] Unlike the profit allocation based on the ALP, a wide variety of policy rationales can be imagined that can support different formulas in various circumstances, therefore, the choice of one or more of these factors is much more likely to create a feeling of arbitrariness. Stated in a different manner, what is the rationale for the choice of one or more of the factors?

Needless to say, levelling the global playing field amid the current societal, environmental, and economic geopolitical pressures that the world economy faces is fertile soil for thinking of alternatives.

Formulary, apportionment for both the full pool and the residual profit (or parts thereof such as under Pillar One) may be ideal in a world where multilateralism fully reigns. That may be difficult to achieve in the current geopolitical context. Countries will need to agree on common tax accounting rules to corner the amount subject to the formula in a first instance. Second, they will need to find a common formula and, lastly, they have to cooperate intensively and durably in order to assess the overall amount and the per-state amount of the economic factors that enter the formula.[38]

The view that there is no objectively proper or fair way to allocate profits was reached almost a century ago by the US National Tax Association when it concluded that all methods of apportionment are arbitrary and that the only correct rule is one 'on which several states can and will get together as a matter of comity'.[39]

The authors of this article feel a similar sentiment towards the objective character of the formulary approach of Amount A – the correct rule will be one upon which the OECD/IF countries ultimately can agree. In this respect, it remains uncertain if Amount A's formulary-based approach will fall prey to the same issue that has prevented global formulary apportionment as an international tax standard or whether the OECD/IF countries can find an agreement.

37. A.A. Pepper, J. Coleman & T. Bettge, *Why It's Still Not Time for Global Formulary Apportionment*, 107 Tax Notes International 919 (22 August 2022).
38. U. Schreiber et al., *Why the Arm's Length Principle Should Be Maintained*, International Transfer Pricing Journal 414-415 (November/December 2020).
39. A. Pepper, J. Coleman & T. Bettge, *Why It's Still Not Time for Global Formulary Apportionment*, 107 Tax Notes International 919 (22 August 2022).

3.3 Amount A: How Does It Work?

3.3.1 The Scope of Amount A

Following the description from the OECD in Action One – Tax Challenges Arising from Digitalisation: 'Pillar One will ensure a *fairer* [emphasis added] distribution of profits and taxing rights among countries with respect to the largest MNEs, including digital companies. It would re-allocate some taxing rights over MNEs from their home countries to the markets where they have business activities and earn profits, regardless of whether firms have a physical presence there.'[40] Thus, MNEs falling within the scope of Amount A will have a share of their consolidated profit reallocated to market jurisdictions under certain conditions.

The scope of Amount A is based upon quantitative thresholds, i.e., any MNE that meets the scope thresholds will have to apply the Amount A rules regardless of what industry it performs its activities.[41] The scope of Amount A, therefore, does not refer specifically to the 'digital' economy but encompasses it if the thresholds are met. The scope thresholds comprise two parts targeting MNEs with revenues greater than EUR 20 billion and profitability greater than 10%. These thresholds apply at a group level with the financial data of an MNE's consolidated financial statements as its basis.

Segmentation will occur in exceptional cases which refers to a situation where an MNE does not meet the profitability threshold, but a segment reported in the MNE's consolidated financial statements has revenues greater than EUR 20 billion and profitability greater than 10% on a standalone basis. In that case, solely that disclosed segment will be in the scope of Amount A.[42]

Amount A rules foresee the exclusion of the extractive industry and the Regulated Financial Services industry. It is based upon a predominance test that examines whether 75% of the revenues are related to activities excluded from Amount A.[43] When the 75% excluded revenue test is not met, Amount A rules will still be applicable. The exclusion is applied by removing the revenues and associated costs that are related to activities that are not in the scope of Amount A in order to recalculate the MNE's remaining revenue and profit.

3.3.2 Nexus and Revenue Sourcing Rules

Once an MNE falls within the scope of the Amount A rules, a determination needs to be made of how much revenue it generates in each of its market countries. Amount A

40. OECD Progress Report on Amount A of Pillar One, July 2022, Frequently Asked Questions, Question 5, pp. 2-3.
41. Excluding the out of scope sectors of the extractive industry and the regulated financial services industry.
42. OECD Progress Report on Amount A of Pillar One, July 2022, Frequently Asked Questions, Question 3, pp. 1-2.
43. OECD (2022), Progress Report on Amount A of Pillar One, Two-Pillar Solution to the Tax Challenges of the Digitalisation of the Economy, OECD/G20 Base Erosion and Profit Shifting Project, OECD, Paris, pp. 8 and 38.

profit will only be reallocated to market countries when the MNE meets the new quantitative special purpose nexus test even if no physical presence exists in that market country. This test is satisfied when an MNE generates more than EUR 1 million in revenues in a market country per the revenue sourcing rules. Despite this threshold, the OECD/IF set out to guarantee that smaller countries will also benefit from the implementation of Amount A. In this way, a lower nexus threshold of EUR 250,000 applies when a country's GDP is less than EUR 40 billion.[44]

Revenue sourcing rules will need to be applied to identify the jurisdiction where revenue arises for the purposes of Amount A. This is to be completed on a transaction-by-transaction basis, and the rules are based on categories of transactions (e.g., sales of finished goods, services, etc.) with multiple subcategories. A transaction and not an invoice is the item that generates income. Transactions under multiple categories are sourced depending on their 'predominant character'. The rules are based on a range of indicators and allocation keys using 'reliable method' indicators (e.g., location of customer) and allocation keys (e.g., headcount) specific to the transaction category.[45]

The tax base determination rules establish the profit of in-scope MNEs that will be used for the Amount A calculations to reallocate a portion of their profits to market jurisdictions. The tax base or profit will be determined by reference to financial accounting income with 'a small number of adjustments'. Losses will be carried forward.[46] After determining the tax base for the in-scope MNE, 25% of the residual profit[47] (defined as profit in excess of 10% of revenue) will be allocated to market jurisdictions with a sufficient nexus using a 'revenue-based' allocation key.[48]

3.3.3 *Marketing and Distribution Profits Safe Harbour (MDSH)*

Following the OECD's guidance on the new safe harbour rule, the measure aims to 'adjust the allocation of Amount A for market jurisdictions that already have existing taxing rights over the Group's residual profits'. It is thus primarily designed towards the prevention of double taxation. This may occur if a market jurisdiction has the ability to tax the residual profits of an MNE in two ways, i.e., once through the existing – traditional – profit allocation rules (source and residence-based) and again through Amount A allocations.[49]

44. Countries with a GDP lower than EUR 40 billion include: Estonia, Burkina Faso, Cameroon, Senegal, etc.
45. OECD (2022), Progress Report on Amount A of Pillar One, Two-Pillar Solution to the Tax Challenges of the Digitalisation of the Economy, OECD/G20 Base Erosion and Profit Shifting Project, OECD, Paris, p. 13.
46. OECD (2022), Progress Report on Amount A of Pillar One, Two-Pillar Solution to the Tax Challenges of the Digitalisation of the Economy, OECD/G20 Base Erosion and Profit Shifting Project, OECD, Paris, p. 15.
47. To avoid any misinterpretation, the term 'residual profit' is used in a different context than the term that is used under a residual profit split methodology.
48. OECD (2022), Progress Report on Amount A of Pillar One, Two-Pillar Solution to the Tax Challenges of the Digitalisation of the Economy, OECD/G20 Base Erosion and Profit Shifting Project, OECD, Paris, p. 16.
49. L. Eden, *The (Not So) Simple Analytics of the New Amount A*, 107 Tax Notes International 1491 (1487-1501) (26 September 2022).

To prevent this, an additional step is included in the calculation of Amount A. A capping mechanism is introduced to reduce the profit reallocated to a specific country by the amount of residual profit already taxed there. This mechanism accords with the same jurisdictional and qualitative approach also used in connection with the elimination of double taxation. Thus, this includes a formula to determine the precise amount of the reduction for each market jurisdiction and quantitative criteria to identify residual profits already taxed in a market country.[50]

The safe harbour should apply to all profit earned by an MNE's subsidiaries and PEs in a market jurisdiction.[51] As a result, the original name of the 'safe harbour for routine marketing and distribution activities' has become obsolete as Amount A now includes all industries except for the regulated financial and extractive sectors. To alleviate this confusion, a change of name may be in order particularly because the MDSH is based on tangible assets and payroll factors and not on marketing and distribution.

It is important to note that the Amount A allocations and the interaction of this adjustment with the elimination of the double taxation mechanism are still under development at the moment of writing this chapter.

A remaining question is: who will benefit from the safe harbour, jurisdictions or MNEs? That is also unclear at the moment of writing this chapter.

3.3.4 The Prevention of Double Taxation

Based upon the latest documents published on Amount A, the obligation to eliminate double taxation that would otherwise be suffered by an MNE will be allocated among countries using a quantitative approach. It is designed to ensure that the obligation is borne by the countries in which the MNE earns its residual profits. Those countries will be divided into tiers based upon the MNE's profitability in each of them (measured by reference to a new profit indicator, i.e., the return on depreciation (of tangible assets) and payroll (RODP) relative to the MNE's overall profitability. Double taxation would first be relieved by countries identified in the highest profit tiers. This relief mechanism has been labelled as the 'waterfall and pro rata approach'. Currently, the tiers are determined as follows:[52]

- tier 1: jurisdictions where the RODP is greater than fifteen times the RODP of the group;
- tier 2: jurisdictions under tier 1 and other jurisdictions where the RODP is greater than 1.5 times the RODP of the group;

50. OECD (2022), Progress Report on Amount A of Pillar One, Two-Pillar Solution to the Tax Challenges of the Digitalisation of the Economy, OECD/G20 Base Erosion and Profit Shifting Project, OECD, Paris, p. 7.
51. L. Eden, *The (Not So) Simple Analytics of the New Amount A*, 107 Tax Notes International 1491 (26 September 2022).
52. OECD (2022), Progress Report on Amount A of Pillar One, Two-Pillar Solution to the Tax Challenges of the Digitalisation of the Economy, OECD/G20 Base Erosion and Profit Shifting Project, OECD, Paris, p. 19.

- tier 3A: Tier 2 jurisdictions and other jurisdictions where the RODP exceeds 40% of the elimination threshold of the RODP of the group. The elimination value is set at 10% of the group's in-scope third-party sales divided by its depreciation and payroll (equals the routine or non-residual profits under Amount A); and
- tier 3B: Other jurisdictions where the RODP is greater than the elimination threshold mentioned above.[53]

Double taxation is relieved in the following manner. First, the jurisdictions in the scope of tier 1 are relevant. The jurisdictions are ranked by order of tier; the highest ratio in the tier comes first. The amount allocated to the first jurisdiction on the list of tier 1 is limited to what would reduce its RODP to the level of the second jurisdiction on the list if need be (if the relief to be given has not yet been exhausted), and so on. If the tier 1 jurisdictions cannot fully relieve double taxation, then the tier 2 jurisdictions become a factor until their residual profits are exhausted. Any remaining amount is then allocated to jurisdictions under tier 3A and, if needed, under tier 3B.[54]

Confused? Have another read ... and, be assured ... you are not the only one.

3.3.5 *Evolution and Aim: Is Pillar One Amount A Still Aligned with Reaching the Goals Originally Set Out by the OECD in Its First Blueprint?*

It becomes apparent when consulting the OECD blueprint that the original purpose of Pillar One was to reconcile the current international tax rules with the new developments of an increasingly digital world. The key obstacle that effectuated Pillar One can be described as follows: 'In an increasingly digital age, in scope businesses are able to generate profits through participation in a significant/active and sustained way in the economic life of a jurisdiction, beyond the mere conclusion of sales, with or without the benefit of local physical presence.'[55]

This obstacle of businesses generating profit without the benefit of a local physical presence cannot be overcome by the current income allocation rules. The dual approach of source taxation by host countries combined with residence taxation by home countries have either the physical presence of the MNE in a country, i.e., MNE global profits are either taxed where the profits are earned through a physical presence (subsidiary or PE) or where the MNE shareholders or headquarters are located as their basis.[56] The OECD's proposal on Amount A would drastically novelize the current

53. OECD Progress Report on Amount A of Pillar One, July 2022, Frequently Asked Questions, Question 9, p. 4.
54. OECD Progress Report on Amount A of Pillar One, July 2022, Frequently Asked Questions, Question 9, p. 4.
55. OECD (2020), Tax Challenges Arising from Digitalisation – Report on Pillar One Blueprint: Inclusive Framework on BEPS, OECD/G20 Base Erosion and Profit Shifting Project, OECD Publishing, Paris. https://doi.org/10.1787/beba0634-enp. 8.
56. L. Eden, *The (Not So) Simple Analytics of the New Amount A*, 107 Tax Notes International 1500-1501 (26 September 2022).

system as it would envision shifting a certain amount of the MNE's global profits from source and residence jurisdictions to market jurisdictions.[57] Reflecting further on the concept of profit allocation to market jurisdictions could lead to a hasty conclusion of a seemingly perfect fit to the nexus problem. The introduction of this concept would allow jurisdictions to capture part of the MNE's profit for which they have no claim under the current distributive rules.

After having discussed the objective of Amount A and the methodology with which it aims to achieve it, an important question to ask is, after the long development process, is Amount A still aligned with the original goals of Pillar One as set out by the OECD in its original blueprint?

To answer this question, the key objective of 'businesses being able to generate profits beyond the mere conclusion of sales, with or without the benefit of local physical presence' is assessed from the framework of the OECD's original blueprint on Pillar One and compared with the latest rules present in the OECD's July 2022 progress report.[58]

When conducting the analysis of the new Amount A rules, several other key issues or concerns are revealed. One of these is the increased obscurity of who will ultimately benefit from the introduction of Amount A rules. Based upon the OECD's blueprint, it was clear that Amount A would generate the most benefits to tax jurisdictions where foreign MNEs have a major market presence but declare little profits. Examples of such entities include MNEs with large destination-based sales that have no taxable presence in those foreign countries, i.e., having no subsidiary, foreign branch, or PE or only a subsidiary or PE that earns limited returns (e.g., low-risk distributors).[59]

A shift in reasoning is being observed as the project proceeds. Where the focus was previously on MNEs' destination-based sales activities in the form of exports and in-country sales by their affiliates, the approach now no longer includes that focus as the word 'sales' in the formula has been replaced with the word 'revenues' throughout the progress report. Correspondingly, a core driver of the Pillar One Amount A project, i.e., the situation in which MNEs are substantially profiting from sales in market jurisdictions without a physical taxable presence there has collapsed by shifting from global in-scope destination-based sales (GIDS) to revenues.[60]

Important elements of the initial Amount A proposal are hence seemingly left behind. Indeed, Amount A provides less of a tailored response to the key objectives than those set out in the 2020 OECD blueprint. Additionally, the ambiguity surrounding who would ultimately benefit[61] from the implementation of Amount A can bring into question its chances of successful adoption by countries (at least in its current form).

57. OECD, 'Progress Report on Amount A of Pillar One: Two-Pillar Solution to the Tax Challenges of the Digitalisation of the Economy', p. 8.
58. OECD, 'Progress Report on Amount A of Pillar One: Two-Pillar Solution to the Tax Challenges of the Digitalisation of the Economy'.
59. L. Eden, *The (Not So) Simple Analytics of the New Amount A*, 107 Tax Notes International 1496-1497 (26 September 2022).
60. L. Eden, *The (Not So) Simple Analytics of the New Amount A*, 107 Tax Notes International, 1491 (26 September 2022).
61. It is very likely that the United States – when it adheres to the MLC – will have to surrender a significant part of its existing taxing rights on profits of MNEs. Following the OECD/G20 BEPS

Amount A, as defined in the OECD/IF's July 2022 progress report differs from the version originally described in the 2020 Blueprint as Professor Dr Lorraine Eden describes: (i) it is less aligned with the original goals of Pillar One; and (ii) it is more difficult to estimate, implement, and administer; offers greater opportunities for manipulation; and is more likely to benefit low-income countries with a large market.[62]

Another question is whether the proposed system under Amount A is future proof. Only time can tell of course, but it may be wondered, e.g., whether the Metaverse does not command radical thinking on a new distributive rule. The OECD and EU Commission are considering taxation of non-fungible tokens (NFT), cryptocurrencies, and digital ledger technologies. Will those find a fit in the Amount A approach, or is Amount A already outdated before it commences? Support for Amount A as a key feature of the international taxation system for the next 100 years is diminishing.

3.3.6 Tax-Base-Relieving Process

The new Amount A rules provide less clarity on the jurisdictions that would ultimately benefit from its implementation. An important element to assess which jurisdictions will gain from Amount A is the tax-base-relieving process. It determines who will ultimately bear the cost for Amount A which consequently affects the administrative and dispute settlement costs.

The tax-base-relieving system of Amount A is built on the premise of the jurisdiction providing tax-base relief by effectively transferring its taxing rights to a specific portion of the MNE tax base in perpetuity to other jurisdictions. This transfer is to be completed without knowing which jurisdictions are receiving that base or what will be levied on it. In this way, each tax base relieving jurisdiction must commit to waiving its taxing rights over a specific portion of the MNE tax base. Somewhat ironically, the OECD/IF refers to the system as the relief of double taxation by giving up a part of the taxing rights to other jurisdictions. The political question once again arises. Jurisdictions will, of course, count their dues. If the result is negative to a large extent, the question is whether the jurisdiction will be easily lured to sign up for the MLC. A new one would indeed be created to enforce that commitment in order to ensure the effective working of this process despite that it may remain a difficult process to convince governments to forfeit part of their sovereign rights to tax.

Over the last decade, the OECD Model Convention framework has placed the ownership of intangible assets and connected senior headcount involvement (under the Development, Enhancement, Maintenance, Protection and Exploitation (DEMPE) acronym) at the foreground of determining the allocation of the system profit of entities. Consequently, MNEs' system profits in the current global market are closely

Action 1 – Tax Challenges Arising from Digitalisation – under the Two-Pillar project, it follows that 'Under Pillar One, taxing rights on more than USD 125 billion of profit are expected to be reallocated to market jurisdictions each year.' *See* International community strikes a ground-breaking tax deal for the digital age, available at https://www.oecd.org/tax/international-community-strikes-a-ground-breaking-tax-deal-for-the-digital-age.htm.

62. L. Eden, *The (Not So) Simple Analytics of the New Amount A*, 107 Tax Notes International 1500-1501 (26 September 2022).

associated more with their intangible assets and less with their property, plants, and equipment or (some of their) labour costs. Following this, it is difficult to establish a linear connection between a jurisdiction's share of taxable profit and its share of the direct product cost (DPC) of an MNE. Therefore, the question of who will ultimately bear the cost for Amount A will remain both highly uncertain and uneven in any formula based on the DPC.[63]

The authors praise the efforts by the OECD/IF to make the international tax rules *better* and would hate to cry wolf with cynics who see similarities between Pillar One, Amount A rules, and a Rube Goldberg machine.[64] This being stated, objectively, the feeling cannot be set aside that it has become increasingly convoluted resulting in less certainty regarding what the impact will be of the implementation and who would benefit or lose the most from that implementation. It becomes apparent that the focus has shifted away from the original aim of Pillar One, i.e., the taxation of the digitalization of the economy.

3.3.7 Dispute Resolution

Based on the convoluted nature of Pillar One Amount A rules, dispute prevention and dispute resolution are both important aspects for determining the robustness of the Pillar One framework. The Global IFA/ICC Webinar on Preventing and Resolving International Tax Disputes provided additional insight into the dispute resolution process as of 2024.[65] As indicated in the public consultation document on a tax certainty framework for Amount A,[66] a three-tiered approach is considered for dispute prevention and resolution: (1) a scope certainty review to give certainty that an MNE is not in the scope of Amount A;[67] (2) an advance certainty review to provide *ex ante* certainty over the Amount A methodology that an MNE used;[68] and (3) a comprehensive certainty review[69] to provide an MNE *ex post* binding multilateral certainty over its application of the Amount A rules. As the OECD Secretariat indicated during the Global IFA/ICC Webinar, parallels can be drawn between the existing mechanisms and the Amount A certainty processes. An 'Advanced Certainty Review' would find its roots in advanced pricing agreements (APA). Furthermore, a 'Scope Certainty review' would parallel the cooperative compliance programme. Lastly, a 'Comprehensive Certainty

63. OECD (2020), Tax Challenges Arising from Digitalisation – Report on Pillar One Blueprint: Inclusive Framework on BEPS, OECD/G20 Base Erosion and Profit Shifting Project, OECD Publishing, Paris. https://doi.org/10.1787/beba0634-en, p. 8.
64. A chain reaction type machine intentionally designed to perform a simple task in an overcomplicated way that is named after its investor who is an American cartoonist.
65. The Global IFA/ICC Webinar on Preventing and Resolving International Tax Disputes, 26 January 2023.
66. OECD Public Consultation Document Pillar One – A Tax Certainty Framework for Amount A.
67. OECD Public Consultation Document Pillar One – A Tax Certainty Framework for Amount A, p. 5.
68. OECD Public Consultation Document Pillar One – A Tax Certainty Framework for Amount A, p. 6.
69. OECD Public Consultation Document Pillar One – A Tax Certainty Framework for Amount A, p. 6.

Review' would be achieved through audits. Dispute resolution will adhere to the MAP procedure and review, and determination panels will be established through the MLC. Suggested rules for the composition of the review panel and determination panel were described in the consultation document and would consist of, i.e., the lead tax administration, relieving countries, and affected countries. They would be smaller in composition than determination panels. When the review panel does not reach an agreement or when an agreement proposed by the panel is not accepted by the competent authority of any concerned party, disagreements will be referred to a determination panel for a final outcome. However, not all parties would be represented on the review or determination panels.

The scope of the dispute resolution process is rather limited. The advance certainty framework outlined in the consultation document does not address advance certainty to a group's approach beyond revenue and segment reporting. It is expected that this limitation will lead to increased use of the comprehensive certainty process. The authors suggest applying advance certainty to all methodology-based elements of computing Amount A and applying it on a case-by-case basis depending on each group's particular facts and circumstances.[70]

In today's world that is marked by increased real-time cooperation between taxpayers and tax authorities, the dispute resolution process through an MAP misses an opportunity by limiting the role of the MNE in the proceedings. Per the consultation document, the role of the MNE is limited to making the request for a MAP and the dispute resolution panel, responding to questions from the competent authorities, and providing the necessary information. The MNE does not have the right to be heard either by the competent authorities or by the dispute resolution panel. The authors believe that greater involvement by the MNE is necessary and will expedite the solutions and increase the transparency of the process.[71]

A red flag that continues through the Pillar One Amount A framework is the complexity of the process. The dispute prevention and resolution rules are no exception to this. The authors propose to simplify the procedure where possible and welcome additional guidance for both the tax authorities and the MNEs.

3.3.8 Problems with Adoption?

There is a lack of clarity stemming from the OECD Pillar One reports, discussion drafts, and estimates (and even realism) regarding the national sovereignty and self-interest behaviours of countries combined with the difficulties of administering Amount A in today's global economy. MNEs and governments are assumed to abide by the rules. Furthermore, the balancing exercise of exerting influence on Amounts A and B between larger jurisdictions with many MNEs in scope and small jurisdictions that are

70. OECD Public Consultation Document on Pillar One – A Tax Certainty Framework for Amount A, Comments by PwC, 10 June 2022, p. 2.
71. OECD Public Consultation Document on Pillar One – A Tax Certainty Framework for Amount A, Comments by European Business Initiative on Taxation – EBIT, 9 June 2022, p. 3.

less able to impact the rules of the game remains difficult. As an example, pharmaceutical companies are in scope for Amount A but regulated financial services are not. Both industries may be earning *above-normal returns* and are highly regulated, however, one is excluded while the other is not. This will affect the distribution of winners and losers.[72] The argument of high regulation used for the exclusion of regulated financial services may not be overly convincing, particularly when looking at the straight jacket-type of a regulatory framework in which the pharma sector operates. Similar thoughts are echoed in other sectors such as in the consumer goods sphere.

Drafting an Amount A framework that is endorsed by multiple stakeholders will be a delicate balancing act. Indeed, an inherent risk of Amount A becoming a new form of protectionism wielded by source countries is imminent.[73]

3.4 TP Issues

The OECD/IF seeks to resolve this nexus issue by introducing a third principle as the basis of income allocation. Next to the arm's length income allocation approach giving tax rights to resident states and source states, Amount A will allocate a certain amount of profits to market jurisdictions (i.e., jurisdictions where MNEs conduct sales activities but have no physical presence).

The TP rules have been an important feature of the international tax system for about a century. However, due to the global expansion of MNEs, increased complexity of shortened supply chains leveraging rapid technological advancement and sustained divergence in countries' tax rates, the determination of where groups should pay tax has become increasingly contested.

Amount A brings with it a shift from an income allocation system that is centred around a revenue and source-based approach to a dual system combining these long-established rules with a destination-based approach. As the OECD/IF set out in their blueprint, this system 'would restore stability to the international tax system'.[74] This stability is achieved by maintaining the tried-and-true core principles of the arm's length standard and TP rules and emboldening them with new income allocation rules catered towards the digitized economy.[75]

However, some have less faith in the compatibility of these two systems and view the implementation of Amount A as an existential threat to the arm's length standard and TP as it is currently known. It remains true that Amount A stems from a different philosophical perspective promoting a destination-based rule to taxation, representing a formulaic approach to allocating taxing rights and using the country-per-country

72. L. Eden, *The (Not So) Simple Analytics of the New Amount A*, 107 Tax Notes International 1492 (26 September 2022).
73. L. Eden, *The (Not So) Simple Analytics of the New Amount A*, 107 Tax Notes International 1499-1500 (26 September 2022).
74. OECD Progress Report on Amount A of Pillar One, July 2022, Frequently Asked Questions, Question 1, p. 1.
75. J. Coleman et al., *The Arm's-Length Standard after the Pillars*, 107 Tax Notes International 1514-1515 (26 September 2022).

income rather than a separate entity. Nonetheless, the discussions on Amount A also provide evidence as to why moving away from the ALP may not be a realistic option.[76]

Amount A applies as an overlay system to the existing profit allocation rules based on the arm's length standard. The choice for this type of system can be considered as an implicit endorsement of the ALP to the detriment of a move to full formulary apportionment.[77]

Finally, through the tax base relieving system, an entity of an MNE that falls into one of the four tiers providing the relief may ultimately be taxed in its residence state on an amount that is less than at arm's length. In particular, questions may arise with regard to the remuneration of the DEMPE functions. These functions may command the highest returns (or losses) under the ALP (once they follow a likewise contractual allocation of risk[78]). Through the Amount A mechanism, part of those returns remunerating the higher risk is shifted to the market states. Advocates of Amount A will defend that only 25% of the excess above 10% profitability is being shifted to the market/users' state. Still, it is a clear break from the principle agreed upon under BEPS 1.0 that TP outcomes should be aligned where value is created. The million-euro question is whether the amount allocated to market/users' states is in sync with the alleged value creation in that state.

3.5 A Solution for DSTs

The importance of successful adoption of Pillar One is inseparably linked to the lack of alternatives that exist to date. In the absence of an IF agreement, a significant risk exists that the failure of Pillar One will not only result in the proliferation of DSTs but also in the adoption of other measures and practices that are fundamentally inconsistent with the ALP.[79] The IF has therefore taken the following precautions.

The IF Statement of 8 October 2021 requests the withdrawal of all DSTs and similar measures and commits to not introduce such measures in the future – at least until 31 December 2023 or the entry into force of the Multilateral Convention introducing Amount A (MLC).[80] Just before the 2022 December holiday season, the OECD/IF launched a public consultation[81] on two draft provisions to be embedded in the MLC

76. J. Coleman et al., *The Arm's-Length Standard after the Pillars*, 107 Tax Notes International 1514-1515 (26 September 2022).
77. J. Coleman et al., *The Arm's-Length Standard after the Pillars*, 107 Tax Notes International 1514-1515 (26 September 2022).
78. An in-depth analysis of the 6-step framework to risk in the OECD TPG is outside the scope of this chapter.
79. J. Coleman et al., *The Arm's-Length Standard after the Pillars*, 107 Tax Notes International 1517 (26 September 2022).
80. OECD / IF – Statement on a Two-Pillar Solution to Address the Tax Challenges Arising from the digitalisation of the Economy 8 October 2021, p. 3.
81. OECD – Public Consultation Document – Pillar One – Amount A: Draft Multilateral Convention Provisions on Digital Services Taxes and other Relevant Similar Measures – 20 December 2022-20 January 2023.

containing the features of the unilateral measures that have to be withdrawn. These features that should all be met are:[82]

- the measure should be determined primarily by reference to the location of the customers or users (or similar criteria – the destination element);
- the measure should be facially discriminatory (applicable almost exclusively to non-residents or non-resident owners); and
- the measure should not be an income tax.

Several taxes or levies, such as VAT, transaction taxes, withholding taxes under a double tax treaty, or rules countering tax abuse are not considered DSTs.[83]

The authors wonder whether this will be sufficient as the proposed provisions leave ample opportunity for circumventing the prohibition to apply a DST. The European Commission's initiative on a digital levy may very well illustrate certain things. According to the inception document, the initiative wants digital companies to pay their fair share and will support revenue generation and help the sustainability of Member States' public finances as well as positively affect the (perceived) social fairness of the tax system. For now, the idea of the digital levy has not moved but could certainly surface.

Countries have introduced or were in the course of introducing DSTs. It might only be a small effort to modify the characteristics of the unilateral measures to fit the conditions to be carved out. In addition, the authors wonder whether the public consultation on the withdrawal of unilateral measures captures all possible DSTs. In particular, the reference to withholding tax carve out might prove to be somewhat problematic. Further, the proposed MLC text on withdrawal seems to leave the choice to countries to either opt for Amount A and receive a part of the Amount A profit or renounce it and maintain the freedom to (continue) to levy DSTs or similar taxes.[84] Such optionality would be contrary to the IF Statement of 8 October 2021 and would not remove what the cynically enhanced might call the DST chaos.

3.6 And What about the European Union?

Pillar One is linked to Pillar Two. Achieving consensus on Pillar Two was not a walk in the park. At least one Member State wanted to have a link between Pillar One and Pillar

82. OECD – Public Consultation Document – Pillar One – Amount A: Draft Multilateral Convention Provisions on Digital Services Taxes and other Relevant Similar Measures, pp. 2 and 5.
83. OECD – Public Consultation Document – Pillar One – Amount A: Draft Multilateral Convention Provisions on Digital Services Taxes and other Relevant Similar Measures, pp. 2 and 6.
84. OECD – Public Consultation Document – Pillar One – Amount A: Draft Multilateral Convention Provisions on Digital Services Taxes and other Relevant Similar Measures, pp. 4 and 5: Article 38(1): Any Party for which a digital services tax or relevant similar measure, or a measure listed in Annex A (List of Existing Measures Subject to Removal), is in force and in effect during a Period:

    a. shall not be allocated any profit under [the MLC provision allocating Amount A] with respect to that Period; and
    b. shall not impose tax with respect to that Period under any domestic law provision implementing the provisions of [the MLC provision allocating Amount A].

Two. The preamble of the Pillar Two Directive[85] and its Article 57 provide that link. That article provides that the EC will inform the Council with an assessment report on the situation regarding the implementation of Pillar One by 30 June 2023 and, if appropriate, submit a legislative proposal to address those tax challenges in the absence of the implementation of the Pillar One solution.

If it is considered that the proceeds of Amount A would be entirely allocated to the EU Member States, then things would need to be rethought. The European Commission is indeed planning to use the potential proceeds of Amount A partly for its own resources. This could already be read in last year's edition of Transfer Pricing Around the World.[86] In its turn, the European Parliament approved the plan of the EC on 23 November 2022 to use part of Amount A for its own resources budget. It is now up to the Council and parliamentary ratification by the Member States.[87]

3.7 Interim Conclusion Amount A

Substantial political capital has been built on the promise to skim part of the *disproportionate* economic rents generated by companies from consumers who are happy to open their wallets without (sufficient) compensation for the countries in which they surf, stream, search, buy online, etc. Looking at the figures then, the return of 25% of the excess above 10% PBT to be allocated to market or user states could lead to a relatively meagre benefit for most countries. The impact assessment presented on 20 January 2023 indicated that approximately USD 100 billion of profit could be reallocated under Pillar One. This would lead to revenue gains between USD 5 and USD 12 billion.[88] These revenue gains have to be divided over the countries entitled to the Amount A allocation. For the OECD, low and middle-income countries would gain the most. However, according to the OECD impact assessment, everyone is a winner except investment hubs (in particular due to Pillar Two). Nonetheless, the USD 200 billion taxing right shift must be offset somewhere else in order to arrive at the zero-sum game. Unfortunately, the impact assessment does not go into that level of granularity. Some countries are probably bound to lose.

The Pillar One Amount A rules have become increasingly convoluted resulting in less certainty on two fronts. On the one hand, it is unclear what the impact will be of the implementation of Amount A while, on the other hand, there is an absence of clarity on which jurisdictions would benefit or lose the most from that implementation. It becomes apparent that the focus has shifted away from the original aim of Pillar One, i.e., taxing the digital economy or digitization of the economy. Instead, it is now among

85. Council Directive (EU) 2022/2523 of 14 December 2022 on ensuring a global minimum level of taxation for multinational enterprise groups and large-scale domestic groups in the Union – 22 December 2022 – OJ L 328/1, p. 7.
86. M. Lang & R. Petruzzi (eds), *Transfer Pricing Developments Around the World 2022* (2022).
87. M. Thompson, *EU Parliament Approves Pillar One as Funding Source for Bloc*, Law 360.
88. OECD Webinar: Economic impact assessment of the Two-Pillar Solution – 18 January 2023 – https://www.oecd.org/tax/beps/webinar-economic-impact-assessment-two-pillar-solution.htm.

the approximately 100 biggest and most profitable MNEs irrespective of the industry in which they are involved (except regulated financial services and extractive industries).

The starting point of Amount A are the consolidated accounts with some adjustments. Its approach mirrors the complexity of Pillar Two but with some divergences in the adjustments to be made to calculate the PBT. The complexity of the in-scope MNE is likely to grow and result in a greater number of burdensome compliance issues.

Another issue that, at the moment of writing this chapter is uncertain, is the question of how many countries will sign up for the MLC introducing Amount A. As an alternative to adopting it, countries might still apply DSTs. In practice, the authors believe that a sour cocktail of Amount A and DSTs might be seen as countries risk being lured towards regimes that generate the juiciest tax revenues. MNEs will be left behind with an amalgam of complex compliance obligations and double burdens.

The discussions on Amount A also provide evidence of why moving away from the ALP risks being cumbersome.[89] As Amount A is an overlay to the existing distributive rules, the ALP stays at the very heart of the action. Therefore, it may be premature to throw away your copy of the OECD TPG yet!

4 AMOUNT B

4.1 Introduction

There are certain dichotomies in the Pillar One project. While the previous section has proven the politically controversial and tumultuous nature of Amount A, Amount B has not yet been scrutinized in the same manner.[90] This could be argued based on the absence of almost any public discussion, including among academia. The authors highly welcome work on Amount B being taken forward. When properly designed and implemented, it spares tax authorities and taxpayers from substantial work when verifying or supporting (as the case may be) millions of transactions for which little amounts risk remaining untaxed. The consultation document on Amount B released by the OECD/IF on 8 December 2022 has certainly initiated the discussion as it brought forward the points of discussion that have been simmering on the back burner.[91] In this line of thinking, the question could be asked if Amount B is controversial. This section will attempt to answer this question mainly based on the consultation document.[92] This introductory part, besides giving the general framework of Amount B, will focus on the goals and envisaged benefits of enacting this policy. In a second section, the primary building blocks of Amount B will be discussed from a high-level perspective. Afterwards, the main lessons learned will be discussed that will address, among others,

89. J. Coleman et al., The Arm's-Length Standard after the Pillars, 107 Tax Notes International 1514-1515 (26 September 2022).
90. As Robert Goulder would joke that the B in Amount B signifies '*boring*'; R. Goulder, *What If Amount B Is All There Is?*, 109 Tax Notes International 281 (9 January 2023.
91. G.S. Cooper. *Building on the Rubble of Pillar One*. 75 Bulletin for International Taxation, IBFD 533 (2021); I.F. Dykes & L.H. Keegan, *The OECD Pillar One Blueprint: Why Amount B Matters*, 75(3) BIT (2021).
92. OECD Public Consultation Document Pillar One – Amount B, § nos 5 and 7.

whether the envisaged benefits are achieved and also some critical notes. Lastly, based on these takeaways, this section will propose a number of recommendations to take up in the future.

Moreover, it should be noted that the authors do not address the specific questions brought up in the consultation document. It is a secretariat paper and represents no consensus (yet) at the OECD/IF level.[93] This chapter refers to the document, however, as if it were written by the OECD/IF.

The goal of Pillar One Amount B is to implement a standardized, simplified, and streamlined solution to determine the remuneration of baseline marketing and distribution activities.[94] It is also noticeable that it actually focuses on buy-sell functions, i.e., a local entity purchases goods from a related party (for example, a manufacturer) for resale to third-party clients.[95] There are other main background elements and much attention is being devoted to the accurate delineation of the actual transaction.[96] Furthermore, the OECD /IF indicates that the suggested approach is in accordance with the ALP.[97] In this regard, it has to be noted that Pillar One Amount B heavily relies on the existing guidance in the OECD TPG which is apparent throughout the consultation document. Some examples are the continued references to the accurate delineation of the transaction, as already mentioned above, and the reliance on the risk assessment analysis of the OECD TPG.[98] The latter might have some implications contrary to the objectives of Amount B, as will be discussed later in this chapter.

The OECD/IF also heavily emphasizes the benefit of the approach for low-capacity jurisdictions which is another term for developing and emerging economies.[99] The consultation document expands on this matter as it mentions that the administrative burden for tax administrations may be disproportionate to the amounts of tax involved. Moreover, the document reiterates the needs and lack of resources of these low-capacity jurisdictions in administering the ALP.[100] In this context, the reasons for the low number of MAP procedures ongoing in developing countries must be considered. This is due to a couple of factors. First, there is the issue of evoking MAP provisions or allowing access to a MAP (leading to no guaranteed outcome). The second cause of this phenomenon can be attributed to the tax treaty network of developing countries. The problem is twofold: On the one hand, their treaty networks are fairly limited while, on the other hand, the tax treaties actually may not always contain a MAP article, or they may have limited (or no) experience with the MAP. Lastly, there are fewer complex TP cases in these low-capacity jurisdictions due to some domestic factors, such as limited

93. OECD IF Public Consultation Document Pillar One – Amount B, p. 5.
94. OECD IF Public Consultation Document Pillar One – Amount B, § nos 1-3.
95. OECD IF Public Consultation Document Pillar One – Amount B, § no. 7.
96. OECD Public Consultation Document Pillar One – Amount B, On the accurate delineation of transactions, *see* § nos 8, 16, 17, 18, 22, 27, 33, Box 3.1, 87; On the risk assessment analysis, *see* § nos 83, 88, 89.
97. OECD / IF – Statement on a Two-Pillar Solution to Address the Tax Challenges Arising from the digitalisation of the Economy 8 October 2021, p. 3; OECD Public Consultation Document Pillar One – Amount B, § no. 5.
98. OECD Public Consultation Document Pillar One – Amount B, § no. 5.
99. OECD Public Consultation Document Pillar One – Amount B, p. 3.
100. OECD Public Consultation Document Pillar One – Amount B, § no. 43.

resources, shortage of (local) comparables, and lack of enabling legislation in place. Taking into account these circumstances, it is clear how these low-capacity jurisdictions could potentially benefit from an overall simplification and streamlining policy such as Amount B. It would permit them to focus their resources on cases that are more complex or on treaty renegotiations because of the alleviated burden on the administration.

It is still unsure at the moment of writing this chapter what approach the OECD/IF is going to take. Will the work be implemented through safe harbour rules, as a rebuttable presumption, or yet another format? The instrument of implementation remains unknown. Some possibilities are, for example, a simple incorporation as guidance in the OECD TPG (soft law approach), through treaty changes possibly through a modification of existing double tax treaties, or through a multilateral instrument or convention or even both.[101] The option of a multilateral instrument could effectively be combined with Amount A into a true *Pillar One* MLC. However, the same problems might arise as those under the BEPS MLI including late ratification and implementation, among others.[102] Perhaps these questions can be answered by mid-2023 as the final approach is to be released by that time. On a final note, technically, Amount A and Amount B are not Siamese twins and can be implemented separately.

The impact of Amount B can be quite considerable as it will affect all MNEs. Contrary to Amount A (MNE with revenue of more than EUR 20 billion and profitability of 10%) or Pillar Two (MNE with revenue of more than EUR 750 million), Amount B does not have a threshold, therefore, many more MNEs can or will be affected by it.

4.2 What Is Amount B?

4.2.1 Scope

The detailed scoping criteria in Paragraph 18 of the consultation document are based on quantitative and qualitative criteria. The primary scope is 'buy-sell arrangements where the tested party purchases goods from one or more associated enterprises resident in other jurisdictions for wholesale distribution to unrelated parties primarily in its local market'.[103] Moreover, one of the primary issues is whether this scope should be extended to also cover commissionaires and sales agents when they reveal economically relevant characteristics similar to the baseline distributor. Some countries took the position that these structures resemble buy-sell arrangements in the scope of Amount B and should hence be included. Other countries considered that differences occur and they should not be in its scope on the basis of the accurate

101. R. Goulder, *What If Amount B Is All There Is?*, 109 Tax Notes International 283 (9 January 2023).
102. J. Rohmer, *Does the MLI Achieve More Justice and Equality?*, in *Justice, Equality and Tax Law* 80 (Cincin & Rield eds, 2022).
103. S. De Baets in PwC Tax Bites Podcast, Episode 33, 16 December 2022 https://news.pwc.be/tax-bites-podcast-discussion-draft-on-pillar-one-amount-b-published/ (consulted 10 January 2023).

delineation of the actual transaction.[104] At the time of drafting this chapter, no decision has yet been taken on whether to include commissionaires and sales-agents structures. To the authors, it would seem reasonable that these could also benefit from some simplified measure like Amount B, possibly with a twist in terms of remuneration as *value added* through their functionality should be the ultimate criterion rather than how a party is earmarked. It does not seem logical that even a less value-adding structure than baseline marketing and distribution could not benefit from a simplified approach while, at the same time, structures that are more complex could.

If a transaction fits the description of baseline marketing and distribution, secondary scoping criteria should be analysed.[105] Before discussing these, a few general remarks come to mind. First, the link between Amount B and the OECD TPG is confirmed as the criteria strive to be consistent with the principles set out in Chapter I OECD TPG and in line with the accurate delineation of the actual transaction.[106] For example, whether a transaction should be considered as baseline marketing and distribution has to be assessed based on established facts and circumstances and not on the labelling of transactions.[107]

Second, these scoping criteria intend to simplify the application of Amount B. To achieve this, they are qualitative and quantitative in nature. The former measures test whether the economically relevant characteristics are present to identify an in-scope distributor. The latter criteria goals are twofold. The first goal of introducing these criteria is to identify whether an in-scope transaction is present or is pursued. The criteria to achieve this are based on indicia present in the financial statements of the relevant entity. Similar to the qualitative criteria, the quantitative criteria attempt to analyse whether the relevant economic characteristics are present in the transaction.

The second aim of quantitative conditions is to test whether a transaction is excluded from Amount B. This is the case, for example, when annual net sales of the relevant distributor to end consumers through physical and online stores exceed a certain percentage of those sales. Another condition provides that sales to one single customer cannot exceed a certain threshold. It is not clear, however, what is meant with one single customer. Could this be an independent legal entity, a single legal entity within the MNE, or several associated legal entities part of the same MNE?

Furthermore, as for the qualitative criteria, the same approach of excluding transactions is used. If one of the boxes concerned is checked, the transaction is to be excluded from Amount B. For instance, a distributor is to be disqualified if it performs – a combination of – certain activities that include manufacturing, research and development, procurement, and financing. This condition emphasizes that an entity has to be a true baseline local market distributor. To further ensure this, the consultation document states that certain economic risks should also not be assumed by the distributor.[108] Notably, this document links some qualitative criteria to quantitative

104. OECD Public Consultation Document Pillar One – Amount B, § no. 14.
105. OECD Public Consultation Document Pillar One – Amount B, § no. 15.
106. OECD Public Consultation Document Pillar One – Amount B, § nos 23, 24.
107. OECD Public Consultation Document Pillar One – Amount B, § no. 16.
108. OECD Public Consultation Document Pillar One – Amount B, § no. 17.

ones, i.e., based on information verifiable in the financial statements, for example, operating expenses are tied to net sales. This seems to be an attempt to use mechanical approaches to assist in the risk analysis.

One notable point of discussion is the question of whether a written contract is necessary. The consultation document discusses this at some length.[109] The proposed guidance requires taxpayers to properly document the division of responsibilities, obligations, and rights as well as the assumption of the economically significant risks associated with the distribution functions in a written contract. Thus, as in the TPG, if there is a written contract, it should be used as the starting point to the assessment that is confirmed by the functional analysis. However, two remarks should be made. First, in the case that the written text contains insufficient information or content that is not in accordance with economic reality, further information contained in other documents should be considered.[110] Second, in the absence of a written contract, the relevant tax authorities are able to assert that a controlled transaction is a qualifying transaction whenever the criteria are met.[111] Furthermore, even if there is a written contract, whenever it is inconsistent with economic reality, the authorities can assert the relevant transaction to be in or out of scope.[112] This could be a precursor to what appears to be one of the problems of the suggested approach on Amount B, i.e., the many conditions that must be fulfilled before an entity may be in the scope of Amount B may incite potential conflict. In such a case, the dispute would change from a pricing issue (non-arm's length return) to a scoping conflict (the transaction is or is not in scope). An idea could be to leverage the six-step analysis of risk in the current OECD TPG in order to achieve a streamlined approach for Amount B purposes:[113]

- identification of the economically significant risks;
- identification of the contractual assumption of risks;
- undertaking a functional analysis in relation to the identified risks; and
- determining whether the tested party is capable of managing the risks that it contractually bears. If so, the transaction should be respected; if not, the risk may be reallocated.

4.2.1.1 Some Particularities

Controlled transactions involving possible baseline marketing and distribution activities subject to bilateral and multilateral advance pricing agreements (BAPA/MBAPA) are excluded from Amount B application. This is based on the fact that both Amount B and the MAPAs/BAPAs share a common purpose, i.e., the prevention of disputes.[114] Their exclusion actually makes sense as the transaction has been thoroughly examined

109. OECD Public Consultation Document Pillar One – Amount B, § no. 16.
110. OECD Public Consultation Document Pillar One – Amount B, § no. 27.
111. OECD Public Consultation Document Pillar One – Amount B, § no. 18 (h)(i).
112. OECD Public Consultation Document Pillar One – Amount B, § no. 18 (g).
113. See also PwC submission to the Consultation Document, p. 4.
114. OECD Public Consultation Document Pillar One – Amount B, § no. 18 (d) and (j).

by the tax authorities concerned before reaching an agreement under them. Hence, there is no need to apply Amount B. Stated differently, Amount B yields to the BAPA/MAPA. The authors consider, however, that this exclusion should not be interpreted as they cannot contain an Amount B approach for in-scope transactions.

The OECD/IF is also discussing the use of the most appropriate method and possibly excluding the application of Amount B under certain circumstances.[115] Because Amount B is based on a TNMM pricing methodology, certain countries consider that, based on facts and circumstances, a method other than the TNMM could be considered the most appropriate TP method (e.g., a comparable uncontrolled price (CUP) method). The following considerations can be made in this regard. First, a clash can be seen between the objectives of Amount B (standardizing, streamlining, and simplifying a relatively simple low-risk transaction) and the application of a full-blown TP analysis, including the accurate delineation of the transaction and the selection of the most appropriate TP method. The objectives of administration, simplification, and dispute prevention would be undermined as it would permit both taxpayers and particularly tax administrations to question the appropriateness of the TNMM under Amount B. The OECD Consultation Document on Amount B predicates that it follows the ALP.[116] Applying it implies utilizing the most appropriate method available. To choose one over the other might suggest abandoning some of the goals or principles set out in the OECD Consultation Document on Amount B leading to a simplified approach. Alternatively, it is still uncertain whether the OECD/IF, helped by the comments received during the public consultation, is able to reconcile both opposing sides. In any way, it is highly recommended that a compromise be found between administrability and simplicity, on the one hand, and accuracy, on the other, for baseline marketing and distribution activities that can be considered low-risk transactions. Amount B represents a highly welcomed, unique balance between administrability and simplicity versus accuracy for a low-risk transaction, and this should not be hampered by a high administrative burden.

4.2.1.2 Local Market Comparables

It is very common for taxpayers, for a wide variety of reasons as enumerated in Chapter 3 of the OECD TPG, to use regional comparables samples and to make pragmatic decisions about functional comparability. It is equally not overly surprising for tax authorities to (routinely) disregard these samples, to insist that local comparables be used, to reconfigure samples or to argue that their territory is peculiar, and to assert that a high point in the comparable range should be adopted. The latter situation appears to prevail in the OECD Consultation Document on Amount B. As certain studies have already indicated,[117] differences between local comparables searches and

115. OECD Public Consultation Document Pillar One – Amount B, box 3.4.2, § nos 6-9.
116. OECD Public Consultation Document Pillar One – Amount B, box 3.4.2, § no. 3.
117. Is Europe One Market? A Transfer Pricing Economic Analysis of Pan-European Comparables Sets https://taxation-customs.ec.europa.eu/system/files/2016-09/europe_one_market_white_paper_feb18.pdf, pp. 43-44, and Study on Comparable Data used for transfer pricing in the EU – Final Report, p. 15.

international comparables searches tend to be negligible. Additionally, in the case of low-capacity jurisdictions, the use of local comparables risks giving a distorted view of the acceptable return for baseline marketing and distribution. Countries with only a few comparables tend to arrive at a higher return for distributors than countries for which more comparables can be retrieved. All of the above combined with the lack of certainty adversely affects the appeal of Amount B in comparison to the application of the ALP under the OECD TPG. On the contrary, allowing the application of local market comparables under an Amount B approach is a recipe that will fuel TP disputes.

With regard to commodities, there is also no consensus yet on whether they should or should not be included in Pillar One Amount B.

4.2.2 Pricing Methodology

The pricing methodology should be aligned with the ALP.[118] Building thereon, the Amount B approach has a few policy objectives in itself including reducing resource constraints, ensuring consistency, and mitigating risk of disputes as well as being readily available and up to date and adaptable.[119] Especially the first two goals very well accommodate the desires of low-capacity jurisdictions.

When assessing the overall pricing solution offered by the approach in the OECD Consultation Document on Amount B, it could be assumed that the TNMM is the standard methodology as it has a predominant place there.[120] However, the document also refers to the selection of the most appropriate profit indicator under the TNMM. These criteria for selection have been duplicated from the four criteria mentioned in the OECD TPG on the selection of the most appropriate method.[121] Reference is made to various profit indicators, such as return on sales (ROS), Berry ratio, return on assets (ROA), and ROS/Berry ratio, respectively, a floor and a cap as a guardrail or even a combination of profit indicators.[122] These are all TNMM methodologies. However, it has to be kept in mind that there is not (yet) an explicit definitive profit level indicator or even methodology selected because of the ongoing above discussions on the most appropriate method and the availability of local market comparables (cf. *supra* section 4.2.1.1).

Then, moving forward, the OECD Consultation Documents on Amount B suggests two ways to approach the pricing question, i.e., (i) a matrix approach, and (ii) a mechanical approach. In the former, as the name itself indicates, a matrix has to be conceived based on the methodology (e.g., TNMM ROS) where several factors have to be considered (e.g., industry, geographical elements, and similar markets) to lead to somewhat different returns.[123] This results in several ranges within this matrix in

118. OECD Public Consultation Document Pillar One – Amount B, § no. 46.
119. OECD Public Consultation Document Pillar One – Amount B, § no. 47.
120. OECD Public Consultation Document Pillar One – Amount B, § nos 67-70.
121. *See* OECD TPG 2022, § 2.2.
122. OECD Public Consultation Document Pillar One – Amount B, § no. 70.
123. OECD Public Consultation Document Pillar One – Amount B, § no. 62.

which the most appropriate point of return should be pinpointed.[124] In the latter, which is more formulaic in nature, a few ranges would be determined and, when in range, the return would be considered at arm's length under Amount B. When the return does not fall within these predetermined ranges, corrections would need to be made.[125] At the time of writing this chapter, no agreement on the use of the matrix approach or the mechanical pricing tool has been reached.

The OECD Consultation Document on Amount B also refers to common benchmarking criteria in order to introduce a type of standardized process on how to come to an agreeable comparable set. This would subsequently underpin the Amount B pricing solution. However, the document also indicates that further work is needed.[126] Another area where no agreement has been reached (yet) is, for example, on the use of comparability adjustments and whether such adjustments for inventory, receivables, and payables are actually needed. Countries have diverging views on the need and use of these types of changes.[127]

4.2.3 *Documentation*

It is no understatement to say that there is already quite a bit of discussion on documentation in the OECD TPG. With this in mind, the question related to Amount B remains whether it would lead to an extra layer of documentation upon that already provided in the OECD TPG. It can already be noted that, according to the consultation document, the information request should be aligned with the Local File (LF). However, robust and comprehensive documentation is requested as it constitutes an essential element of Amount B.[128] Moreover, it should not be forgotten that individual countries always have the right to ask for more, and more, and even more. TP documentation is typically left to domestic tax law.

The section on documentation in the consultation document sets out all of the requirements that could be useful. For example:

- a statement that all of the information relating to Amount B is *true, accurate and complete*[129] though this is likely not the kind of element that would require the most work;
- an explanation on the delineation of the baseline marketing and distribution functions;
- financial information from key customers;
- sales to associated and third-party customers with a segregation per product per jurisdiction;
- sales to end customers and wholesale retailers (which may be particularly cumbersome);

124. OECD Public Consultation Document Pillar One – Amount B, § no. 62.
125. OECD Public Consultation Document Pillar One – Amount B, § no. 66.
126. OECD Public Consultation Document Pillar One – Amount B, § no. 58.
127. OECD Public Consultation Document Pillar One – Amount B, § nos 76-78.
128. OECD Public Consultation Document Pillar One – Amount B, § nos 83-86.
129. OECD Public Consultation Document Pillar One – Amount Bt, § no. 87(a).

- commercial and financial relationships within the group that could affect Amount B;
- annual account of the tested party if it is not the taxpayer;
- how Amount B affects the pricing of the controlled transaction and its results;
- written contracts. Moreover, the OECD Consultation Document on Amount B already specifies what needs to be written in the contract. The question could be posed on how to combine this with the freedom of conclusion of contracts; and
- all other rulings besides all unilateral and multilateral advanced pricing arrangements

Needless to say, *good* documentation is of paramount importance to enable all TP stakeholders to *do their job* in the most effective way. There should be few compromises on that (if any) whatsoever. It may be wondered, however, whether there is not an excessive opportunity cost stemming from the substantive documentation requirements for low-risk transactions in the OECD Consultation Document on Amount B. The fact that an MNE opts for use of Amount B, however, could be a useful entry in the Master File (MF).

The documentation package of Amount B is said to build on the guidance in Chapter V of the OECD TPG. It ties in with the MF and LF approach.[130] For the authors, the Amount B documentation should be capped by what is requested under the MF or LF. Therefore, extra filing requirements as a part of Amount B should be avoided. Additionally, tax authorities should refrain from asking the taxpayer to submit information that has already been submitted to the authorities or requesting them to submit it in another format.

Taking all of this into consideration, it would probably not be inaccurate to say that this is, in fact, an extra layer of documentation to the already substantial red tape requirements that MNEs must confront.

4.2.4 *Tax Certainty*

For the OECD/IF, implementing Amount B should lead to increased tax certainty.[131] The way it would do so would be two-fold. First, there is the scoping exercise that delivers a common and consistent framework and, second, there is the pricing solution. Furthermore, to prevent any dispute between a taxpayer and administration, in particular on the scoping exercise, the OECD Consultation Document on Amount B suggests keeping robust and comprehensive documentation in line with what is already suggested (cf. *supra* section 4.2.1).[132]

On the issue of dispute prevention, the OECD Consultation Document on Amount B refers to existing mechanisms available and used in practice and discussed in the OECD TPG. Among others, it suggests the preference for using a bilateral or multilateral APA

130. OECD Public Consultation Document Pillar One – Amount B, § nos 88-89.
131. OECD Public Consultation Document Pillar One – Amount B, § no. 98.
132. OECD Public Consultation Document Pillar One – Amount B, § no. 99.

over unilateral ones and the usefulness of the MAP.[133] It has to be noted that the OECD Consultation Document on Amount B suggests that these mechanics are more suitable for controlled transactions that are more complex and more sophisticated than for the transactions in the scope of Amount B. It would indeed be strange to insist on concluding a BAPA or MAPA for relatively straightforward and low-risk transactions. In that respect, the authors wonder whether it is not a missed opportunity that the tax authorities have not made use of the Draft Memorandum of Understanding for low-risk distribution services created when the guidance on safe harbours in the OECD TPG was revised.[134] It is also not clear whether the OECD/IF is implying that using the documentation package as suggested in the OECD Consultation Document on Amount B would suffice.

When addressing dispute resolution, the same themes return as the 'classic' solutions for the prevention and resolution of double taxation that are already available.[135] These are Article 9(2) OECD Model Convention (MC) corresponding adjustment, initiating a MAP based on Article 25 OECD MC, and finally activating the arbitration provision where available. A few points need to be clarified in this regard. First of all, the OECD/IF clarifies the effect of Amount B on MAP procedures. Already settled matters should not be reopened and reassessed based on Amount B. Ongoing matters and prospective MAP procedures should be solved using Amount B as guidance.[136] Second and perhaps a more interesting point is the impact of Amount B on the MAP outcome. That is, whenever a MAP remains unresolved (competent authorities only 'endeavour' to resolve the case) and no arbitration is available, the taxpayer bears the brunt. Ideally, Amount B should warrant that no such cases remain unresolved for baseline marketing and distribution. Stated otherwise, it could serve as a type of arbitrage approach.

On this last note, it can only be concluded that the tax certainty aspect of Amount B almost fully relies on already existing instruments. Its main innovation suggests a more robust documentation package. This is actually quite surprising as one of the main objectives and *selling points* of Amount B is the reinforced tax certainty. For example, as indicated earlier in this chapter, disputes on whether an entity is in the scope of Amount B will arise, but no guarantee for a definite solution is available.

4.3 Main Takeaways

4.3.1 Tax Certainty/Simplification/Streamlining/Standardization

The OECD/IF efforts devoted to Amount B deserve high praise as they have enormous potential to make the pricing and auditing of millions of transactions easily manageable

133. In line with 4.141 OECD TPG; OECD Public Consultation Document Pillar One – Amount B, § nos 101-102.
134. Sample Memoranda of Understanding on Low Risk Manufacturing Activities – OECD – Revised Section E on Safe Harbours in Chapter IV of the Transfer Pricing Guidelines and OECD TPG – 2022 – Annex I to Chapter IV.
135. OECD Public Consultation Document Pillar One – Amount B, § nos 103-107.
136. OECD Public Consultation Document Pillar One – Amount B, § no. 107.

to many in the *TP trenches*. In multiple places, the OECD/IF indeed points to Amount B's simplification and certainty goals.[137] For low-capacity jurisdictions, in particular, it would constitute substantial aid as resource-constraint tax authorities would be permitted to focus on higher-risk outcomes.[138] However, Amount B as drafted in the consultation document risks a failure to deliver. Ultimately, the focus of disputes is likely to shift from pricing the transaction to whether the entity falls in its scope. In such a case, nothing will be gained, on the contrary, there will be an extra cost of compliance.[139] The authors also wonder whether low-capacity jurisdictions will actually use a simplified, streamlined approach. A parallel could be drawn with the guidance on low value-adding intra-group services discussed in Chapter VII of the OECD TPG.[140] Several developing/emerging economies (for which corporate taxes represent a large portion of overall tax income) refrain from using that approach for fear of losing some tax revenue and hence adhere to a *hardcore* TP analysis. Attributes of such an attitude can also be seen in the OECD/IF suggestions by way of the numerous elements to be dealt with regarding whether an entity or transaction could fall into the scope of Amount B, the references to the accurate delineation of the transaction, and the references to the most appropriate TP methods. This leads the authors to question whether the way in which Amount B is currently presented is actually the kind of simplification and streamlining that would be expected for low-risk transactions, such as baseline marketing and distribution.[141]

The glass, however, may be rather half full instead of half empty. The authors follow those who claim that obstacles do not seem insurmountable. It may be good to once again evaluate the exclusions in general. Moreover, these exclusions could use more quantitative and, accordingly, more objective criteria that are based on accounting statements.[142] Undoubtedly, this will help to improve certainty as it affords governments and taxpayers fewer opportunities to dispute the applicability of Amount B. Passing a certain threshold based on a 'you're in or out' principle also makes the rules easier to administer. The question still lingers, though, whether the added compliance burden is worth the hassle even if the scoping issues would be solved. Lastly, the OECD/IF could also be maintained in place as a permanent forum to discuss the impact of the pillars and tax certainty.

137. For example, OECD Public Consultation Document Pillar One - Amount B, § nos 7-10, 63, 73, 76 and others.
138. R. Finley, *Amount B Proposal Holds Promise, but It Needs Work*, 109 Tax Notes International 18 (2 January 2023).
139. R. Finley notices the same ultimately in his article. R. Finley, *Amount B Proposal Holds Promise, but It Needs Work*, 109 Tax Notes International 23 (2 January 2023),.
140. OECD TPG, Chapter VII, Section D. - Low Value-Adding Intra-Group Services - §§ 7.43-7.65.
141. It must be kept in mind what *streamlining* and *simplification* actually mean. The Cambridge dictionary indicates that streamlining has to be understood as making a business, process, activity, etc., simpler and more effective by reducing costs and the number of people involved in it. Simplification is the process of making something less complicated and therefore easier to do or understand or the thing that results from this process. It is then not unimaginable to state that scoping as it is presented now is certainly not simplified and doubts certainly remain on the actual streamlining.
142. Ryan Finley, *Amount B Proposal Holds Promise, but It Needs Work*, 109 Tax Notes International 18 (2 January 2023).

4.3.2 ALP and Impact on Companies

As mentioned in the introduction, one of the main dichotomies of Amount B's main guiding principle is the ALP. It could be said that Amount B applies (or intends to apply) the ALP while it abandons it at the same time through the upfront cornering of returns for in-scope activities. Even more seemingly contradictory is that the OECD/IF admits this fact in box 3.2 of the consultation document by stating that the solution offered by Amount B needs to walk a fine line between accuracy and efficiency/simplification. Well, the whole purpose of the ALP is to only closely approximate market conditions,[143] and some inaccuracies in pricing intercompany transactions seem unavoidable even under *hardcore* TP. The approach under Amount B should be kept relatively simple. Therefore, even if it is not entirely accurate, this should not be too much of a preoccupation as long as it closely approximates the open market. As said, the level of detail suggested by the OECD/IF – although there is still no full consensus – seems precisely to (risk to) miss that point.

4.3.3 Impact on Business and TP Models

Stating that there are as many TP models as there are business models would be slamming an already open door. That does not mean, however, that discussing them would be without merit. It is quite the contrary. The OECD Consultation Document on Amount B is a work in progress, hence, there is a need to unlock its potential to fulfil the expectations of simplifying, streamlining, and standardizing the TP for baseline marketing and distribution activities. An Amount B approach will be very helpful for reducing the number of disputes for what are essentially low-risk activities. Amount B has the ability to introduce an arm's length methodology that all jurisdictions, including low-capacity jurisdictions, can apply relatively easily thereby generating arm's length revenue without double taxation and hence actually saving resources that can subsequently be devoted to more tax risk incurring taxpayers.

How can this be achieved? The public consultation on the Pillar One Blueprint already offered some inspiration. In the PricewaterhouseCoopers' (PwC) submissions, a pragmatic way of how Amount B could offer a workable solution was already explained, that it can serve as a foundation to build further.[144]

The first hurdle to overcome is the issue of what is considered as being in or out of scope. Instead of attempting to develop a definition of in-scope enterprises (carrying with it the danger of excluding many enterprises and not achieving the goals of Amount B mentioned above), the baseline marketing and distribution entities could be in or out

143. OECD TPG, §§ 1.14, 3.55, 4.99.
144. PwC's comments in relation to the Reports on the Pillar One and Pillar Two Blueprints in light of the consultation document of 12 October 2020, p. 19. The comments are available at https://www.oecd.org/tax/beps/public-comments-received-on-the-reports-on-pillar-one-and-pillar-two-blueprints.htm.

of Amount B on the basis of whether they can be characterized as *benchmarkable*. The idea is that, when the marketing and distribution transaction cannot be benchmarked, it does not come in its scope. If an activity is *benchmarkable*, it does not already contain any element of residual profit in the sense of Amount A or even under a mainstream TP approach. If an affiliate performs functions, owns assets, or assumes risks representing a unique contribution to the transaction, then no benchmark will be found. This way of looking at it would indeed represent a substantial simplification and could cover a wide range of taxpayers. The reasoning behind this is that, when a distributor has sufficient bargaining power to capture the economic rents and it assumes the accompanying risks, performs the necessary functions, and owns or uses the appropriate assets, it is very likely, not *benchmarkable*. In the opposite scenario, it should be *benchmarkable*. One of the criteria to select the TNMM is precisely that the tested party does not capture the economic rents on the basis of its functions, assets, and risks.

The authors would like to refer to a benchmarking exercise using dynamic dashboards that was performed around the same period as the public consultation on the Pillar One Blueprint.[145] In the accompanying article, the two developers of the benchmarking exercise demonstrate *there is a place for broad-based comparables searches and for reference samples*. Strong arguments in favour of the Berry ratio were found as well as a solution for determining Amount B:

- the Berry ratio is a direct measure of functional activity (as indicated by Professor Berry himself; if the firms are fairly comparable, then there should not be a big difference in the level of costs in terms of the functions performed[146]); and
- the Berry ratio might be an appropriate profit level indicator for low-risk distributors (this argument, acknowledged by the EC, was used in the state aid case that the EC initiated against Ireland on Apple).[147]

Countries would need to abandon their discretion to deal with baseline marketing and distribution activities on a case-by-case basis. What can work is a trade-off between simplicity and administrability versus very strict compliance with the ALP for the in-scope activities. Some could see this as a shift towards a more formulaic approach. The authors rather see this as a practical and pragmatic application of the ALP but not an abandonment thereof. If a case-by-case approach is not abandoned, the authors fear that Amount B would not be able to fulfil the expectations.

145. I.F Dykes & L.H. Keegan, *OECD/International – The OECD Pillar 1 Blueprint: Why Amount B Matters*, 75(3) Bulletin for International Taxation 9-14 (2021).
146. C. Berry, *Berry Ratios – Their Use and Misuse*, Journal of Global Transfer Pricing 20 (April-May 1999).
147. Commission Decision (EU) 2017/1283 of 30 August 2016 on State aid SA.38373 (2014/C) (ex2014/NN) (ex 2014/CP) implemented by Ireland to Apple (notified under document C(2017) 5605).

The PwC submission on the latest OECD Consultation Document on Amount B draws from an updated benchmarking study to underscore the usefulness of dynamic dashboards.[148]

4.4 Amount B and the EU

There is no formal EC position with regard to Amount B. The EC regularly refers to the virtues of simplification and reducing compliance burden for enterprises, but it seems to put its eggs in the Business in Europe – Framework in Taxation (BEFIT) basket. It is unnecessary to say that Amount B is said to be within the ambit of the ALP while the EC is moving (again) towards formulary apportionment. Its first attempt through the Common Consolidated Corporate Tax Base (CCCTB) received only lukewarm support left and right rather than a unanimous endorsement. Amount B could now be seen as a hybrid bridging between the ALP and formulary apportionment, particularly when the mechanical approach to pricing is applied.

4.5 Interim Conclusion

To finally answer the question that was posed at the beginning of this section on whether Amount B is controversial: No, it is not, except when it is introduced as a *cast in stone* floor and/or cap. There is more to Amount B than is perceived and, most of all, it is a work in progress. There are quite some uncertainties left at this stage, and the risk of overcomplication is always imminent. As a consequence, irrespective of the amazing opportunities it offers to all parties grappling with the TP, there is an expectation gap looming with respect to tax certainty, simplification, and streamlining. The authors hope that the public consultation will bring resolution because the Amount B policy cannot be ignored as the impact on certain business models is disruptive. Let the work of the commentators to the public consultation serve as an effective and helpful membrane to create a superb osmosis with the efforts of the OECD. This is likely to be a prerequisite to achieving a result that is fit for purpose.

There is no doubt that international agreement on search strategies and profitability for low-risk and less complex transactions is unambiguously beneficial to both taxpayers and tax authorities.[149]

What is not discussed so far in the publications of the OECD – be it in the blueprint or in the OECD Consultation Document on Amount B – is the height of the return under Amount B. It should not serve as a *holy grail* generating tax revenue in abundance as the absence of impact assessment on Amount B might illustrate. Expectation monitoring is a key success factor.

148. PwC's comments in relation to OECD's Public Consultation on Amount B of Pillar One, Appendix F, p. 38. The comments are available at https://www.dropbox.com/s/f4jssaabg2xwocr/public-comments-design-elements-amount-b-pillar-one-transfer-pricing.zip?dl = 0&file_subpath = %2FPublished + 30 + January + 2023 + (Morning) %2FPwC + .pdf.

149. I.F Dykes & L.H. Keegan, *OECD/International – The OECD Pillar 1 Blueprint: Why Amount B Matters*, 75(3) *Bulletin for International Taxation* 15 (2021).

5 CLOSING COMMENTS

The Pillar One discussion is part of a project that is too important to let fail.

Professor Pistone[150] questions the validity of the proxies and the criteria that states have used for over a century in their domestic law and tax treaties to determine the boundaries of their tax jurisdiction and allocate taxing rights at the international level.

The issue of remote economic activity and hence value creation serves as a catalyst for change in international tax law. A comprehensive reconsideration of domestic and treaty rules on income from activities is then a plausible option towards a balanced intervention that preserves the fair allocation of taxing rights.

Putting the focus of this debate on Pillar One, the overall result is now that traditional businesses are being targeted under Amount A. Although the number of MNEs currently in its scope seems to slightly exceed 100, the scope will be reviewed in seven to eight years. It is not unlikely that – should the system work well from a tax authority perspective – the scope is extended by either lowering the revenue threshold, lowering the profitability threshold, or lowering both.

It is still unclear how many countries will be interested in signing and ratifying the MLC implementing Amount A. When countries begin counting their dues, it might be that they find they would be on the relieving (or paying) side of the spectrum. They might also start calculating what brings in the most tax revenue, i.e., A DST or Amount A. The former might be here to stay[151]. It is not excluded that creative solutions can be found by legislators to have a combination of both.

The Amount A implementation and relieving mechanism as well as the tax certainty approach also seem to be complex. Direct link with the ALP is also not very clear. It is an *overlay*, but that is all that is said. In the authors' opinion, the ALP should be applied first. Indeed, an MNE's entity situated in a certain state and earmarked as a relieving entity will end up with a taxable result in that country that is below arm's length after the Amount A allocation. It is plausible to assume that, if the remuneration is at arm's length before that, then such a remuneration should not be revisited because of Amount A. In the absence of such a course of action, double taxation is unavoidable. Nothing has been written from an OECD/IF perspective in that respect. After all, *surrendering* is a term that carries a torturous connotation.

Amount B is said to simplify, streamline, and standardize the TP for baseline marketing and distribution. Whenever there is an attempt to simplify tax rules, one way or another, there is a risk of ending up with a more complex system. This appears to be the case as well with Amount B. Despite the great intentions of the OECD/IF, the perils of *real-life* marketing and distribution are left unaddressed under a plethora of options and loose ends. There is an urgent need to address a fair accuracy/efficiency trade-off.

---

150. P. Pistone, *Chapter 8: The Faltering Legitimacy of the Place of Physical Presence as a Tax Nexus for Active Income*, in *Building Global International Tax Law: Essays in Honour of Guglielmo Maisto* 159-179 (P. Pistone ed., 2022).
151. G. Kofler, *The Future of Digital Services Taxes*, EC Tax Review 51 (2021/2).

Until now, (too) little attention has been awarded to Amount B despite the potential impact it might have on the returns of the entities involved. As such, it might also have an impact on the system profit of the enterprise and where to allocate it. Depending on the details of the mechanics of the eventual pricing solutions, returns may become due to low-risk entities that are not commensurate with functions, assets, and risks.

There are a few ideas that can fuel optimism around the viability of Amount B. First, it should be a measure that is optional for the taxpayer. Upon election by the taxpayer - and, of course, provided certain conditions are fulfilled - the tax authorities should not question or challenge its application. This is in the style of the low-value adding intra-group services guidance. Further, the remuneration matrix (if it can be called as such) should be kept as simple as possible with only a few differentiators (for example, broad industry categories, broad geographical regions, etc.). Finally, local comparables should not serve as a benchmark for Amount B. More is less, so to speak.

Perhaps a pilot project could help obtain a gradual buy-in from all stakeholders. That could be feasible via modelling with the help of dynamic dashboards as explained above. The OECD could work out an approach to rationally stress test the system to ensure that the process and outcome align with the agreed policy objectives and is supported by IF Members. In 2021, the PwC submission suggested some testing for a certain period with a small number of MNEs and tax administrations (e.g., International Compliance Assurance Program (ICAP) volunteers) followed by an intense review for six months (or so) of the technical framework based on the profit reallocation pilot with resulting recommendations subject to IF approval.[152]

Praise is due to the work that has been done on both Pillar One - Amount A and Amount B - and on Pillar Two as well. Very important topics are also waiting to be thoroughly addressed, such as environmental and carbon taxation, ESG, cryptos and NFT, or the Metaverse. One can only hope that the OECD Secretariat and delegates of the IF refrain from rushing over the final hurdles of Amount A and particularly Amount B. The latter specifically could be a game changer, but it might not be realized (yet).

152. PwC's comments in relation to the Reports on the Pillar One and Pillar Two Blueprints in light of the consultation document of 12 October 2020, p. 5. The comments are available at https://www.oecd.org/tax/beps/public-comments-received-on-the-reports-on-pillar-one-and-pillar-two-blueprints.htm.

CHAPTER 3

Transfer Pricing Aspects of Pillar Two

Andrea Tolley, Kevin Perry & Charles Havisham

1 INTRODUCTION

The OECD Inclusive Framework's programme of work following its original Base Erosion and Profit Shifting (BEPS) Project (referred to here as BEPS 1.0) continued to consider the tax challenges arising from the digitalization of the economy and has culminated into a new two-pillar international tax reform package (referred to as BEPS 2.0).[1] Pillar Two, the key component of which is a global minimum tax of 15% on all multinational enterprises (MNEs) with an annual revenue over EUR 750 million[2] is the focus of this article.

1. OECD, *OECD/G20 Inclusive Framework on BEPS – Progress report September 2021 – September 2022* 2 (2022).
2. OECD, *Statement on a Two-Pillar Solution to Address the Tax Challenges Arising from the Digitalisation of the Economy 8 October 2021* 3-4 (2021).

The introduction of a global minimum tax represents a radical shift in the international taxation system that will have far-reaching economic consequences. Given the broad repercussions of Pillar Two, this article first considers what the role of transfer pricing is in a post-Pillar Two world by discussing whether there is still a need for transfer pricing if tax rates are converging. It will then move on to how transfer pricing and the arm's length principle (ALP) will be impacted by Pillar Two as tax authorities grapple with the taxation of the digitalized economy. There is a concern that, while a core objective of BEPS 2.0 was to drive international consensus and tax certainty,[3] transfer pricing in a post-Pillar Two world will be characterized by a declining international consensus from differing and aggressive interpretations of the ALP leading to a lack of certainty for taxpayers.

The chapter then considers the direct and indirect impacts of Pillar Two on transfer pricing and the ALP. As part of the calculation of the global minimum tax rate, Article 3.2.3 of the Global Anti-Base Erosion (GloBE) model rules requires transactions between group entities to be priced consistent with the ALP.[4] This chapter discusses this provision and whether timing differences will cause difficulties for tax authorities and MNEs alike and other areas where there is a direct interaction with Pillar Two. Finally, it examines areas in which Pillar Two will indirectly impact MNEs and tax authorities' approaches to transfer pricing, i.e., how MNEs structure their operations; incentive regimes; and data collection.

2 THE ROAD TO PILLAR TWO: WHY A GLOBAL MINIMUM TAX

After the BEPS 1.0 Project, there was a widely held view that it did not adequately address the tax challenges presented by the digitalization of the economy.[5] As a result of this, many countries such as France and Spain implemented unilateral digital taxes.[6] Additionally, the OECD continued its work on BEPS Action 1 considering tax challenges arising from digitalization in a bid to address these concerns and develop international consensus.

The BEPS 1.0 Project was the result of a political desire to target tax planning strategies that resulted in little to no corporation tax being paid – the OECD estimated that global revenue losses resulting from BEPS were up to USD 240 billion annually.[7]

3. OECD, *supra* n. 1.
4. OECD, *Tax Challenges Arising from the Digitalisation of the Economy – Global Anti-Base Erosion Model Rules (Pillar Two): Inclusive Framework on BEPS* 16 (2021).
5. KPMG, *BEPS 2.0: What You Need to Know* 1 (2022).
6. *Présentation de la taxe sur les services fournis par les grandes entreprises du secteur numérique*, Direction générale des Finances publiques (République Française) (July 2019), https://www.impots.gouv.fr/actualite/presentation-de-la-taxe-sur-les-services-fournis-par-les-grandes-entreprises-du-secteur; *Ley 4/2020, de 15 de octubre, del Impuesto sobre Determinados Servicios Digitales*, Agencia Estatal Boletín Oficial del Estado (15 October 2020), https://www.boe.es/eli/es/l/2020/10/15/4/con.
7. *Action 11 – BEPS data analysis*, OECD, https://www.oecd.org/tax/beps/beps-actions/action11/; KPMG Luxembourg, *Base Erosion and Profit Shifting* 2 (2014).

The international action here that was coordinated through the OECD, as a supranational body, was essential as the targeted BEPS often took advantage of differences in the interpretation of tax rules across different jurisdictions.[8]

The 15 Actions resulting from BEPS 1.0 covered a wide range of topics aimed at restricting BEPS by improving the operation and supporting the consistent interpretation of aspects of the international tax system, including transfer pricing and the ALP.[9] One core concept of BEPS 1.0 was that taxing rights should be more closely aligned with the location of 'value creation', and this was addressed by changes made to the OECD Transfer Pricing Guidelines pursuant to Actions 8-10.[10]

In contrast to the other BEPS 1.0 Actions, the deliverable for Action 1 - Tax Challenges Arising from Digitalization - was conspicuous in the absence of clear implementable outcomes. While the finalization of the BEPS deliverables for the other Actions resulted in changes to double tax treaties, OECD Transfer Pricing Guidelines, and domestic laws, the Action 1 report recommended that the digital economy should not be ring-fenced. This is because it is increasingly becoming the economy itself and no new direct tax, such as: (i) a new nexus in the form of a significant economic presence; (ii) a withholding tax on certain types of digital transactions; or (iii) an equalization levy was recommended.[11] More widely, the report anticipated that the measures developed in the other Actions of the BEPS Project should have a substantial impact on issues previously identified with the digital economy and left the choice open for countries to introduce any of the three options in their domestic taxation system.[12] Unsurprisingly, countries adopted these or other unilateral measures to protect their tax base in the absence of (or at least pending) international agreement on how to tax the digitalized economy.

This perceived deficiency of Action 1 due to the lack of uniformity on how to tax the digitalized economy may be overly harsh and characterizes the other individual actions very broadly if considering the aims of BEPS 1.0 and the approaches taken by individual tax authorities and the relatively short amount of time following the implementation of the BEPS 1.0 deliverables. BEPS 1.0 was a set of practical steps aimed at improving the existing rules in order to address arbitrage on differences in tax implementation across various jurisdictions.[13] The BEPS 1.0 Project was therefore possibly not adequately equipped to deal with the radical changes that businesses have undergone as a result of digitalization.

The extent to which the BEPS 1.0 Actions could be an effective tool for taxing the digital economy was further limited by the amount of time given to determine the relative merits of the Actions. Given that the OECD Transfer Pricing Guidelines were

8. KPMG Luxembourg, *supra* n. 7.
9. *BEPS Actions*, OECD, https://www.oecd.org/tax/beps/beps-actions/.
10. *Actions 8-10 Transfer Pricing*, OECD, https://www.oecd.org/tax/beps/beps-actions/actions8-10/.
11. OECD, *Addressing the Tax Challenges of the Digital Economy, Action 1 - 2015 Final Report* 54 and 137 (2015).
12. OECD, *supra* n. 11, at 137.
13. OECD, *supra* n. 1.

only updated for Actions 8-10 in 2017,[14] although many tax authorities had implemented them earlier as they were published on 5 October 2015, relatively little time has elapsed during which the revised guidelines have been in force. The areas covered in Actions 8-10, especially concepts such as risk control and development, enhancement, maintenance, protection and exploitation (DEMPE) activities, are complex refinements of the ALP that is a principle that is inherently open to a range of different interpretations. Taxpayers and tax authorities had to explain and apply these changes. In this regard, it is not particularly surprising that the complex new concepts found within the revised OECD Transfer Pricing Guidelines following Action 8-10 report are not yet being uniformly implemented by tax authorities and why OECD Working Party 6 is reviewing certain elements of these BEPS changes.[15]

Finally, when considering the extent to which the ALP addresses the tax challenges presented by the digital economy, tax authorities should not be seen as passive actors given that their actions shape how the ALP is applied. It is not applied in a vacuum; countries will inevitability act in their own economic interests to maintain their tax base. Classic examples of this are 'market premiums' and 'location savings' of which both have been used by tax authorities in relation to a number of different activities to receive high returns for seemingly routine activities.[16] At the same time, there has been a proliferation of unilateral tax measures that operate outside the established treaty framework such as the UK's Diverted Profit Tax and Australia's Multinational Anti-Avoidance Laws[17] as well as different digital taxes.[18] By asserting unilateral taxing rights, the international tax framework is made less effective.[19] While Pillar Two may address this proliferation of unilateral taxes to a certain extent, it is key that the international tax community does not overlook the importance and individual merits of the BEPS 1.0 Actions when implementing Pillar Two.

However, it must be recognized that the digitalization of the economy drove a fundamental change in how businesses operate and interact with customers to which the international tax framework is still struggling to adapt. As more and more of the world becomes digital, this leads to a fundamental challenge to the international tax framework.[20] As MNEs' business models have become digitalized, companies are able to move more of their operations online which alleviates the need for a 'brick and

14. OECD, *OECD Transfer Pricing Guidelines for Multinational Enterprises and Tax Administrations 2017* 4 (2017).
15. Jessie Coleman et al., *The Arm's-Length Standard after the Pillars*, 107(13) Tax Notes International 1513, 1513 (2022).
16. Coleman et al., *supra* n. 15.
17. Her Majesty's Revenue and Customs (HMRC), *Diverted Profits Tax* 1 (2014); *Combating Multinational Tax Avoidance: A Targeted Anti-avoidance Law*, Australian Taxation Office (12 April 2021), https://www.ato.gov.au/Business/International-tax-for-business/In-detail/Doing-business-in-Australia/Combating-multinational-tax-avoidance---a-targeted-anti-avoidance-law/.
18. Direction générale des Finances publiques (République Française), *supra* n. 6; Agencia Estatal Boletín Oficial del Estado, *supra* n. 6.
19. KPMG Luxembourg, *supra* n. 7.
20. OECD, *supra* n. 11, at 16.

mortar' presence that has historically been how a taxable presence has been determined. This consequently resulted in an erosion of taxable profits in market jurisdictions. It is these concerns that have underpinned and driven Pillar Two. Jurisdictions are unable to effectively assert taxing rights on large parts of an MNE's value chain.[21] While the BEPS 2.0 programme of work rests on the other pillar, Pillar One does address some of these considerations directly by providing expanded taxing rights to market jurisdictions. Pillar One only applies to 100 or so of the very largest MNEs, and its implementation continues to be highly uncertain.[22] The Pillar Two mechanism does not directly address the concerns that countries are unable to tax profits earned by MNEs to the same extent as has historically been done; rather, it smoothens the edges. It is aimed at ensuring that profit will be subject to a minimum level of tax no matter where the income is recognized.[23] Pillar Two does not offer a solution to the concerns about nexus, data, or characterization as defined in Action 1[24] or more widely consider the suitability of the current international framework in being able to tax an appropriate level of MNE profit in the digitalized economy. Rather, it operates as a release valve by ensuring that the profits generated by MNEs are taxed somewhere.

However, the question continues of what is the role of transfer pricing and the ALP in a post-Pillar Two world. Whether, following a global minimum tax that enables the taxation of MNE profit no matter where it arises, the same level of importance will not be placed on MNEs' transfer pricing arrangements or whether the ALP remains one of the primary tools through which tax authorities are able to assert taxing rights.

3 THE ALP IN A PILLAR TWO WORLD

In considering transfer pricing and the ALP in a Pillar Two world, it is important to recognize that the Pillar Two rules as a minimum tax do not directly determine the actual tax base of an entity other than through the calculation of its tax base under the GloBE rules. The pricing of intercompany transactions may be critical in determining this. Indeed, Article 3.2.3 of the GloBE rules specifically states that transactions between group entities are to be priced consistent with the ALP and recorded at the same price for GloBE purposes for all constituent entities that are parties to the transaction[25] (this is considered in detail later in this chapter). Therefore, the GloBE rules exist in conjunction with and inclusive of transfer pricing and not instead of it. What this means is that the GloBE rules are a complex set of rules that present an additional compliance burden for the taxpayer, but it is not expected that they will directly result in a corresponding alleviation of the taxpayer's transfer pricing compliance burden.

In recent years, transfer pricing has been at the forefront of tax authority enquiries, and announcements on its compliance show that taxpayers' compliance burden for transfer pricing is increasing. Examples of this in the last six months include Germany

21. OECD, *supra* n. 11, at 79.
22. KPMG Luxembourg, *supra* n. 7, at 2.
23. Coleman et al., *supra* n. 15, at 1517.
24. OECD, *supra* n. 11, at 18.
25. OECD, *supra* n. 4.

reducing the length of time to submit documentation during an audit,[26] Denmark implementing mandatory submission of documentation,[27] and the United Arab Emirates implementing documentation requirements.[28] Additionally, the United Kingdom will, for the first time, certainly require the preparation of a Local File and Master File for MNEs meeting the country-by-country (CbCR) reporting threshold and may implement additional reporting requirements in the form of a summary audit trail questionnaire or an international dealings schedule in the future.[29]

It is also not anticipated that the Pillar Two rules will reduce or even contribute to a decrease in the level of tax authority scrutiny and challenges on the transfer pricing of MNEs.[30] Conceptually, transfer pricing disputes are concerned with the taxation of an MNE's profits in accordance with the ALP, and this acts as a tool by which countries can protect and expand their tax bases.[31] MNEs can often have a lower effective tax rate (ETR) than the global minimum tax rate of 15% in jurisdictions with a headline corporate income tax rate above 15%, for example, due to incentive regimes[32] (this is why countries like the United Kingdom with headline rates higher than the global minimum tax rate of 15% are introducing a qualifying domestic minimum top-up tax (QDMTT)[33]). Historically, some of the largest transfer pricing disputes for MNEs have taken place between developed countries that have headline tax rates higher than the 15% GloBE rate as these are disagreements in relation to the tax base of an MNE rather than the tax rate applied to its profits.[34] The GloBE rules will not directly prevent or limit these disputes, and it is anticipated that transfer pricing will remain a fundamental focus of tax authorities across the globe as transfer pricing enables countries to maintain and expand their tax base which the Pillar Two rules do not. The ALP, however, is continually being eroded and put under strain. The BEPS 1.0 Actions partially addressed the concerns outlined above in relation to the taxation of the digitalized economy. As detailed earlier, the BEPS 1.0 Actions were inadequately equipped to address the wholesale change brought by the digitalized economy,

26. *Gesetz zur Umsetzung der Richtlinie (EU) 2021/514 des Rates vom 22. März 2021 zur Änderung der Richtlinie 2011/16/EU über die Zusammenarbeit der Verwaltungsbehörden im Bereich der Besteuerung und zur Modernisierung des Steuerverfahrensrechts vom 20. Dezember 2022*, Bundesfinanzministerium (28 December 2022), https://www.bundesfinanzministerium.de/Content/DE/Gesetzestexte/Gesetze_Gesetzesvorhaben/Abteilungen/Abteilung_IV/20_Legislaturperiode/2022-12-28-Gesetz-zur-Umsetzung-der-Richtlinie-EU-2021-514/4-Verkuendetes-Gesetz.pdf?__blob=publicationFile&v=2.
27. *L 28 Forslag til lov om ændring af selskabsskatteloven og forskellige andre love*, Folketinget (3 December 2020), https://www.ft.dk/samling/20201/Lovforslag/L28/index.htm.
28. *Federal Decree-Law No. 47 of 2022 on the Taxation of Corporations and Businesses*, UAE Ministry of Finance (9 December 2022), https://mof.gov.ae/wp-content/uploads/2022/12/Federal-Decree-Law-No.-47-of-2022-EN.pdf.
29. *Policy paper: Transfer pricing documentation*, HMRC (20 July 2022), https://www.gov.uk/government/publications/new-transfer-pricing-documentation-requirements-for-uk-businesses/transfer-pricing-documentation.
30. Coleman et al., *supra* n. 15, at 1517.
31. Coleman et al., *supra* n. 15, at 1517.
32. KPMG, *Tax Incentives Revisited: Initial Observations of OECD Report on Tax Incentives and the Global Minimum Tax* 1 (2022).
33. KPMG, *Autumn Statement 2022* 1 (2022).
34. Coleman et al., *supra* n. 15, at 1517.

however, in specific ways, the BEPS Actions refined and better equipped the ALP for tackling the taxation challenges presented by the digitalized economy. Action 7 enabled tax authorities to establish a taxable presence and assess taxes through attribution of profit on certain low-intensity, low-nexus digitalized activities in distribution functions by extending the definition of a dependent agent permanent establishment (DAPE).[35] Actions 8-10 required that returns are aligned with the DEMPE functions in relation to intangibles and control of economically significant risks.[36] When intangibles and the corresponding assumption and control of economically significant risks in relation to these intangibles are drivers of value for the business, parties will be rewarded for these activities commensurately with the value of their contributions under Actions 8-10 and the OECD Transfer Pricing Guidelines.[37] Given the fundamental importance of intellectual property (IP) in digitalized industries, this should provide tax authorities with a framework to identify any tax returns on digitalized businesses while covering aspects of the policy challenges raised by Action 1.[38]

Despite these, the proliferation of unilateral measures demonstrates that tax authorities perceived that they lacked the tools to effectively tax large parts of an MNE's value chain. This was rooted in the view that the digitalized nature of MNEs' value chains was such that Actions 8-10 of BEPS 1.0 did not enable countries to apply taxing rights to markets in which revenue is sourced if the key business risks are controlled above the market. This is due to them limiting the mobility of income arising directly from the exploitation of intangibles through the risk control framework focussing on the location of people controlling economically significant business risks.[39] In this regard, the ALP was not an adequate tool for addressing all of the tax authorities concerns.

This perceived inadequacy has led to some contortions as tax authorities have attempted to counter unwelcome outcomes with the tools available, i.e., the ALP. For example, recent years have seen a drive towards increasing the use of the profit split method that some commentators have called excessive.[40] The OECD Transfer Pricing Guidelines provide indicators as to when a profit split is likely to be applicable, broadly when having accurately delineated the transaction, there are 'unique and valuable contributions by each party to the controlled transaction' or there is a 'high level of integration of business operations to which the transactions relate and/or the shared assumption of economically significant risks'.[41] Concerns have been raised that tax

35. OECD, *Preventing the Artificial Avoidance of Permanent Establishment Status, Action 7 – 2015 Final Report* 25 (2015).
36. OECD, *Aligning Transfer Pricing Outcomes with Value Creation, Actions 8-10 – 2015 Final Reports* 64 (2015).
37. OECD, *supra* n. 36, at 64-65; OECD, *OECD Transfer Pricing Guidelines for Multinational Enterprises and Tax Administrations 2022* 284-286 (2022).
38. OECD, *supra* n. 11, at 91.
39. KPMG, *supra* n. 36, at 6.
40. KPMG, *supra* n. 36, at 12; Andrew Hickman, *Arm's Length Principle Mutations: Control of Risk in the OECD Guidelines and Variations in Practice*, MNE Tax (13 January 2021), https://mnetax.com/arms-length-principle-mutations-control-of-risk-in-the-oecd-guidelines-and-variations-in-practice-42047.
41. OECD Transfer Pricing Guidelines, at 131.

authorities have favoured a profit split in circumstances of control functions relating to economically significant risks but which arguably fail to assume such risks.[42]

Consistency in the application of the ALP is essential for the international tax framework to operate from a transfer pricing perspective and for MNEs to be able to function with certainty. The more countries that align their domestic transfer pricing legislation with the OECD Transfer Pricing Guidelines, the more the level of alignment across the globe on transfer pricing and the ALP should increase. In this regard, it is a positive move that Brazil has issued draft legislation to align its unique transfer pricing system with the OECD Transfer Pricing Guidelines.[43] Furthermore, the digitalization of economies does not apply only to MNEs. Tax authorities in certain countries that may historically have struggled to collect data to apply the ALP may now find that they are able to do so.[44] When returns based on a bespoke analysis of the functions, assets, and risks of the parties would previously have represented too great a burden and, instead, fixed returns based on financial indicators were applied, tax authorities may now find that they have the tools to be able to apply such methodologies in accordance with the OECD Transfer Pricing Guidelines.

It is hoped that providing an additional tool in the kit will help Pillar Two to relieve some of the excess pressure placed on the ALP by overly aggressive interpretations. The flip side will be to ensure that taxpayers are not faced with an excessive compliance burden under Pillar Two while facing difficult tax authority approaches to transfer pricing at the same time.

4 SPECIFIC CONSIDERATIONS IN RELATION TO PILLAR TWO

The second half of this article considers the GloBE Rules,[45] as well as the Commentary on the GloBE Rules[46] and its interplay with transfer pricing. Ostensibly, Pillar Two now appears to be another compliance exercise to be completed by qualifying MNEs. However, as stated previously, Pillar Two fundamentally relies on transfer pricing and particularly the ALP being applied and applied correctly to the allocation of profits across the group in accordance with the MNE's functions, risks, assets and its DEMPE.

This covers Article 3.2.3 which considers the arm's length requirements for cross-border transactions,[47] the impact of the GloBE rules on MNEs that have operated a PE and the impact of the CbCR safe harbour; at this point, further safe harbours are still to be developed, thus this remains an ongoing issue.[48] Transfer pricing explicitly plays a

42. Hickman, *supra* n. 40.
43. *Medida Provisória Nº 1.152, de 28 de Dezembro de 2022,* Presidência da República (Brasil) Secretaria-Geral (28 December 2022), https://www.planalto.gov.br/ccivil_03/_ato2019-2022/2022/mpv/mpv1152.htm.
44. KPMG, *BEPS Actions 8-10: Current State of Play* 7 (2019).
45. OECD, *supra* n. 4, at 1.
46. OECD, *Tax Challenges Arising from the Digitalisation of the Economy – Commentary to the Global Anti-Base Erosion Model Rules (Pillar Two), First Edition: Inclusive Framework on BEPS* 1 (2022).
47. OECD, *supra* n. 4.
48. KPMG, *Inclusive Framework BEPS Agreement Administrative Guidance of Pillar Two under BEPS 2.0* 3 (2023).

fundamental role in Article 3.2.3 but will also be a key consideration when calculating the ETR of PEs under the GloBE rules and the CbCR safe harbour. The chapter now moves on to consider how Pillar Two will affect the operations of MNEs more generally and consider the influence on their operating models; how MNEs that benefit from IP box type regimes will be impacted; and how the compliance requirements under Pillar Two may impact other reporting requirements affected by transfer pricing.

4.1 The Impact of Pillar Two on MNE Value Chains

Actions 8-10 placed significant emphasis on the location of functions being performed in relation to the DEMPE of intangibles and the control of economically significant risks.[49] The focus on key functions performed by MNEs has led to them operating so that key employees responsible for controlling economically significant risks are located in global or regional hubs. Their activities can, though not necessarily, enable higher returns for the hub location on an arm's length basis. Such models are predominant in IP-intensive industries such as life sciences or technology given their likely critical role in an MNE's value chain.[50] However, all industries are evolving and developing critical centralized IP in either technical know-how, brand, or technology, and this is driving market differentiation, significant profits, loss of competitiveness, and the ultimate exit from the market. These models inherently rely on certain employees being located in the hub location and may, as such, impose restrictions on the location of certain roles and where decision-making forums can take place. This proposition has already been challenged by the COVID-19 pandemic and the ability and preference of employees to work remotely.[51]

At a global level, countries have promoted MNEs setting up such models through the use of lower tax rates or incentives to attract businesses and primarily their senior workforce.[52] Examples of this include Belgium,[53] Ireland,[54] Singapore,[55] Switzerland,[56] and the United Arab Emirates.[57] Tax regimes of this nature reflect the implicit principle of the BEPS 1.0 action plan that countries may use tax as a competitive lever provided that the MNE's activities in the lower tax location are underpinned by economic

49. OECD, *supra* n. 36.
50. OECD, *Tax Incentives and the Global Minimum Corporate Tax: Reconsidering Tax Incentives after the GloBE Rules* 11 (2022).
51. Tim Sarson, *Travel Bans and Tax Risks: A Few Thoughts*, LinkedIn (4 March 2020), https://www.linkedin.com/pulse/travel-bans-tax-risks-few-thoughts-timothy-sarson?trk=portfolio_article-card_title.
52. OECD, *supra* n. 50.
53. KPMG, *New Belgian Expatriate Tax Regime: Key Takeaways from Our May 2022 Webinar* 1 (2022).
54. KPMG in Ireland, *RD&I Grants* 1 (2019).
55. KPMG, *Global R&D Incentives Guide* 137 (2021).
56. KPMG, *Tax Incentives to Promote Innovation in Switzerland: Additional Deduction for R&D and Patent Box as Tax Opportunity* 1 (2020); Benjamin Bellwald, *KPMG Switzerland: Innovation Tax Incentives in Pharma, BioTech & MedTech* 1 (2022).
57. KPMG Lower Gulf, *Corporate Tax in the UAE: A New Federal Corporate Tax (CT) System in the UAE* (2022); *Free Zones*, United Arab Emirates Ministry of Economy, https://www.moec.gov.ae/en/free-zones.

substance.[58] The GloBE rules, as a global minimum tax, do not follow this principle.[59] The benefit of the lower tax rate that an MNE would pay by having a hub and an accompanying transfer pricing model in such a location may have been a driver in the MNE setting one up in such a location.[60] The GloBE rules will limit the tax benefit of such hubs.[61] The rate applied under the GloBE rules of 15% will usually still be lower than the rate applied in potential headquarters locations that have higher tax rates such as France, Germany, the United Kingdom, or the United States, and the viability of such hub locations is often the result of a number of factors. These include the cost of the location, talent available in the marketplace, employee willingness to live/relocate to that location, and the tax rate. A marked shift in the relative tax benefit of a location could be enough to make the business case for operating out of such a location no longer compelling. This is the stated intent of Pillar Two: to reduce the incentive for taxpayers to engage in profit shifting and establish a floor for tax competition among jurisdictions.[62]

Financing arrangements may be subject to similar considerations. In the context of loan agreements, decisions controlling economically significant risk include whether to enter into a loan, its quantum, and the applicable interest rate. This relatively low level of intensity in decision-making lent itself to financing companies being set up in lower tax rate jurisdictions. Again, the business case for setting up financing companies in specific locations will be impacted by a number of factors but, given that such operations have often been subject to very low tax rates, it is likely that many MNEs will be reviewing their intra-group financing arrangements.

The ability of countries to set rates and rules on the tax base to attract MNEs to invest in the country has led to MNEs operating hubs that are regional or global headquarters in locations where they may not have otherwise been located.[63] However, it is important to note that, in practice, tax is generally only one factor that is considered when setting up these types of hubs. The tax consequences arising from the chosen operating model are heavily dependent upon the governance arrangements and working practices in place and the ongoing commitment of the business to adhere to these. MNEs' desire to have the flexibility to recruit the best person for a senior role wherever they may be based in the world was already a factor prior to the COVID-19 pandemic. With the acceleration of remote working post-pandemic, operating models which are evolving as MNEs try to accommodate flexible working conditions and implement remote working policies. It is likely that centralized 'above market' decision-making structures will remain, but the big challenge from a tax perspective will be managing the consequences of geographically dispersed management teams. In reducing the tax benefits available from locating activities in low-tax jurisdictions, the GloBE rules are likely to see greater adoption of multi-territory centralized operating models that may become increasingly virtual. If MNEs withdraw from locations in

58. OECD, *supra* n. 50, at 16.
59. OECD, *supra* n. 50, at 43.
60. OECD, *supra* n. 50, at 12.
61. Bezhan Salehy, *Pillar 2 and the Future of Tax Incentives*, Issue 1582 Tax Journal 1, 3 (2022).
62. OECD, *supra* n. 50, at 50.
63. OECD, *supra* n. 50, at 11.

which they previously had operations, it will be necessary for them to consider their position in relation to exit charges (and any specific local rules in relation to such restructurings, e.g., transfer taxes) and the post-restructuring transfer pricing. The impact of Pillar Two here may therefore be to increase disagreements between tax authorities on transfer pricing and other international tax matters.

4.2 The Impact of Pillar Two on Tax Incentive Regimes

Over the past two decades, jurisdictions have offered a range of incentive regimes usually to promote R&D activity and ownership of associated intellectual property rights in that jurisdiction.[64] The availability of incentive regimes is a further factor for MNEs in considering the location of their R&D operations. One of the most common types of incentive regimes is an 'IP box' regime that provides a lower ETR on qualifying income. The UK's patent box regime is an example of such a regime under which a corporate tax rate of 10% is paid on profits earned from patented inventions.[65] The number of jurisdictions in the OECD offering support for innovation-related income was five times greater in 2021 than it was in 2000.[66]

The GloBE rules level the playing field in this regard as tax incentive regimes that reduce covered taxes impact the jurisdictional ETR calculations and will impact the top-up tax calculation.[67]

It is worth noting that the enhanced benefits under incentive regimes such as super-deductions on qualifying expenditures are often available to smaller companies such as start-ups.[68] These benefits should not be diluted by the GloBE rules. Nevertheless, the impact of the GloBE rules on IP box regimes and the contrasting treatment of the Qualified Refundable Tax Credits mean that it is difficult not to envisage a change in governments' policies on incentive regimes. The GloBE rules may lead governments to adopt incentive regimes that operate through grants or are closer to grants in substance, e.g., the Research and Development expenditure credit.[69] Given that IP box-type regimes are impacted by the GloBE jurisdictional ETR calculations, they are likely to be less attractive to governments; however, this does not necessarily mean that such regimes will no longer exist. Countries that use IP box regimes, such as the United Kingdom and the Netherlands, use them to foster innovation and maintain tax competitiveness despite their higher headline rates.[70] The GloBE minimum ETR does not change this proposition other than in scenarios where the incentive regimes cause an entity's ETR to fall below the minimum tax rate of 15%. These tax regimes may

64. OECD, *supra* n. 50, at 11.
65. HMRC, *Guidance – Use the Patent Box to Reduce Your Corporation Tax on Profits* 1 (2020).
66. OECD, *supra* n. 50, at 11.
67. OECD, *supra* n. 50, at 50.
68. OECD, *supra* n. 50, at 50.
69. Salehy, *supra* n. 61, at 3.
70. HMRC, *supra* n. 65; *How to use the innovation box in your vpb*, Tax and Customs Administration, Belastingdienst, https://business.gov.nl/running-your-business/business-taxes/filing-your-tax-returns/how-to-use-the-innovation-box/.

likely still provide value to MNEs as they can still avail themselves of the benefits of the regimes to the point that a 15% ETR is reached. From a transfer pricing perspective, royalties and other IP-related payments by group entities to an IP owner taxed under an IP box regime may still be viable. The value of such regimes could even be viewed to be strengthened as smaller countries are unable to compete against such regimes by offering lower headline rates.

To comply with the GloBE rules, MNEs will have to carefully review their ETR but, while such IP box regimes remain, they may operate as a tool by which an MNE can reduce and possibly control its ETR to the global minimum ETR so that, if preferable, the MNE does not have to apply the qualified domestic minimum top-up tax. The pricing of royalties, and by proxy, the valuation of IP has always been a contested area in transfer pricing but, while IP box regimes remain, royalty pricing will remain a tool through which MNEs can manage their tax exposure, so they will likely be a focus of MNEs and tax authorities alike.

The GloBE rules application of a global minimum tax represents a fundamental shake-up of the established international tax framework. The all-encompassing nature of these rules means that knock-on impacts on the government's tax policy and how MNEs operate are inevitable. The GloBE rules will impact MNEs' decision-making, where to locate their operations and the benefits of different types of operating models. This, coupled with greater flexibility in working locations post the COVID-19 pandemic could drive significant changes to MNEs' operations and require changes to existing transfer pricing arrangements.

4.3 Article 3.2.3: Alignment with the ALP

Notwithstanding the substantial changes to the international tax system represented by Pillar Two, the long-standing ALP is retained. Article 3.2.3 of the GloBE Model Rules requires transactions between group entities to be priced consistent with the ALP and to be recorded at the same price for GloBE purposes for all affected constituent entities.[71]

Example 1

- Country 1 implements the GloBE rules that apply to Country 2 and Country 3 where the intermediate parent has two subsidiaries.
- An intra group transaction between Subsidiary 2 (resident in Country 2) and Subsidiary 3 (Resident in Country 3) is not priced at arm's length in the entity accounts of either entity with the price understated by USD 35 million.
- For GloBE purposes, Subsidiary 2's income is increased by USD 35 million and Subsidiary 3's income is reduced by USD 35 million which pushes Country 2 below a 15% ETR.

71. OECD, *supra* n. 4.

Situations where transactions may not align with the ALP:

- Transfer pricing rules not applied in Country 2 or 3.
- Transactions reported at a different price in financial statements.
- Transactions not recognized/permitted by the tax administration in Country 3.

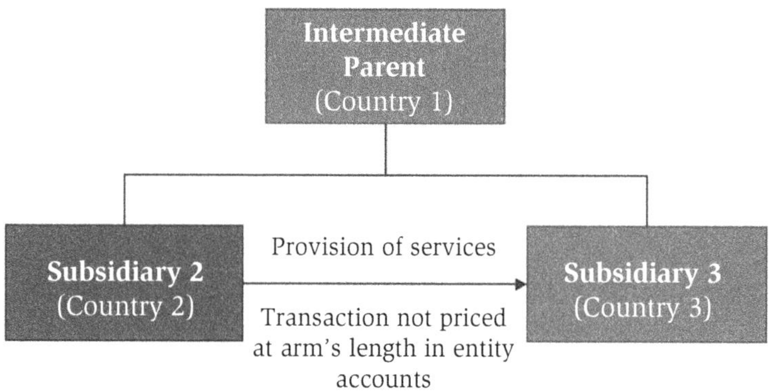

	$m
Accounting Income	100
ALP adjustment	35
GloBE Income	135
Tax ($100m @ 20%)	20
GloBE ETR	14.8%

	$m
Accounting Income	100
ALP adjustment	(35)
GloBE Income	65
Tax ($100m @ 20%)	15
GloBE ETR	23.1%

First, it is worth noting, however, that the definition of the ALP in the GloBE model rules differs from the definition in the OECD Guidelines. The former defines the ALP as 'the principle under which transactions between Constituent Entities must be recorded by reference to the conditions that would have been obtained between independent enterprises in comparable transactions and under comparable circumstances'.[72] However, the OECD Guidelines define it by reference to Article 9 of the OECD Model Tax Convention:

> conditions are made or imposed between the two enterprises in their commercial or financial relations which differ from those which would be made between independent enterprises, then any profits which would, but for those conditions, have accrued to one of the enterprises, but, by reason of those conditions, have not

72. OECD, *supra* n. 4, at 53.

so accrued, may be included in the profits of that enterprise and taxed accordingly.[73]

To add further complexity, this definition differs from that used for the attribution of profits to a PE which is per Article 7. The difference in definition between the OECD Guidelines and the GloBE model rules will enable countries whose transfer pricing legislation is not aligned with the OECD Guidelines to have consistency in their national legislation when implementing the GloBE rules. It also risks greater uncertainty. After the implementation of the GloBE rules, there may be various definitions of the ALP within a country's national law (this will be a certainty when an OECD member country's obligations under their double tax treaty network are taken into account). This could lead to tax authorities taking conflicting positions when applying the different definitions of the ALP. Here, as is the case across transfer pricing, consistency in approach is important to enable certainty, and this difference in definition risks creating inconsistencies.

When transactions are not priced consistently as defined in Article 3.2.3, an adjustment must be made such that the arm's length price is reflected. The OECD's published Commentary on the GLoBE model rules recognizes that such adjustments may result in an asymmetry in the following circumstances:

- under a unilateral advance pricing agreement (APA);
- when a domestic (tax-only) transfer pricing adjustment is made by one or more of the constituent entities; or
- as the result of a tax authority audit.[74]

Article 3.2.3 then provides for a compensating adjustment 'where necessary to prevent double taxation or double non-taxation under the GloBE Rules' except for 'under-taxed' jurisdictions.[75]

Example 2

- Unilateral transfer pricing adjustments result in a corresponding adjustment to the GloBE income or loss for all counterparties.
- An exception is when the adjustment increases or decreases the taxable income of a group in a jurisdiction with a nominal tax rate below 15% or that was a low-tax jurisdiction for the group in the prior two years (an under-taxed jurisdiction).
- In this example, Country 2 has a nominal tax rate below 15% which means that the unilateral downward transfer pricing adjustment in Country 2 is ignored for GloBE purposes.
- This reduces Country 2's GloBE ETR as GloBE income includes income that is not subject to tax in Country 2.

73. OECD, *Model Tax Convention on Income and on Capital Volume I and II (Updated 21 November 2017)* M-32 (2017).
74. OECD, *supra* n. 46, at 62.
75. OECD, *supra* n. 4.

- The objective is to prevent double non-taxation whereby unilateral transfer pricing adjustments could avoid tax under the GloBE and in Country 3.

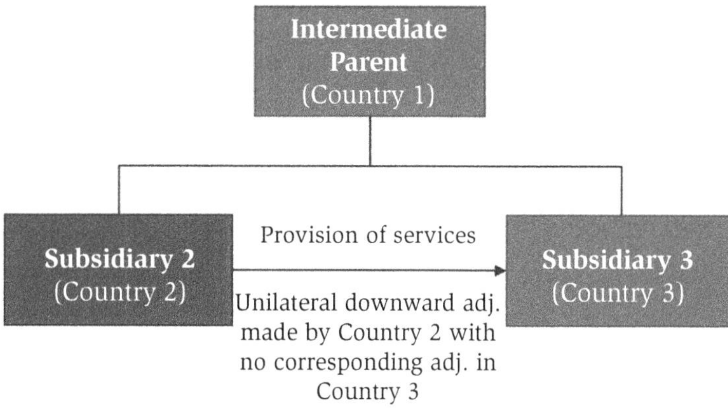

	$m
Accounting Income	100
TP adjustment	(35)
GloBE Income	100
Tax ($65m @ 10%)	6.5
GloBE ETR	6.5%

	$m
Accounting Income	100
TP adjustment	-
GloBE Income	100
Tax ($100m @ 25%)	25
GloBE ETR	25%

These are important considerations in reconciling Pillar Two with existing transfer pricing rules, but they are not comprehensive. The mechanisms for adjusting GloBE profits implicitly assume that the extent and timing of an adjustment are known in time for an adjustment to the GloBE computation to be made. This will often not be the case. Bilateral APAs are already a useful tool for taxpayers to achieve certainty on intercompany transactions. The overlay of Article 3.2.3 enhances the value of bilateral (although not unilateral) APAs as, through providing certainty on the intercompany transactions, the APA can also do so on the intercompany transactions in relation to Pillar Two. The helpfulness of APAs in supporting taxpayers to achieve certainty on Pillar Two will be limited to the extent that there is (i) a double tax treaty between the two relevant countries and (ii) a working competent authority relationship. It is also worth noting that the timeframe for a bilateral APA is typically two to three years, and certain tax authorities have restrictions on the type of transactions that can enter their APA programme. This means that achieving certainty on specific transactions may take time or not be available at all. Transfer pricing adjustments stemming from tax authority audits are rarely agreed within three years of the end of the relevant financial year. It is also possible that the relevant tax authorities may disagree on the adjustment to be made in order to restore the ALP. While the adjustment itself may be subject to a competent authority mutual agreement under the mutual agreement procedure (MAP) article of a treaty between the relevant countries, a provision should be made to extend its effect to a consequential GloBE adjustment. It would be preferable for such a provision to fall under the terms of a multilateral instrument as the taxing jurisdiction under the income inclusion rule (IIR) may not be either of the two jurisdictions involved in the transfer pricing adjustment. The terms of such an instrument would need to allow for the time delay noted above. Working through a simple example, a local audit may take three to five years to complete and then a potential MAP on top of this, therefore, it could easily be six to eight years before a dispute is resolved. Add to this the complexity of the GloBE rules, and tax certainty may not be reached within ten years.

Example 3

- The facts are similar to Example 1 except that the intra-group transaction between Subsidiary 2 and 3 is not priced at arm's length because there is a subsequent transfer pricing adjustment.
- As a result, Subsidiary 2's income is increased, and Subsidiary 3's income is decreased for tax and GloBE purposes, hence, the GloBE ETR should align with the country's tax rate.

Issues to consider:

- Transfer pricing adjustments agreed through MAP will need to be reflected in a group's GloBE calculation and in an amended GloBE return where adjustments are material.
- There is a risk that domestic laws could impose penalties for such amendments (though it does not appear to be the OECD's intention that such adjustments should result in penalties).

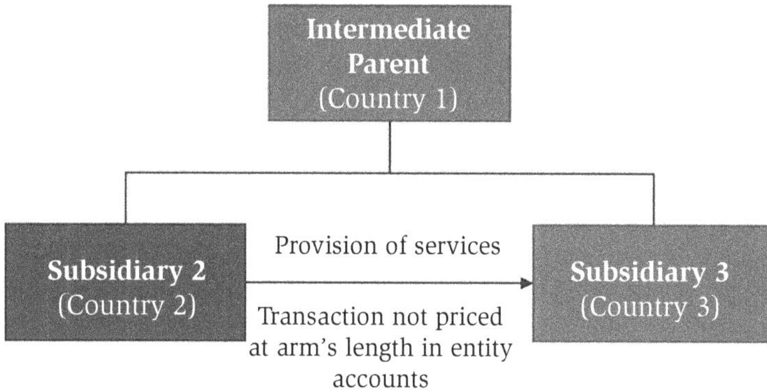

	$m
Accounting Income	100
TP adjustment	35
GloBE Income	135
Tax ($135m @ 20%)	27
GloBE ETR	20%

	$m
Accounting Income	100
TP adjustment	(35)
GloBE Income	65
Tax ($65m @ 15%)	10
GloBE ETR	15%

Both transfer pricing and the GloBE will be important to ensure that the interaction between the two is consistent and in accordance with objectives will be critical to the success of the new regime. The introduction of the GloBE rules adds to the arguments for further improvements in transfer pricing dispute prevention and resolution.

4.4 Permanent Establishments

Pillar Two represents an increased compliance burden for MNEs in relation to PEs. They may have been historically unwilling to closely examine their PE position due to the tax at risk being immaterial and due to the cost of compliance. In a way, Pillar Two does not change this. If an MNE is not correctly self-assessing a PE position, Pillar Two is only adding a further layer of compliance that the MNE is failing to meet. Nevertheless, when combined with a generally higher level of PE risk due to increased employee flexibility, this increased compliance burden in light of the Pillar Two rules may compel MNEs to assess their PE position and PE identification compliance process. When MNEs are already recognizing PEs, Pillar Two levels a considerable compliance burden requiring them to prepare an analysis in relation to the PEs that would not be currently prepared under the normal course of business.

Article 10.1 defines a PE for the purposes of the GloBE rules and details four situations under which a PE exists for them.[76] To summarize, the four situations under the GloBE rules in which a PE may be found are when:

- a PE exists in accordance with an applicable tax treaty in force;
- a PE exists in accordance with the domestic law in force;
- if there is no corporate income system, a PE would exist assuming there were domestic rules on PEs based on the OECD Model Tax Convention; or
- a place of business that is not already described in the scenarios above through which operations are conducted outside the jurisdiction where the entity is located provided that such jurisdiction exempts the income attributable to such operations.[77]

The key takeaway is that the scope of what is a PE for the purposes of the GloBE rules is broad and does not depend on whether there is a de facto PE under the laws of the source jurisdiction which means that MNEs cannot rely exclusively on their current PE analysis.

The treatment of certain industries under the GloBE rules exacerbates this tension. Article 8 of the OECD Model Tax Convention states that profits of an enterprise from the operation of ships or aircraft in international traffic shall be taxable only in the state where that enterprise is resident.[78] Article 8 generally takes priority over Article 7 on business profits so the effect of the treaty is that, if there is a PE, then the state where it is located would not have taxing rights over profits attributable to it that are from the operation of ships or aircraft in international traffic.[79]

Article 3.3 of the GloBE rules excludes international shipping income.[80] However, for airlines, while the MNE will not have a taxable PE as a result of its international travel under Article 8 of the OECD Model Tax Convention,[81] this position may not be replicated under the GloBE rules. In a scenario, for example, when an aircraft is operated for international travel in a jurisdiction that has no corporation tax system but would be treated as establishing a PE under the OECD Model Tax Convention, the operation of an aircraft would establish a PE under the GloBE rules.

Having identified a PE under the GloBE rules, income must then be allocated to it. Per Article 3.4 of the GloBE rules, the financial accounting net income or loss of a constituent entity that is a PE is the net income or loss reflected in its separate financial accounts when these have been prepared and adjusted to the arm's length position if necessary.[82] However, in practice, MNEs may not maintain separate financial accounting information for their PEs with the attribution of profit being an 'offline' exercise performed for corporate tax compliance purposes. In some dependent agent cases, no physical branch will exist even when a PE is deemed for tax purposes. When accounts

76. OECD, *supra* n. 4, at 63.
77. OECD, *supra* n. 4, at 63.
78. OECD, *supra* n. 73, at M-30.
79. OECD, *supra* n. 73.
80. OECD, *supra* n. 4, at 18.
81. OECD, *supra* n. 73.
82. OECD, *supra* n. 4, at 19.

have not been prepared, it will be necessary for MNEs to compile quasi accounts in accordance with the ultimate parent entities accounting standard and the ALP. They will compute the amount that would have been reflected in the financial accounts (had they been prepared). This requirement represents a considerable compliance burden for MNEs in addition to the already increased compliance with the GloBE rules.

The GloBE rules also mean that MNEs will have to consider transfer pricing in scenarios where transfer pricing has historically been less important, i.e., jurisdictions that do not have a corporate tax regime. An example would be an MNE that has a small presence in the United Arab Emirates covering the Middle East region and providing local support to the HQ locations. Given that there historically has not been a corporation tax regime there, an approach taken by MNEs has been to not apply any specific transfer pricing or attribute any profit.[83] If such an operation meets the definition of a PE then, under the GloBE rules, in addition to having to prepare accounts for the newly established PE, the MNE will also have to determine an arm's length attribution of profit.[84] To the extent that such countries have implemented the GloBE rules (or indeed implemented a corporate tax regime as a result of the GloBE rules), there will now be a compliance requirement in countries where MNEs have not historically had reasons to consider the local direct tax consequences of operations in that area. The complexity of the draft Globe Information Return that is required to document these decisions is a cause for concern over the compliance burden facing MNEs.

4.5 A Driver of Behaviours

The Pillar Two rules operate as a complex set of prescriptive requirements. The safe harbours (both transitional and, it is expected, permanent) operate formula-based tests that can remove compliance obligations under the GloBE rules.[85] To take the CbCR safe harbour where the simplified ETR of the MNE is above a set percentage (proposed to reduce from 17% to 15% over the first few years of operation), the top-up tax will be deemed to be zero.[86] The simplified ETR is calculated by dividing the jurisdiction's income tax expense as reported on the MNE's financial statement by its profit or loss before income tax as reported in the MNE's CbCR for that jurisdiction.[87]

The two inputs to the CbCR safe harbour, i.e., financial statements and the profit or loss before income tax, include an entity's related party transactions. There may be a risk here that MNEs are incentivized to enter into arrangements through transfer pricing or other means in order to produce results that are still arguable as arm's length but more generally favourable under the safe harbours or under the application of Pillar Two. For example, an MNE could structure its transfer pricing to raise the jurisdiction's

83. KPMG, *UAE: Transfer Pricing Implications with Introduction of a Corporate Income Tax Regime* 1 (2022).
84. KPMG, *supra* n. 83.
85. OECD, *supra* n. 4, at 47-48.
86. OECD, *supra* n. 4, at 47.
87. OECD, *supra* n. 4, at 28-29.

ETR under this safe harbour. Any such transactions would certainly have an impact on actual tax paid, but the blanket prescriptive nature of the safe harbours and rules may create a risk that the GloBE rules themselves become a driver for tax planning through artificial arrangements when the BEPS 1.0 Project significantly curbed such activities.

4.6 Domestic Transfer Pricing Requirements

The application of transfer pricing rules to domestic-related party transactions is a relatively recent development (leaving aside its application to transactions between constituent states in federations, such as in US interstate trade). The main reason for this is not difficult to identify; in many cases, the overall tax effect of non-arm's length pricing will sum to zero, or approximately so, such that the fiscal risk is too small to justify when set against the additional compliance burden that would be involved. When domestic rules have been introduced, it is often for reasons of non-discrimination between residents and non-residents or to counter policy-driven asymmetries in domestic tax treatment for transactions into incentive schemes (IP boxes, for example). When no such concerns arise, the compliance burden on domestic transactions, even those required to be priced at arm's length, is often intentionally reduced. An example here is the UK's exclusion of most domestic transactions from the scope of its new mandatory Local File documentation requirements for members of large groups.

The GloBE rules do not require the implementation of domestic transfer pricing rules as the rules require a consolidated view on a country-by-country basis and, therefore, the pricing of such transactions should not impact the amount of GloBE income determined for each country. However, there are two exceptions to this that create an implicit domestic transfer pricing requirement and hence the need to establish and support arm's length pricing:

- First, transfer pricing and the ALPs needs to be applied to in-country asset transfers. This is primarily to avoid artificial losses being created and moved within groups.
- Second, the ALPs must be applied to in-country transactions where one of the entities is either an excluded entity or an entity – such as an investment entity or a minority-owned constituent entity – that has its GloBE ETR calculated separately from the rest of the group.[88]

4.7 An Unexpected Benefit?

One of the most complex parts of the Pillar Two requirements is the access to and collation of data – not just the amount of data but also the sources from where data needs to be drawn. At a theoretical level, this sounds relatively simple, i.e., pull

88. OECD, *supra* n. 46, at 63.

information from the local generally accepted accounting principles (GAAP) statutory accounts and pull data and information for the group GAAP from the consolidated accounts. This has been a significant operational transfer pricing issue faced by MNEs for a number of years. It is technically complex from a systems perspective, there is often no real-time data in the local GAAP accounts, and the governance and rigour between the two sets of financial information often fall between the gaps of the finance business partner, the central consolidation team, and the local finance teams or shared services teams. Tax authorities often require that returns on a local GAAP basis must be in line with benchmarking so MNEs have no choice but to run calculations on the local GAAP basis, and such data tends to get locked down later as the priority is initially group consolidation accounts. The GAAP adjustments can create material differences in the profitability in the local GAAP accounts as well as in the business unit segmentation and profitability, resulting in potential mismatches and further reconciliations.

This inconsistency and inability to look at data were highlighted with the implementation of the CbCR requirements pursuant to Action 13 of the BEPS 1.0 Project. As this reporting requirement was implemented at a national level, MNEs spent a significant amount of time and a number of iterations working through how best to comply with the OECD's CbCR requirements and trying different methods for system solutions to support them. Two general approaches were adopted and implemented, i.e., the 'top down' approach working from the group reporting data in the group GAAP to a local country level and the 'bottom up' working from the local statutory accounts to a country level. However, it was soon identified that the two were extremely difficult to implement in the existing Enterprise Resource Planning (ERP) system and finance processes, and a reconciliation, while it could be calculated on a country-by-country basis in principle, in reality, is very complex and time-consuming, requires multiple data sources and data points, and therefore is not completed unless required. The data requirements for Pillar Two depend on data from a group and a local GAAP position. It is estimated that the determination of the CbCR uses less than 20 separate data elements whereas the Pillar Two requirement is over 150 data elements; this is a significant level of additional required data.

At the same time, many MNEs are in the midst of ERP or significant finance transformation projects that, for the first time, acknowledge that the corporate tax requirements are a critical part of these transformations, and there is an opportunity to develop technology solutions to support the tax teams in the ERP system, particularly with the compliance of Pillar Two. This gives MNEs the opportunity to think more widely about the system transformation and incorporating transfer pricing requirements, CbCR, and other tax compliance needs from different sets of accounts. Additionally, they can broaden their approach to the reconciliations between the two creating potential opportunities for finance and ERP transformation to create central data repositories for all tax reporting requirements. However, although this might look like a potential positive for transfer pricing, it is important to remember that these transformations take three to five years to implement, so the full benefit of tax requirements in ERP transformations is a long-term benefit for transfer pricing.

5 CONCLUSION

The concept of a global minimum tax of 15% is a simple and well-intentioned idea, yet the implementation is far from simple and relies on two key principles: (i) global implementation and recognition and (ii) global consistency. If both of these principles are not met, countries may find that it is not driving the required outcomes while taxpayers may be caught between differing levels of implementation and interpretations of the rules. The current rules are designed to create an even playing field and reduce tax competition between countries, but they crucially rely on transfer pricing and the application of the ALP. There are several challenges with this with one of the key ones being that the ALP is simply that, i.e., a principle and a range of results leading to differences of interpretation. The assumption that the component transactions of an entity's tax base are carried out at arm's length, a foundation on which the GloBE calculation stands, may be found to be a shaky one. Challenges to this tax base will arise well after the GloBE compliance period and leave taxpayers not only facing bilateral disputes between tax authorities on their transfer pricing but also the additional burden of having to manage the impact on the GloBE filings that will likely not only involve the two countries subject to the dispute.

CHAPTER 4

Transfer Pricing and Big Data

Mukesh Butani, Seema Kejriwal & Kriti Chawla

1 INTRODUCTION

Big data is a booming business globally. The 'big' here refers to the large data sets that are analysed to reveal trends in consumer behaviour. Its creation and gathering process comes from sources that include feeds posted on social media,[1] wholesale or retail transactions, e-commerce data, shipping, audio and video logs, text messaging, internet search queries, satellite imagery and Global Positioning System (GPS) data, and stock-market activity and financial transactions. Data is also flooding in from the Internet of Things[2] that spans a host of connected devices. These include intelligent home gadgets, industrial machines, wearables, smart cities, and more. It is likely that there will be approximately 27 billion connected IoT devices by 2025.[3]

An enormous amount of big data generates tremendous economic benefits for businesses. As an example, 'Every 60 seconds, 510,000 comments are posted, 293,000 statuses are updated, 4 million posts are liked, and 136,000 photos are uploaded on Facebook.'[4] When analysed meaningfully, this data is a treasure trove of business customer information that can be used for both explicit and implicit monetization. The former is the result of the direct sale or sharing of data,[5] while the latter could result indirectly through the enhancement of in-house data-based products.[6]

Annexure 1 provides a list of the information that Facebook collects about its users.[7] Apart from other uses, Meta utilizes this to deliver targeted ad services by providing numerous parameters that advertisers can choose before they must pay for a click on their advertisement. This is an example of explicit monetization. For instance, the premise of Netflix's first show, i.e., the David Fincher-directed political thriller 'House of Cards' had its roots in big data. Netflix invested about USD 100 million in the show's first two seasons because consumers who watched it also watched movies directed by David Fincher and starring Kevin Spacey. Executives correctly predicted that a series combining all three would be a hit.[8] This is an example of implicit monetization.

Another relevant example is the Formula 1 (F1) race. Here, the margin between winning and losing is measured in split seconds. F1 teams would not be able to compete without the real-time insight that is gained through telemetry data supplied by

1. Facebook, Instagram, Whatsapp, Youtube, Linkedin, etc., are examples of social media networks.
2. Big Data Companies and Data Analytics, Brian Deagon, accessed at https://www.investors.com/news/technology/big-data-companies-data-analytics-stocks-to-watch/.
3. State of IoT 2022: Number of connected IoT devices growing by 18% to 14.4 billion globally, Mohammad Hasan, May 2022 accessed at https://iot-analytics.com/number-connected-iot-devices/.
4. Facebook Statistics and Facts, 2022 accessed at https://kinsta.com/blog/facebook-statistics/.
5. Example of such a business model includes Facebook, Google, Amazon, etc.
6. Example of such a business model could include Netflix, Uber, etc.
7. Meta, Privacy Policy accessed at https://www.facebook.com/privacy/policy.
8. Companies use big data to predict the next best step for Industries, accessed at https://builtin.com/big-data/big-data-examples-applications.

hundreds of car sensors. These sensors can generate a billion data points in a single race weekend.[9]

1.1 What Is Big Data?

The OECD defines 'Big Data' as data that cannot be processed using standard data processing tools and techniques because they are too large or complex[10] and differs from traditional data in a significant way. While big data systems involve an increasing amount of semi-structured and unstructured data being collected, the scope of traditional data is limited to structured data.[11]

Structured data is used by traditional database systems in which records are divided into well-defined 'fields' (such as 'name', 'address', etc.) that can be easily searched, classified, and sorted according to certain criteria. On the other hand, unstructured data such as image data, Twitter updates, etc., lack a clearly defined format. Semi-structured data is a combination of structured and unstructured data. While certain aspects of the data may be defined (typically within the information itself, for example, location data appended to social media updates), it lacks the rigidity associated with structured data.[12]

In 2001, Doug Laney[13] described the '3V' model in order to define big data using three dimensions, specifically:

(i) *Volume*: Size and scale of big data typically starting at tens of terabytes to transform into meaningful information.
(ii) *Velocity*: Frequency at which data is generated and processed. For instance, most organizations expect data to be available within twenty-four hours of being captured and processed.[14]
(iii) *Variety*: Indicating the wide variety of unstructured data types frequently stored in big data systems, including the different forms and ranges of the data that is analysed. This may include pictures, videos, audio recordings, email messages, documents, books, presentations, tweets, etc.

Over the years, this has expanded to now include 7Vs with the rest being under:

(iv) *Variability*: Variability is different from variety. A coffee shop may offer six different blends of coffee, but if you get the same blend every day and it

9. Geoff McGrath, managing director of the Applied Technologies division at F1 team McLaren, The white book of big Data: The definitive guide to the revolution in business analytics accessed at https://www.fujitsu.com/se/imagesgig5/WhiteBookofBigData.pdf.
10. OECD Guidelines for Collecting, Reporting and Using Data on Innovation, 4th Edition, Glossary of Terms.
11. Bill Franks, *Taming the Big Data Tidal Wave* (2012).
12. Ian Mitchell, *The White Book of Big Data* 9 (2012), accessed at https://www.fujitsu.com/se/imagesgig5/WhiteBookofBigData.pdf.
13. Doug Laney, *3D Data Management: Controlling Data Volume, Velocity and Variety*, Gartner, file No. 949, 6 February 2001.
14. Collaborative research survey conducted by the IBM Institute for Business Value and the Saïd Business School at the University of Oxford.

tastes different every day, that is variability. The same is true of data. If the meaning constantly changes, it can significantly impact your data homogenization.

(v) *Veracity*: Veracity ensures the data is accurate which requires processes to keep the insufficient data from accumulating in systems. The simplest example is when contacts enter a marketing automation system with false names and inaccurate contact information. How many times have you seen Mickey Mouse in a database? It's the classic 'garbage in, garbage out' challenge.

(vi) *Visualization*: Visualization is critical in today's world. Using charts and graphs to visualize large amounts of complex data is much more effective in conveying meaning than spreadsheets and reports chock-full of numbers and formulas.

(vii) *Value*: Value is the end game. After addressing volume, velocity, variety, variability, veracity, and visualization - which takes a lot of time, effort, and resources, there must be an assurance that an organization is getting value from the data.

Big data and analytics technology help businesses achieve valuable insights in many areas. This includes in-depth customer research, product development, cost management, and competitive analysis. Big data also provides operational intelligence that enables companies to investigate, monitor, analyse situations, and then react and respond. For retailers, big data helps companies better understand customers and the most effective ways to keep them coming back. As a result, manufacturers can solve problems faster and make business decisions that are more agile. In addition, bankers use it to help minimize risk and fraud.

The application of data analytics affects organizations across practically every industry and takes an active part in developing strategies for their success. Four main types of data analysis can be valuable for businesses, including when handling big data, i.e., descriptive, diagnostic, predictive, and prescriptive:

- *Descriptive analysis*: shows what is happening now based on incoming data, often via a real-time dashboard or email reports.
- *Diagnostic analysis*: looks at past performance to determine what happened and why often in the form of an analytic dashboard.
- *Predictive analysis*: forecasts likely scenarios of what might happen.
- *Prescriptive analysis*: reveals what actions should be taken and usually results in rules and recommended next steps.

The businesses that use big data most effectively have a reliable data management strategy, insightful reporting, and focused analysis of the areas that matter.

1.2 Sources of Big Data

There are two types of big data sources, i.e., internal and external. Data is internal if a company generates, owns, and controls it. Its sources are corporate enterprise resource planning (ERP) modules, internal documents, sensors, controllers, in-house call centers and website logs. External data is public data or data generated outside the company; correspondingly, the company neither owns nor controls it. Big data environments often incorporate it on consumers, financial markets, weather and traffic conditions, geographic information, scientific research, and more. Images, videos, and audio files are also forms of big data, and many big data applications involve streaming data that is processed and collected on a continual basis.

1.3 Uses of Big Data

1.3.1 Big Data and Data-Driven Decision-Making

OECD Report on Analytics for Integrity[15] depicts how the data that is collected is used for effective decision-making.

Figure 4.1 The Data Value Chain

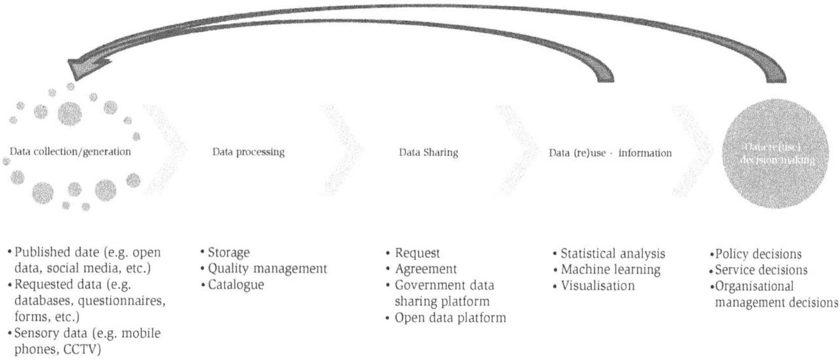

1.3.2 Examples of Data-Driven Decision-Making

1.3.2.1 Leadership Development at Google

Google focuses heavily on what it refers to as 'people analytics'. As part of one of its well-known people analytics initiatives, Project Oxygen, Google mined data from more than 10,000 performance reviews and compared the data with employee retention rates. Then, it used the information to identify common behaviours of high-performing managers and created training programmes to develop these competencies. These efforts boosted median favorability scores for managers from 83% to 88%.

15. OECD 2019, Analytics for Integrity: Data-Driven Approaches for Enhancing Corruption and fraud Risk Assessments, accessed at https://www.oecd.org/gov/ethics/analytics-for-integrity.pdf.

1.3.2.2 Real Estate Decisions at Starbucks

After hundreds of Starbucks' locations were closed in 2008, then-CEO Howard Schultz promised that the company would take a more analytical approach to identify future store locations. It now partners with a location-analytics company to pinpoint ideal store locations using data like demographics and traffic patterns. The organization also considers input from its regional teams before making decisions that Starbucks uses to determine the likelihood of success for a particular location before taking on a new investment.

1.3.2.3 Driving Sales at Amazon

Amazon uses data to decide which products they should recommend to customers based on their prior purchases and patterns in search behaviour. However, Amazon uses data analytics and machine learning to drive its recommendation engine rather than blindly suggesting a product. McKinsey estimated that, in 2017, 35% of Amazon's consumer purchases could be tied back to the company's recommendation system.[16]

Collecting, extracting, formatting, and analysing insights for enhanced data-driven decision-making in business was once an all-encompassing task that naturally delayed the entire data decision-making process. However, today, the development and democratization of business intelligence software empower users without deep-rooted technical expertise for analysing and extract valuable conclusions from their information. As a direct result, less information technology (IT) support is required to produce reports, trends, and visualization that facilitate the data decision-making process.

Data comes in two distinctive types, qualitative and quantitative, and both are critical for making a data-driven decision. Qualitative analysis focuses on data that is not defined by numbers or metrics, such as interviews, videos, and anecdotes. It is based on observation rather than measurement. Here, it is crucial to code the data to ensure that items are grouped together methodically and intelligently. The quantitative analysis focuses on numbers and statistics. The median, standard deviation, and other descriptive stats play a pivotal role here. This type of analysis is measured rather than observed. Both qualitative and quantitative data should be analysed to achieve smarter business decisions.

1.3.3 Big Data Industry

The big data industry thus comprises several players:

(1) Companies that analyse customer data at their disposal and use it for, *inter alia*, targeted advertising that is their primary source of revenue are large companies like Facebook and Google.

16. The advantages of data-driven decision making, Tim Stobierski, 26 August 2019 accessed at https://online.hbs.edu/blog/post/data-driven-decision-making.

(2) Companies that analyse customer data at their disposal and use it for both improved customer experiences and other commercial uses are those such as Netflix, Uber, Airbnb, and Unilever.[17]
(3) Raw data collectors and sellers include companies with customer interactions that collect consumer data and commercially disseminate the same. These could be all companies with access to a wide variety of customer data.
(4) Big Data Analytics companies comprise those that convert big data into meaningful analytical information for use by businesses.
(5) Big Data Intermediaries are data intermediaries that serve as a mediator between those who wish to make their *data* available and those who seek to leverage that *data.*
(6) Consumers virtually include all businesses today.

1.4 Localization Requirements under Privacy Laws: Impact on Ownership and Utilization of Big Data

With exponential growth and widespread acceptance of the benefits of big data, various challenges and risks are associated with its collection, protection, and utilization. It shall be important to address these risks lest they outweigh the benefits derived from big data transactions.

With the din of the absence of a comprehensive data protection law globally, there have been many developments in privacy and data- protecting space over the last decade. In the European Union (EU), the General Data Protection Regulation (GDPR) lays down a baseline set of standards that companies must comply with when dealing with the data of EU citizens. This includes requiring the consent of data subjects[18] for processing their information, anonymizing the data collected to protect the privacy of data subjects, provisions for safe transfer of data across borders, etc. It is significant to note that the GDPR is not just applicable to organizations operating in the EU but rather takes a sweeping approach in that it protects all data of EU citizens even when such information is processed by a foreign organization.[19,20]

Borrowing flavours of the EU GDPR, the (Indian) Digital Personal Data Protection Bill, 2022 (PDP, 2022) recognizes the right of individuals to protect their digital

17. What does Unilever do with AI at 27 of its data centres worldwide, Soumik Roy, 10 April 2019, accessed at https://techwireasia.com/2019/04/what-does-unilever-do-with-ai-at-27-of-its-data-centers-worldwide/.
18. As per Article 4 (Definitions) of the EU GDPR, a 'data subject' is referred to as an 'identified or identifiable natural person'; an identifiable natural person is one who can be identified, directly or indirectly, in particular by reference to an identifier such as a name, an identification number, location data, an online identifier, or one or more factors specific to the physical, physiological, genetic, mental, economic, cultural, or social identity of that natural person.
19. Chapter 5: Article 44 of the EU GDPR.
20. In other words, the criteria is not limited to those organizations operating in Europe but includes all organizations that handle and process data of EU citizens (including those based and operating overseas).

personal data and the need to process such data within lawful bounds.[21] It brings several significant changes compared to the earlier iterations[22] of the proposed law. This includes expanding the scope of law[23] to cover the processing of digital personal data within India when such data is: (i) collected online or (ii) collected offline and is digitized. It will also apply to the processing of personal data outside India if it is for offering goods or services or profiling individuals in India. In this context, the central government shall establish the Data Protection Board of India to adjudicate non-compliance with the provisions of the bill.

The Indian Government has also introduced significant changes for data protection and privacy, such as a data localization mandate issued by the Reserve Bank of India (RBI),[24] banking regulations on card data storage, introducing industry standards for privacy assurance,[25] and introducing tighter security measures in the digital payments[26] sector apart from the data protection bill.

21. Preamble, Digital Personal Data Protection Bill, 2022, accessed at https://www.meity.gov.in/writereaddata/files/The%20Digital%20Personal%20Data%20Potection%20Bill%2C%202022_0.pdf.
22. This is the fourth iteration of the data protection law in India. The first draft of the law, i.e., the Personal Data Protection Bill 2018, was proposed by the Justice Srikrishna Committee set up by the Ministry of Electronics and Information Technology (MeitY) with the mandate of setting out a data protection law for India. The government made revisions to this draft and introduced it as the Personal Data Protection Bill 2019 (PDP Bill, 2019) in the Lok Sabha in 2019. On the same day, the Lok Sabha passed a motion to refer the PDP Bill 2019 to a joint committee of both of the Houses of Parliament. Due to delays caused by the pandemic, the Joint Committee on the PDP Bill, 2019 (JPC) submitted its report on the bill in December 2021. The report was accompanied by a new draft bill, specifically, the Data Protection Bill 2021 that incorporated the recommendations of the JPC. However, in August 2022, the government withdrew the PDP Bill.
23. The bill removes the classification relating to 'sensitive personal data or information' and introduces the definition of the term 'personal data'. A wider definition has also been given to the term 'data' in the new Bill 2022 as a representation of information, facts, concepts, opinions, or instructions in a manner suitable for communication, interpretation, or processing by humans or by automated means.
24. The RBI is India's central bank and regulatory body responsible for regulation of the Indian Banking System.
25. The Bureau of Indian Standards, towards mid-2021, made available to the public its new standards for data privacy assurance, i.e., IS 17428. The standard seeks to provide a privacy assurance framework for organizations to establish, implement, maintain, and continually improve their data privacy management system. It comprises two parts with one being prescriptive for which the requirements are to be mandatorily implemented by anyone applying the standard. The other part is the suggestive part with detailed best practices to aid in implementing the requirements of the prescriptive part.
26. In January 2021, the RBI had constituted a working group to study digital lending activities in light of increasing disruption by online lending apps. The report of the working group on 'Digital Lending including Lending through Online Platforms and Mobile Apps' observed that numerous lapses regarding privacy occurred across digital lending apps. Inadequate transparency, lack of choice of the user to manage or delete their data after a loan has been paid, non-disclosure of partner banks or non-banking financial companies (NBFCs), and misuse of borrowers' sensitive data to harass them and their family/friends were identified as some of the major concerns. Through this report, the working group of the RBI gave some recommendations related to technology including recommendations that data should be stored in servers locally in India and that it should only be collected 'from the borrower/prospective borrower with prior information on the purpose, usage and implication of such data and with explicit consent of the borrower in an auditable way'.

In April 2018, the RBI introduced a directive on payment system data storage in India (Notification).[27] The Notification placed the onus to store payment data within India on 'system providers' (i.e., banks and payment system operators (PSOs). The motivation behind it was to ensure the ready availability of payment data in India for regulatory oversight purposes, thereby making it easier for the RBI to conduct fraud, money laundering, and other investigations.[28]

Further, the RBI also introduced 'Guidelines on Regulation of Payment Aggregators and Payment Gateways' to license and regulate payment intermediaries facilitating and handling payments between users and merchants using electronic/online payment modes. Under these guidelines, the RBI introduced a restriction on payment aggregators and merchants from storing cards and card-related data. As an exemption, the last four digits of the card number and the card issuer's name could be stored for transaction tracking and reconciliation purposes. Tokenization was suggested as a workable solution to comply with the card storage restrictions while maintaining continuity in online payments.

Apart from the above, in line with the TRIPS Agreement[29] and the WIPO Copyright Treaty, the (Indian) Copyright Act 1957 protects databases as collections or compilations of literary and creative works. The fundamental criterion is that a database is the product of its creator's intellectual work and exhibits a sufficient degree of originality.[30]

In India, copyright law subsists over original literary works.[31] While the meaning of the term 'literary works' does not expressly include 'data', 'big data', or 'information' within the ambit of its protection, it includes computer programs, tables, and compilations, including computer databases within its purview.[32]

Thus, it could be argued, while the 'input' is not explicitly protected under the said Act, the output of big data is protected as a copyrightable subject matter. The rationale is that there is a certain level of skill and labour involved in developing the database or the code that generates the database for which a copyright is given to the person[33] who creates the code.

27. The Notification was addressed to banks and authorized PSOs operating under the Banking Regulation Act 1949 and Payment and Settlement Systems Act 2007 (PSS Act) which are the laws empowering the RBI to regulate banks and payment systems, respectively.
28. The RBI, in July 2021, had put an indefinite ban on Mastercard because of the company's failure to comply with local data storage norms that required payment companies to store data related to Indian customers only in the country. The ban has now been lifted.
29. Article 10(2) of the TRIPS Agreement and Article 5 of the WIPO Copyright Treaty provide copyright protection for compilations of data or other materials that constitute an intellectual creation 'by virtue of their selection and arrangement'. Further, Article 2(5) of the Berne Convention provides copyrights on authors' literary and artistic collections 'which constitutes an intellectual creation by reason of the selection and arrangement of their contents'.
30. V.K. Gupta, *Copyright Issues Relating to Database Use*, 17 Desldoc Bulletin of Information Technology (1997) DOI: 10.14429/dbit.17.4.3227.
31. Section 13(1)(a), (Indian) Copyright Act, 1957 defines works in which copyrights subsists.
32. Section 2(o), (Indian) Copyright Act, 1957 defines the meaning of the term 'literary work'.
33. Section 2(d), (Indian) Copyright Act, 1957 provides the meaning of the author in relation to any literary, dramatic, musical, or artistic work that is computer-generated and the person who creates the work.

In light of the above regulatory environment, from a tax perspective, the requirement of the mandatory storage of data on a server or data centre in India could potentially form the basis to tax a foreign company's income in India. A decision of the Advance Ruling authority has held (*MasterCard* case[34]) that, if operational control is vested with the foreign entity, it would create a taxable nexus in India irrespective of ownership of the server. While, for the data protection law, companies may want to exercise control, it could lead to tax exposures.

2 TRANSFER PRICING ANALYSIS OF BIG DATA

2.1 Identifying the Transaction (Interplay with Books of Accounts)

There is no universally accepted set of transactions that companies enter into in the big data context. As has been discussed earlier, sources of big data are both internal and external. To a certain extent, it could be argued that data have been generated internally by businesses for decades now and, to that extent, the value of it or services pertaining to it is captured in the overall function, assets, and risk (FAR) analysis of inter-company transactions. However, the thrust in today's day and age on big data, the investments by businesses in it, and data-driven decision-making all probably warrant looking at the big data ecosystem of a company as a standalone activity warranting an appropriate analysis from both an accounting and transfer pricing standpoint.

A sample picture of a big data infrastructure ecosystem is given in Figure 4.2.

34. AAR No. 1573 of 2014.

Figure 4.2 Example of Real-Time Big Data Analytics Architecture

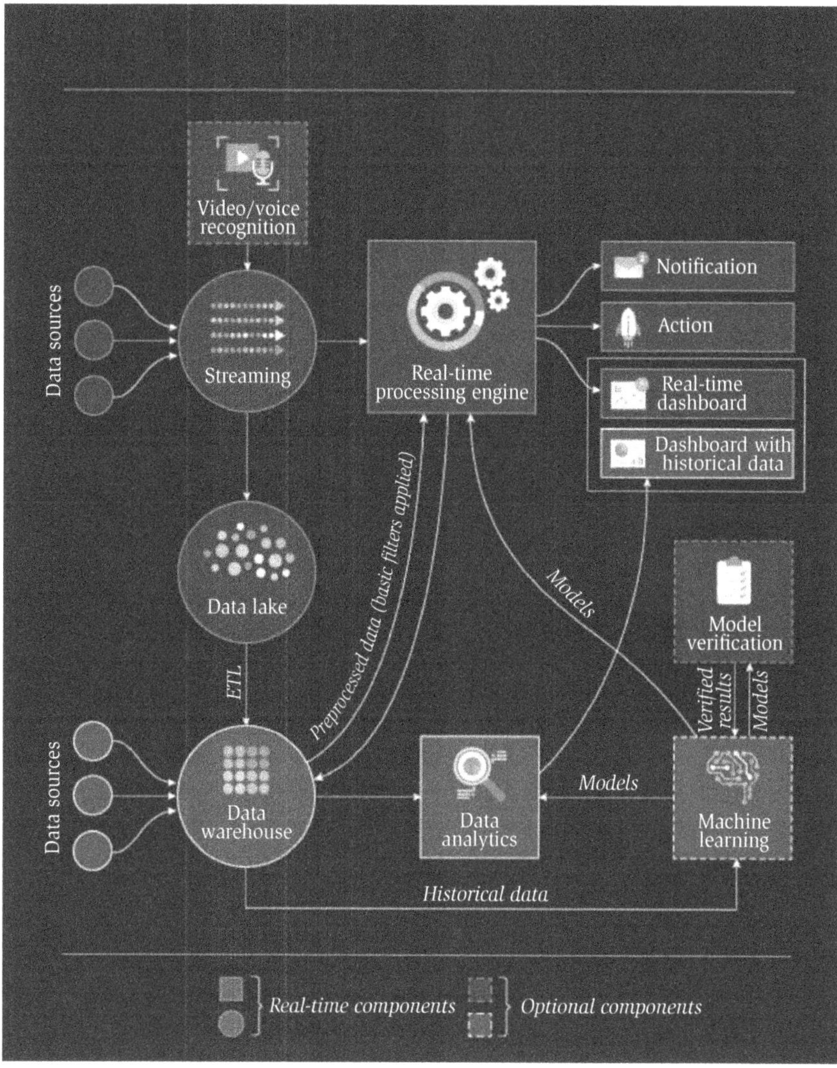

The OECD Guidelines, paragraph 1.42 states that a transaction is the consequence or expression of commercial or financial terms between the parties. It is therefore important that transactions in relation to big data are accurately delineated. The authors opine that inter-company contracts or books of accounts could be the starting point for identifying transactions pertaining to big data in a company. In the absence of any of these, it may be impossible for a transfer pricing practitioner to identify transactions, ascribe values to them, and then arrive at arm's length prices given the complexity of the big data ecosystem (as can be seen from the diagram). In this context, the following excerpt in the context of the digital economy can also be true for analysis of the big data value chain of a business:

> According to Crawford and Joler's 'Anatomy of AI', every step of digital infrastructure and product supply chains should be analysed in terms of labour, resources and data and their joint extraction.
>
> They argue that – similar to neural networks or algorithms – the hidden supply and value chains of the digital economy are currently still black boxes for us and therefore need to be systematically analysed. From such a modular perspective, it follows that not only so-called key value drivers, but also all hidden value contributions necessary to enable the system of the digital economy are considered in the analysis. Resources, data, and work can therefore be understood as an alternative taxonomy for the analysis of the digital economy and the starting point for the following considerations on the actually materialistic value chain.[35]

The authors are of the view that while analysing big data, not only what is referred to as key value drivers but also all hidden value contributions necessary to enable the system of the big data ecosystem need to be considered in the analysis. Nevertheless, the ecosystem notwithstanding, if big data were to be benchmarked on a standalone basis, the following alternatives are possible.

2.1.1 Big Data as a Product

It is possible today to buy big data from third parties. Before doing so, it is necessary to understand how the data is acquired, what method and/or technology is used, what are the measures put in place to ensure the accuracy of the data, how recent is the data collection, what is the degree of quality checking done, etc. Thus, treating big data as a commodity envisages that companies make it available to other group companies in the same way that goods are made available. In cases where companies make big data available to both internal and external users, the analysis would follow the typical benchmarking for the sale of products. This approach would also warrant separate compensation for legal entities involved in the group's data mining and processing activities. The ownership of the data would stay with a single entity within the group, and the returns attributable to such an entity would be determined using a development, enhancement, maintenance, protection and exploitation (DEMPE) analysis.

2.1.2 Big Data as an Intangible

OECD BEPS Action Plans 8-10 defines an intangible asset as 'something which is not a physical asset or a financial asset, which is capable of being owned or controlled for use in commercial activities, and whose use or transfer would be compensated had it

35. The Physical, Human Driven Digital Economy: The Overvaluation of Intangibles and its Effects on Tax and Society, Jan Winterhalter and Lukas Seiling, Mariam Sattorov, 30 March 2023 accessed at https://kluwertaxblog.com/2023/03/30/the-physical-human-driven-digital-economy-the-overvaluation-of-intangibles-and-its-effects-on-tax-and-society/.

occurred in a transaction between independent parties in comparable circumstances'.[36]

For the purpose of transfer pricing, characterizing big data as an intangible asset would require consideration of the following factors:

(i) Is the asset in question a non-physical or non-financial asset? Identifying if big data could be sold or transferred separately will be useful. It shall also be helpful to understand at what stage in the data life cycle the same was transferred.
(ii) Is it capable of being controlled? Which entity in the multinational enterprise (MNE) controls the returns from the data? OECD BEPS Action Plan 8-10 elaborates on the notion of 'control' as an important element in the transfer pricing analysis of intangibles. It involves maintaining and exercising the capability to make significant decisions relating to risks associated with the intangible.
(iii) Would the transfer of big data bring future economic benefits? Identifying if the exploitation of big data will result in incremental revenues or cost savings to an MNE will be beneficial.
(iv) Can the transaction be priced between independent entities? Is big data *something of value* to independent parties such that the transfer would be valued and compensated? For example, in an independent transaction between a buyer and a seller relating to a digital business, a separate price might be attributed to data, i.e., users on the platform. This value can be a useful starting point for transfer pricing analysis.

In addition, individual country's laws have to be considered. As an example, under the Indian transfer pricing regulations, the definition[37] of 'intangible property'[38] is wide

36. The definition as per 2013 OECD Transfer Pricing Guidelines for 'Intangible Property' means 'rights to use Industrial Assets such as patents, trademarks, trade names, designs or models'. It also includes literary or artistic property rights and intellectual property such as know-how and trade secrets. However, the same has been updated under BEPS Action Plan 8-10.
37. Under the Indian transfer pricing regulations, the definition of 'international transaction' under section 92(B) was expanded through the Finance Act, 2012, w.r.e.f. 1 April 2002. This was done specifically to cover certain transactions/arrangements such as the purchase, sale, transfer, lease, or use of intangible property.
38. Explanation (ii) to section 92B(2) of the Act is defined as under:

    (ii) The expression 'intangible property' shall include:
    (a) marketing related intangible assets such as trademarks, trade names, brand names, logos;
    (b) technology related intangible assets such as process patents, patent applications, technical documentation such as laboratory notebooks, technical know-how;
    (c) artistic related intangible assets such as literary works and copyrights, musical compositions, copyrights, maps, engravings;
    (d) data processing related intangible assets such as proprietary computer software, software copyrights, automated databases, and integrated circuit masks and masters;
    (e) engineering related intangible assets such as industrial design, product patents, trade secrets, engineering drawing and schematics, blueprints, proprietary documentation;

enough to incorporate data processing such as proprietary computer software, software copyrights, automated databases, and integrated circuit masks and masters within its purview.

Characterization of Big Data as a Marketing Intangible

The presence of users in a particular jurisdiction contributes heavily to creating a 'brand name' in that jurisdiction. It depends upon the ability of an MNE to "reach into" a jurisdiction either remotely or through a limited local presence to develop a user/customer base and other marketing intangibles. It sees an intrinsic functional link between marketing intangibles and market jurisdiction as manifested in two different ways. First, some marketing intangibles, such as brand and trade name, are reflected in the favourable attitudes in the minds of customers and can be seen to have been created in the market jurisdiction. Second, (and more relevant) other marketing intangibles such as customer data, customer relationships, and customer lists are derived from activities targeted at customers and users in the market jurisdiction. This supports the treatment of such intangibles as being created in the market jurisdiction.[39]

However, even after the implications of OECD BEPS Action Plan 8-10, the situation concerning marketing intangibles is challenging because the link between specific and substantial activities and the return is less readily apparent. Hence, this has been an area of major debate.[40]

(f) customer related intangible assets such as customer lists, customer contracts, customer relationship, open purchase orders;
(g) contract related intangible assets such as favourable supplier, contracts, licence agreements, franchise agreements, non-compete agreements;
(h) human capital related intangible assets such as trained and organized work force, employment agreements, union contracts;
(i) location related intangible assets such as leasehold interest, mineral exploitation rights, easements, air rights, water rights;
(j) goodwill related intangible assets such as institutional goodwill, professional practice goodwill, personal goodwill of professional, celebrity goodwill, general business going concern value;
(k) methods, programmes, systems, procedures, campaigns, surveys, studies, forecasts, estimates, customer lists, or technical data; and
(l) any other similar item that derives its value from its intellectual content rather than its physical attributes.

39. Public Consultation Document Addressing the tax challenges of the digitalisation of the economy, p. 12, accessed at https://www.oecd.org/tax/beps/public-consultation-document-addressing-the-tax-challenges-of-the-digitalisation-of-the-economy.pdf.
40. In India, the tax officer has extensively focused on the creation of marketing intangibles through advertising, marketing, and promotion (AMP) spending by subsidiaries of foreign multinationals. A batch of appeals in this regard is pending before the Supreme Court – the apex court of India. The principal debates around this focus on whether AMP spending can be considered an international transaction for transfer pricing purposes under Indian law, what is the demarcated quantum that should be considered (tax officers usually rely on a bright line or intensity adjustment), and what should be adequate compensation for the creation of such intangibles, if any.

The MNE group's non-routine or residual income[41] that is generated from marketing intangibles and corresponding risks must be allocated to that market jurisdiction. The amount of income attributable to different market jurisdictions can be based on an agreed metric such as the platform users' sales or revenue.[42,43]

2.1.3 Big Data as a Service

Digital Barter

While users take advantage of digital services, they also unwittingly exchange other critical inputs -data on their preferences and activity which can then be used and monetized by a business. Such a digital barter does not require a financial transaction through an online marketplace.

Users instead consume a range of apparently 'free' digital services, for example, browsing websites and reviews for products and services or expressing opinions through 'likes' and 'dislikes'. In reality, they are, of course, not free to the users engaging in multiple micro-barter transactions in which data about their activity and preferences is being incrementally exchanged for a digital service.

Data Transfer Transactions: Service Versus Royalty

It shall also be crucial to identify the characterization relating to data transfer transactions as the distinction between a payment for the provision of services versus a royalty for the grant of rights in an intangible.

As an example, royalty is taxable in India based on payments subject to the source rule of taxation as provided in section 9(1)(vi) of the Act. Accordingly, if the government makes the payments, it is always sourced in India. When an Indian resident makes the payment, it is also sourced in India except when the royalty is payable in respect of any right, property, or information used or services utilized for a business or profession carried out by such a person outside of India or to make or earn any income from any source outside the country. When a non-resident makes the payment, it would be sourced in India only when the royalty is payable in respect of any right, property, or information used or services utilized for a business or profession

41. First, it needs to determine relevant profit, identify routine functions and compensation, deduct routine profit from total profit, and then conclude the final residual profit. Second, non-routine or residual profit need to be allocated in different ways ranging from, e.g., cost-based methods (e.g., costs incurred to develop marketing intangibles versus costs incurred for R&D and trade intangibles) to more formulaic approaches (e.g., using fixed contribution percentages that may differ by business model).
42. Public Consultation Document Addressing the tax challenges of the digitalisation of the economy, accessed at https://www.oecd.org/tax/beps/public-consultation-document-addressing-the-tax-challenges-of-the-digitalisation-of-the-economy.pdf.
43. The OECD draft on Amount B proposes that the scope of Amount B will cover the distribution of tangible goods (including as a sales agent or commissionaire as well as a buy-sell distributor) although it remains under discussion whether this may be expanded to services and software or other digital goods.

carried on by such person in India or to make or earn any income from any source there.[44]

The definition of 'royalty'[45] is wide enough to cover transactions involving 'data', and 'information' whether copyrighted or not within its ambit. To this extent, 'customized electronic data' is treated as part of 'computer software'[46] and taxable as royalty.

In addition, there have been judicial rulings on whether payment for the use of the software is in the nature of royalty. The matter was before the Supreme Court which decided the issue in favour of the taxpayer.[47] Besides, the treaty's supremacy over the Act has been reaffirmed, and it is held that, if the definition under the Double Taxation Avoidance Agreement (DTAA) is narrower, the same shall prevail over the broad definition contained in the Act. In this judgement, the Supreme Court held that, unless an interest in all or any of the rights contained in section 14(b) read with section 14(a) of the Indian Copyright Act is transferred through a licence, it would not amount to the use of the right in copyright and, hence, it cannot be characterized as royalty. The income tax department has filed a review petition before the Supreme Court.

2.1.4 Natural Resource of a Country via Its Population

With largely undefined property rights over personal data and in the absence of legislation governing the collection of or access to data, ownership over user data is implicitly vested in the companies that collect it with no legal obligation to compensate the individuals that have generated this data beyond the digital service for which this data may have been exchanged.

As noted earlier, digital barters are not large, infrequent transactions between businesses but small, high-frequency 'micro' transactions between businesses and consumers across multiple online platforms. For example, social media platforms and search engines record billions of 'likes' and queries daily, respectively. The value of the data being traded in these 'micro barters' is likely to vary significantly, and the current lack of a transparent market or an agreed standardized measure for the value of such data further exacerbates the difficulty in determining and reporting a verifiable person-specific financial value for each exchange.

A more practicable alternative might be achieved if custody over citizens' data was assigned to the government as a proxy. For example, in the case of natural resources, governments typically hold the resources in trust on behalf of their citizens and collect payment for extraction in the form of government revenues. In the case of digital services, data on the behaviour and preferences of a country's citizens would be seen as a collective national asset with compensation for its use payable to the government.

44. Section 9(1)(vi) of the Income-tax Act, 1961.
45. Explanation 2 to section 9(1)(vi) of the Act defines the term Royalty.
46. Explanation 3 of section 9(1)(vi) defines 'computer software' as any computer program recorded on any disc, tape, perforated media, or other information storage device and includes any such program or any customized electronic data.
47. *Engineering Analysis Centre of Excellence (P.) Ltd. v. Commissioner of Income Tax* (Civil Appeal Nos 8733-8734 of 2018) vide order dated 2 March 2021.

Indeed, a government is better placed to exert collective power on behalf of individuals who cannot capture their rents by levying a tariff (e.g., an export tax) on the extraction of data by foreign digital service providers (Hufbauer and Lu, 2018; IMF, 2019).

This arrangement would apply whether data ownership is transferred to the company upon collection or retained by the government, although the arrangement that is chosen (i.e., time-bound access or indefinite ownership) would have implications for the level of compensation. Indeed, while user data is intrinsically tied to an individual, the nature of data collection and the nonlinearly increasing value from user data is often derived not only from aggregating data related to a large number of individuals but also from multiple points in time. This suggests that there is a practical need to centralize ownership in order to coordinate access and compensation.

If such an arrangement developed, companies that wish to collect user information would then need to compensate the jurisdiction in which the data was collected following agreed rules through the corporate income tax system or other tax instruments such as a royalty payment. Such an arrangement still does not prevent the need for clear valuation rules for the data that is collected. Still, it does allow for the possibility of using country-level proxies or formulary methods for determining user value.

User Participation

According to an IMF working paper,[48] an emerging tax concern is that the online customer or 'user' is now considered by many as being a critical driving force behind the value of digital services.

The paper goes on to state that, as a first step to more comprehensively understanding the role that 'user-generated value' can and/or should play in determining the structure of the future corporate tax system, both businesses and government would need to agree and acknowledge that there is such a thing as user-generated value. This remains contentious as some countries and companies claim that user data has no value until it has been processed – before then, it is worthless. In addition, if they agree that value is being created, it needs to be understood how much. It has so far proven tricky to come up with an objective basis for valuing user data and network externalities.

Digitalization has unprecedentedly allowed businesses to harvest data and information about their users. Users provide data on their preferences through their online search, purchase of goods and services, or interactions with others over social media platforms. However, user participation is not recognized under the existing international tax framework as a source of taxable value. As a result, the blurred line between their role in both supply (production) and demand (sales) has – for better or for worse – opened the door to a meaningful conversation about the concepts of source, destination, taxable presence, and profit attribution.

48. Tec(h)tonic Shifts: Taxing the Digital Economy, Aqib Aslam, Alpa Shah, 29 May 2020 accessed at https://www.imf.org/en/Publications/WP/Issues/2020/05/29/Tec-h-tonic-Shifts-Taxing-the-Digital-Economy-49363.

A number of policy proposals have been put forward that seeks to limit the scope of tax avoidance and competition by attempting to predetermine a distribution of taxable profits across countries. Many are predicated – implicitly or explicitly – on the idea that the 'user' has a role to play in value creation, justifying the designation of source-based taxing rights to the jurisdiction in which they are located (*see, e.g.*, European Commission 2018; HM Treasury, 2017). Most prominent among these are the proposals for pure formulary apportionment or a hybrid residual profit allocation alternative that include some measure of user value as an allocation key.

Another related proposal is the allocation of profit to market jurisdictions based on marketing intangibles, that is also justified by the notion that soliciting the sustained engagement and active participation of users is a critical component of value creation. In the interim, several countries have begun to implement user-based turnover taxes targeting specific digitalized industries and activities.

2.2 Identifying the Commercial and Financial Relations

According to paragraph 1.36 of the OECD Guidelines, the economically relevant characteristics or comparability factors that need to be identified in the commercial or financial relations between the associated enterprises in order to accurately delineate the actual transaction can be broadly categorized as follows:

- the contractual terms of the transaction;
- the functions performed by each of the parties to the transaction, taking into account assets used and risks assumed, including how those functions relate to the wider generation of value by the MNE group to which the parties belong, the circumstances surrounding the transaction, and industry practices;
- the characteristics of property transferred or services provided;
- the economic circumstances of the parties and the market in which the parties operate; and
- the business strategies pursued by the parties.

The authors once again reinforce the idea that, for any meaningful analysis of big data transactions, a starting point in terms of an inter-company contract or an accounting entry in the books of accounts is very important. In the absence of such a starting point, identifying transactions, undertaking a FAR/VCA, ascribing values to the transaction, and then benchmarking them would not be in accordance with a conventional transfer pricing analysis. It is also the authors' views that many aspects of a big data ecosystem are not currently being captured in the books of accounts of a company.

2.3 Recognizing the Accurately Delineated Transaction

FAR and Value Chain Analysis

The big data ecosystem in any organization is a complex web comprising all entities, both users and providers of data. Roles such as providers, users, consumers, or intermediaries cannot often be delineated with any level of accuracy. The use of big data in business, especially for data-driven decision-making, poses interesting questions from a transfer pricing standpoint. Some questions here could be:

Transaction / Event	*Group Company Using Data*	*Group Company Supplying Data*	*Comments*
Using data provided by another group company for data-driven decision-making.	Is there an alteration in the risk profile since this entity is no longer making decisions? Who bears the risk for failure of data-driven results?	Should there be an increased return since the entity is taking over the decision-making function? Who bears the risk for failure of data-driven results?	It is also relevant to consider if a group company imposes the mandate to use data-driven decision-making or if the company has made the decision itself. For example, who decides the measure of failure?
Receiving big data analytics from a group company.	What is the arm's length price for accessing proprietary big data analytics?	Should the big data processing segment be as profitable as standalone peers in the industry?	How does sharing proprietary data interplay with accurate delineation? Which entity should leverage big data to benefit from incremental cost savings or sales?
Collating big data from group companies.	Should the company providing the data retain rights to its raw data?	In the open market, raw data would have very little intrinsic value.	
Data localization and regulatory hurdles.	-	-	Which entity should bear the loss if data cannot be accessed outside of a jurisdiction?
Role of back-offices in developing algorithms.	-	-	An accurate DEMPE analysis would be critical.

2.4 DEMPE Analysis

The DEMPE is designed to ensure that the allocation of the returns from the exploitation of intangibles and costs related to the development of intangibles compensate MNE group entities for functions performed, assets used, and risks assumed in the DEMPE of intangibles.[49]

Applying these principles to big data could emphasize the location of business functions about data instead of the location of the origin of the data or simply of the location of the customer for the data-related service.

In the context of a DEMPE analysis for big data, key functions may include the design of the database, software platform, algorithms, ongoing research and development, enhancements to the platform, strategic decisions and creative direction about the database and product offering, decisions and actions to protect the intangible and ensure quality control, marketing functions that enhance the brand value of the intangible product, routine functions such as maintenance of server, troubleshooting, and customer support. All of these functions and services provided by related entities in the group can be compensated at an arm's length basis.[50]

Proper classification of functions relating to the collection, structuring, and exploitation of big data assets through the lens of DEMPE functions would include:[51]

(i) **D**evelopment:
  - Research activities such as the definition of big data strategy, search for data sources, and systems for data collection; and
  - Development activities such as implementation of big data strategy including cloud computing and data collection;

(ii) **E**nhancement: Test runs in connection with IT architecture and data processing;

(iii) **M**aintenance: Measures for keeping the data pool up to date, application management;

(iv) **P**rotection: Implementation of data security measures, licensing, or accessing rights; and

(v) **E**xploitation: Decision-making processes regarding data exploitation (e.g., sales, licensing, processing data)

In summary, a systematic transfer pricing analysis for big data transactions should focus on where value is created rather than on where value-creating activities have their effects.

As explained earlier, the Big Data ecosystem in an organization is complex and highly integrated. An accurate DEMPE analysis would be a highly time-consuming and expensive operation for a business. In addition, the players could change at a concise

49. OECD Action Plan 8-10, para. 6.47.
50. IFA Cahiers 2022, Big data and tax – domestic and international taxation of data driven business, Singapore Report.
51. IFA Cahiers 2022, Big data and tax – domestic and international taxation of data driven business, Switzerland Report.

moment thereby warranting the need for a fresh DEMPE analysis every couple of months.

2.5 Selecting and Applying the Most Appropriate Transfer Pricing Method

The OECD Guidelines state in paragraph 2.12 that, while the selection of a method may not be straightforward in some cases and more than one method may be initially considered, generally, it will be possible to select one method that is appropriate for providing the best estimation of an arm's length price. However, for difficult cases when no one approach is conclusive, a flexible approach would allow the evidence of various methods to be used in conjunction. In such cases, an attempt should be made to reach a conclusion consistent with the arm's length principle (ALP) that is satisfactory from a practical viewpoint to all of the parties involved. It should take into account the facts and circumstances of the case, the mix of evidence available, and the relative reliability of the various methods under consideration.

3 PILLAR ONE AND BIG DATA

3.1 BEPS & Big Data

Articles 5,[52] 7,[53] and 9[54] of the OECD Model Tax Convention[55] form the fundamental basis of the current international tax rules. Performance of functions, employment of assets, and the assumption of risks (FAR analysis) are the critical determinative factors for entitlement of taxing rights to a jurisdiction. However, it is beyond doubt that the current international tax rules have failed to maintain the pace of taxing a digitalized data economy. A digitalized economy displays the following characteristics:[56]

(i) maneuverability of intangibles, users, and business functions;
(ii) data usage and the transformation into big data;
(iii) user interaction and 'network effects';
(iv) use of agglomeration resulting in oligopoly or monopoly of certain services relating directly to the 'network effects'; and
(v) sudden changes in the functioning of the rules because of rapid technological improvements.

---

52. Article 5: Permanent Establishment. This article primarily defines taxing rights of a jurisdiction over the non-resident through the establishment of a PE in that jurisdiction.
53. Article 7: Business Profits. It defines the profits attributable to the PE that could be taxed by the host jurisdiction.
54. Article 9: Associated Enterprises. The transactions between related parties within a group should be undertaken as per the Arm's Length Principle.
55. OECD Model Tax Convention on Income and on Capital.
56. The OECD Public Consultation Document on Addressing the Tax Challenges of the Digitalization of the Economy: Strengths and Weaknesses of the Three Proposals for Revising Profit Allocation and Nexus Rules, Alessandro Samari, IBFD.

On the one hand, the digitalized economy faces a decrease in the significance of a physical presence in the consumer market; on the other hand, the digitalized economy faces the increasing importance of intangibles and their mobility as well as the high degree of convergence in the value chain.[57]

According to the current international taxation framework, the taxing rights of states have been jeopardized for two main reasons. First, nexus rules exclusively rely upon the physical presence, and profit allocation rules focus on substance. Second, significant people functions are not capable of allocating profits even if a nexus is established.[58]

Accordingly, the reallocation of profits and the shift of functions and risks can be easily achieved by companies, especially digital ones, that do not have a significant physical presence in a particular jurisdiction. This problem is usually even more alarming in the case of data-driven companies that rely on generating income exclusively with intangibles. Hence, under the current international tax framework, it is unlikely that the value created by a digitalized business using big data and data mining techniques will be taxed.

Seeking to prevent issues arising due to the absence of a physical presence in the digitalized business framework, the OECD published BEPS Action Plan 1 'Tax Challenges arising from Digitalisation' in October 2015. The OECD identified tax challenges categorized into a nexus for taxation, data use, and the respective attribution of value.[59]

Accordingly, Action Plans 1,[60] 6,[61] 7,[62] and 8-10[63] were proposed to counter abusive tax avoidance practices in this area.

As a development, in 2018, the OECD released Interim Report 2018 on Tax Challenges Arising from Digitalization. It recognized the following characteristics of business in the digital economy:[64]

- cross-jurisdictional scale without mass;
- the importance of intangible assets; and
- the importance of data, user participation, and their synergies with internet protocol (IP).

57. M. Olbert & C. Spengel, *International Taxation in the Digital Economy: Challenge Accepted?*, 9 World Tax J. 1, 3 (2017).
58. OECD/G20, Tax Challenges Arising from Digitalisation – Interim Report 2018: Inclusive Framework on BEPS p. 167, para. 378 (OECD 2018), Primary Sources IBFD; and S. Postler, *The OECD's Work on Profit Allocation and Nexus Rules for a Digitalized Economy – A Potential Improvement of the International Taxation Framework?*, 74 Bull. Intl. Taxn. 2, 76 (2020), Journal Articles & Opinion Pieces IBFD.
59. R. Petruzzi, *International-Transfer Pricing, Users' Participation and Profit Attribution to Digital Permanent Establishments: A Case Study*, 26(2) International Transfer Pricing Journal (2019).
60. OECD BEPS Action Plan 1: Tax Challenges arising from digitalization.
61. Action Plan 6: Prevention of tax treaty abuse.
62. Action Plan 7: Prevent the artificial avoidance of PE status.
63. Action Plan 8-10: Aligning transfer pricing outcomes with value creation.
64. OECD. 2018. Tax Challenges Arising from Digitalisation – Interim Report 2018. Paris: OECD Publishing, para. 130.

It follows that data transformation into information has become one of the most valuable intangibles for multiple digital companies. The importance of data mining has turned the data business into a gold mine. The reason relates to how it is processed and the ability of artificially intelligent systems to automate business processes using data analytics. Moreover, the presence of user data in a jurisdiction surpasses the need for a company to have a physical establishment for effectively conducting business. Hence, the topic of data processing and the fair and effective taxation of data transactions has been increasingly prominent.[65]

Further, in 2019, the OECD and G-20 inclusive framework on base erosion and profit shifting (BEPS) laid out the Programme of Work to Develop a Consensus Solution to the Tax Challenges arising from the Digitalisation of the Economy. Three proposals were devised to expand the taxing rights to market jurisdictions regardless of physical presence:

(i) 'marketing intangibles' proposal;
(ii) 'significant economic presence' (SEP) proposal; and
(iii) 'user participation' proposal.

These proposals all allocate more taxing rights to the customer's and/or user's jurisdiction, i.e., the 'market jurisdictions', in situations when a business activity creates value through (possibly remote) participation in that jurisdiction that is not recognized in the current framework for allocating profits. Further, they have important common policy features as they all agree on the existence of a nexus in the absence of physical presence, consider using the total profit of a business, favour the use of simplifying conventions (including those that diverge from the ALP) to reduce compliance costs and disputes – a feature supported by many commentators at the public consultation who expressed concerns about approaches that would add complexity to existing tax rules – and would operate alongside the current profit allocation rules.[66]

Further work in this area in order to meet its objectives on the taxation of the digital economy included the OECD developing BEPS 2.0 as the 'next step'. In the OECD Public Consultation Report on Digital Economy that was released in February 2019, tentative solutions initially proposed by the Inclusive Framework (as mentioned above) were reflected in a two-pillar proposal.

Pillar One relates to new rules on where tax should be paid (nexus rules) and what portion of profits should be taxed (profit allocation rules). The aim is to ensure that MNEs conducting sustained and significant business in places where they may not have a physical presence can be taxed in such jurisdictions.

Pillar Two aims at addressing the persisting BEPS issues and ensuring that international businesses pay a minimum level of tax.

---

65. P. Valente, *The Data Economy: On Evaluation and Taxation*, 59 Eur. Taxn. 5, 251 (2019), Journal Articles & Opinion Pieces IBFD.
66. OECD Programme of work to develop a consensus solution to the tax challenges arising from the digitalisation of the economy, p. 11, accessed at https://www.oecd.org/tax/beps/programme-of-work-to-develop-a-consensus-solution-to-the-tax-challenges-arising-from-the-digitalisation-of-the-economy.pdf.

3.2 Pillar One and Big Data

The rationale of Pillar One's Amount A is to allocate taxing rights to the jurisdictions in which a company interacts remotely while avoiding the constitution of a physical and traditional permanent establishment (PE). As a solution, new nexus rules are devised.

As per the OECD Public Consultation on Progress Report on Amount A of Pillar One,[67] revenue sourcing rules are contained in Article 4. It determines when revenues derived by a covered group[68] are treated as arising in a jurisdiction for the purposes of this Act.

As per Article 4, revenues derived from the licensing, sale, or other alienation of user data are treated as arising in a jurisdiction where the location of the user associated with the data is in that jurisdiction.

For the above purpose, it has been clarified that the location of the user that is the subject of the data being transferred can be determined using the following indicators:

- user profile information;
- the geolocation of the user's device through which its data is transferred; and
- the IP address of the user's apparatus through which its data is transferred.

The rules, part of the new taxing right, seem to be in line with the allocation of returns to the market jurisdiction.

The unified approach (UA) embodied by Pillar One is structured in the following way:

- Amount A: the creation of new nexus rules; and
- Amount B: the application of a fixed return remuneration for baseline distribution and marketing activities based on the ALP.

While all of this commendable development has been undertaken, the three proposals (as mentioned above, viz., marketing intangibles, SEP, and user participation approach) are three key fundamental principles on which all stakeholders have

67. The Public Consultation can be accessed at https://www.oecd.org/tax/beps/progress-report-on-amount-a-of-pillar-one-july-2022.pdf.
68. As per the public consultation, A Group is a 'covered group' for a period in which both subparagraphs (a) and (b) are met.

The revenues of the group for the period are greater than EUR 20 billion (the revenue test). When the period is shorter or longer than twelve months, the EUR 20 billion amount is adjusted proportionally to correspond with the length of the period.

The pre-tax profit margin of the group is greater than 10% (the profitability test):

(i) in the period (the period test); and
(ii) when the group was not a covered group in the two consecutive periods immediately preceding the period:
    (a) in two or more of the four periods immediately preceding the period (the prior period test); and
    (b) on average across the period and the four periods immediately preceding the period (the average test).

consensus. Moreover, different laws in various jurisdictions[69] all flow back to these principles or practices for the taxation of data in a digitalized economy. Hence, these principles form the cornerstone of analysing big data from the perspective of transfer pricing.

3.3 Application of Tax Treaty Principles to Big Data Transactions

Most tax treaties tax the income of non-residents to the extent the same is attributable[70] to a non-resident's PE.[71] Hence, treaties extend the taxing rights to the nexus rule owing to the presence of a PE.

For data-driven businesses, sensors or data centres could constitute a PE for the non-resident subject to the conditions[72] mentioned in Article 5(1) of the respective DTAA being met. Additionally, it should be ensured that activities carried out through such data centres are not specifically exempt under Article 5(4) of the DTAA. From an Indian standpoint, if the data is hosted on a server in India, it would expose the business to taxation under the domestic tax law[73]and treaties[74] with most countries. However, for this purpose, it shall be essential to prove that the server was 'at the disposal' of the non-resident.

In a few cases, a non-resident does not own a server for parking the data in India but stores the data by leasing a server from a local company that would have also leased it to other companies. Although ownership of a server is not a relevant factor in deciding the existence of a PE, there could be a situation in which many other companies lease the same server, and no specific space is at the company's disposal. In such a situation, the leased server could be argued as not creating a PE in India for failing to pass the disposal test.[75] The decided cases are specific to facts that are on record for the determination of a PE in such situations. However, caution will have to be exercised if there are covenants in the agreement (for leasing the server from third parties) stipulating that the control of the server is with the non-resident, or the server is acting in his capacity or performing functions that an independent agent will not perform.

The OECD has a definitive stand that a server can create a PE of the company that owns the server, so this may be an Internet Service Provider. However, it will not constitute a PE for the companies that merely have websites hosted on such a server.

69. Countries like India and Nigeria have incorporated SEP rules in their domestic tax law. Countries such as Israel and Argentina have also enacted a nexus-based taxable presence test so that foreign entities having a digital presence cannot escape the tax net.
70. Article 7 of the respective DTAAs.
71. Article 5 of the respective DTAAs.
72. For a fixed place PE, it shall be essential to satisfy the following conditions: A fixed place, business activity carried out through that fixed place, and satisfying the 'at the disposal' test, i.e., the fixed place to be at the disposal of the non-resident. Commentary to Article 5 of the OECD Model Tax Convention.
73. Section 9(1)(i) of the Income-tax Act, 1961.
74. Article 5 of respective DTAAs.
75. IFA Cahiers 2022, Big data and tax – domestic and international taxation of data driven business, India Report.

A website is considered an intangible entity that does not have a place of business nor a facility such as premises, etc.[76]

With regards to computer equipment, data, and software, a distinction must be made between data and software used by or stored on computer equipment, on the one hand, and the computer equipment itself on the other. Data and software, e.g., a website or computer code, are not tangible property and therefore cannot qualify as a fixed place of a PE. For example, assume that a company resident in State A is in the business of selling customized beauty products. The company started selling its products in State B through a dedicated website. The website cannot constitute a PE of the company in State B.

Further, it shall also be important to contextualize whether the activity conducted through such a server or sensor is an important element in the data value chain for the MNE or is otherwise preparatory or auxiliary in nature. While this shall be dependent upon a specific purpose and business model for a data-driven business with the core purpose of collecting and selling big data, the same shall not qualify as preparatory or auxiliary.

Considering the importance of a FARM (Functions, Assets, Risks and Market) analysis, even if data processing is the main business purpose, collecting big data from market jurisdictions *may* not qualify as auxiliary in nature, especially for digital businesses. In this case, big data is an inevitable supporting element rather than being classified as mere preparatory or auxiliary.

The question, however, shall always be whether the business is built around data or the data around the business.[77]

3.4 Big Data Implications under Significant Economic Presence Test

If an e-commerce platform gathers data from a jurisdiction and sells it, what would be the transfer pricing consequence of such data?

This question forms the basis of analysing the implications of SEP of an entity in a jurisdiction owing to business functions relating to data.

As per the traditional international tax rules, absent any virtual tax net like the SEP, the entity that is collecting data would have no tax consequence. The value of data may be reflected in the value of the business itself, as with other user contributions, and may be monetized when the business is sold. However, to tax such big data transactions as commercialized through cross-border remote sales, the OECD recommended the concept of the SEP or a significant digital presence. The envisioned concept creates a taxable presence in the jurisdiction where a non-resident entity has substantial and sustained interaction with the economy of that jurisdiction using IT and other automated methodologies.

What is crucial in the context of the SEP relating to big data is to establish a significant nexus with a jurisdiction, and revenue alone cannot be a potential factor.

76. OECD Model Tax Convention on Income and on Capital, Commentary on Article 5, para. 122.
77. IFA Cahiers 2022, Big data and tax – domestic and international taxation of data driven business, Switzerland Report.

Effective interaction of digital technology with the jurisdiction would be established taking additional purposeful factors into consideration. These may include the user base and/or the associated data input and the volume of the digital content derived from the jurisdiction.

Big Data Implications Relating to the SEP under Indian Domestic Law

Historically, India and its domestic law have a concept of a business connection[78] (BC) similar to the concept of the PE. Before dwelling into the nuances of the BC test, it is important to observe that the determination of a PE and attribution of income to it is an outcome of relevant Articles 5 and 7, respectively of the relevant DTAA.

Hence, the notion of the BC under domestic law is relevant only for non-residents with whom India does not have a DTAA. Over the years, the domestic law and the BC test have been subject to interpretation by the courts[79] in general and the Supreme Court in particular that would carry out retrospective amendments in pursuance to the landmark decision in *Vodafone International Holdings B.V.*[80]

Specifically, about the incorporation of the SEP, the domestic law was amended in 2018 to incorporate its concept. This was later omitted by the Finance Act 2020 since the enabling rules to operationalize the application of the SEP was not notified. The decision to not operationalize was partly due to the non-adoption of guidance issued in April 2019[81] for public consultation and also due to India expanding its unilateral levy by extending the equalization levy from business-to-business (B2B) transactions to all forms of transactions.

Hence, in 2020, to coincide with the expansion of the equalization levy, the definition of the SEP was incorporated into domestic law. The concept has two specific components, i.e., the meaning of the term (clause a)[82] and the meaning of the term income attributable to operations carried out in India (clause b).[83]

A plain reading of clause a and clause b suggests that the first part deals with the expansion of a treaty definition under Article 5 for the constitution of a PE, and the

78. Section 9(1)(i) of the Income-tax Act, 1961.
79. *CIT v. R.D. Aggarwal & Co.* [1965 16 ITR 20 (SC)].
80. *Vodafone International Holdings B.V. v. Union of India & ANR* [Civil Appeal No. 733 of 2012].
81. CBDT Report on Attribution of Profits to Permanent Establishments (Proposal for Amendment of Rules for profit attribution to Permanent Establishment) accessed at https://incometaxindia.gov.in/hindi/Lists/Latest%20News/Attachments/261/Report_of_the_Committee_on_Profit_Attribution_to_PE_in_India_18_4_19.pdf.
82. Clause a: [Explanation 2A. For the removal of doubts, it is hereby declared that the significant economic presence of a non-resident in India shall constitute 'BC' in India and 'significant economic presence' for this purpose, shall mean:
    (a) transaction in respect of any goods, services or property carried out by a non-resident with any person in India including provision of download of data or software in India, if the aggregate of payments arising from such transaction or transactions during the previous year exceeds such amount as may be prescribed; or
    (b) systematic and continuous soliciting of business activities or engaging in interaction with such number of users in India, as may be prescribed.
83. Clause b: [Explanation 3A. For the removal of doubts, it is hereby declared that the income attributable to the operations carried out in India, as referred to in Explanation 1, shall include income from:

latter part relates to income attributable to such a PE, like Article 7. A notable aspect of India's domestic law is that the SEP concept was expanded to cover non-digital businesses (refer to clause a), and the income attribution principle targeted digital forms of businesses (clause b).

About the definition of the SEP, in the context of downloaded data or software in India, a threshold of INR 20 million[84] (approximately USD 280,000) has been prescribed. Further, in the case of systematic and continuance solicitation or engagement with a specified number of users, the threshold of 300,000[85] has been prescribed.

Coming to the tax implications on big data, the definition of income attributable to such a SEP assumes significance in light of the definition. Three specific operations undertaken in India assume significance:

(i) advertisement that targets not just a customer residing in India but a customer who advertises the advertisement through an IP address located in India;
(ii) sale of data from the above two categories of customers; and
(iii) sale of goods or services using data collected from the above two categories of customers.

The purpose of this clause is that an advertisement targeting a customer or access to such an advertisement (without triggering a sale) would effectuate business operations. Predictably, the sale of data collected from the Indian resident will be covered even if the non-resident uses an IP address located in India. The third category would cover the sale of goods or services using data collected from residents and non-residents using IP addresses located in India.

It is important to note that a proviso also clarifies that the income attributable to such an SEP would not just cover transactions of sales but also cover activities that need not necessarily result in a sale.

Finally, the definition of the term 'through'[86] that is relevant for advertisement has been expanded to cover 'by means of', 'in consequence of', or 'by reason of'.

The above definition would not impact the definition of a PE as it currently stands under the respective PE clauses in the DTAA that India has signed. It will be interesting to see how the framework evolves.

(i) such advertisement which targets a customer who resides in India or a customer who accesses the advertisement through internet protocol address located in India;
(ii) sale of data collected from a person who resides in India or from a person who uses internet protocol address located in India; and
(iii) sale of goods or services using data collected from a person who resides in India or from a person who uses internet protocol address located in India].

84. Rule 11UD(1) of the Income-tax Rules, 1962.
85. Rule 11UD(2) of the Income-tax Rules, 1962.
86. Explanation 4 to section 9(1)(i) of the Income-tax Act, 1961.

4 CONCLUSION

The big data ecosystem is a complex web within an organization as all group entities feed off of each other as users and providers. All of these are in the overall interest of enhancing the value of the group. A traditional transfer pricing analysis begins with identifying the intra-group transactions and then conducting a value chain or FAR analysis, which seems too unviable as it would involve breaking down the big data ecosystem into thousands, if not millions, of transactions that can be identified on a standalone basis. Then, these would have to be bundled together for the purposes of analysis. Mathematical modelling, which comes with its own sets of assumptions, may not be the optimal solution either.

As businesses become more integrated and it becomes increasingly challenging to identify where value is being created, where control lies, and where the risks lie in the context of every transaction, let alone the challenges in determining what the transaction even is, a traditional transfer pricing analysis must give way to easy-to-manage solutions for both tax administrations and taxpayers.

In the authors' views, safe harbours for entity-level profitability and advanced certainty mechanisms will take centre stage as big data ushers in an era of unprecedented integration in the functioning of multinational companies. Attempts to attribute values for data with uncertain outcomes from a commercial standpoint could be a subjective exercise. Besides, not yielding a fair (arm's length) result could cause uncertainty for MNEs.

CHAPTER 5

Transfer Pricing and Remote Work

Stephan Schnorberger, Benedict Behmenburg, Annabel Buschkämper, Hendrik Menzel & Paulina Witomski

1 TRANSFER PRICING AND REMOTE WORK: AN INTRODUCTION

An everyday impression and the empirical data suggest that working from home and at other places remote from the enterprise is more widespread than ever. There may have been a gradual increase in remote working before the COVID-19 pandemic, but that and the contact limitations imposed by governments have boosted its popularity. In the wake of the pandemic, there is widespread consensus that home office and remote working are now firmly established. Indeed, offering flexible work locations off-site has become a mechanism for attracting personnel in the business world's 'War for Talent'.[1] Rearrangements of supply chains, expansion into new markets and, more generally, virtual organization add to the rise of remote work.

Home offices and remote work create a multitude of compliance and structuring questions in the area of personal income tax, wage tax, social security, and immigration/residence law. This paper focuses on the transfer pricing aspects of remote work. In this area, there are many discussions and analyses about questions of the taxable presence in the form of permanent establishments (PEs). In contrast, comments on profit allocation to existing PEs largely do not seem to go beyond general principles. This chapter approaches this void and addresses questions of profit allocation to these.[2]

2 DEFINITION AND FORMS OF REMOTE WORKING

For purposes of this chapter, it is proposed to define remote working as follows: Remote working is present when an employee of a multinational enterprise exercises his work activity while being physically present somewhere else away from the

1. United Kingdom Office of Tax Simplification, Hybrid and distance working report, December 2022, 27; NBER Working Papers Series, Working from Home and Around the World, Cambridge (Massachusetts), September 2022, 18, 24.
2. The economic principles for the allocation of profits according to Article 7 OECD-MC largely correspond to transfer pricing principles under Article 9 OECD-MC. (Oestreicher /Schnitger/Wellens/*Wellens/Hillmann*, Gewinnabgrenzung nach dem Authorised OECD Approach (AOA), para. 7.161.) Therefore, in line with accepted German terminology, the chapter uses appropriate transfer pricing terminology also in respect of profit attribution/allocation to permanent establishments.

business establishment of the legal or contractual employer, enterprise, or entity.[3] Since transfer pricing is mostly relevant in cross-border situations,[4] the remote working dealt with here shall be present when the place of physical exercise of work activity is in a country where the tax jurisdiction differs from the place of the employer's taxable residence.

Based on this proposed definition, remote working can be seen in many more forms than just home office activity:

- work while travelling on business trips;
- home office;
- secondment to another group entity;
- work under a service arrangement or project of the employers; and
- work in virtually connected teams as opposed to teams meeting physically. This could be international research and development (R&D) teams, virtual organizational units, shared service centres, statutory or non-statutory management committees such as board committees of a stock corporation, or self-established executive management committees comprising board members and other high-ranking managers.

This chapter does not address the phenomenon of digital nomads permanently moving from one country to another. It is not clear that these should be in an employment/dependent work relationship with an employer organization.

It should also be noted that remote working is not possible in occupations where physical closeness to the object of work is indispensable. This relates to personal and medical care; many production, construction, and assembly activities; personal services; driving and piloting, etc.

3 OVERVIEW OF POSSIBLE TRANSFER PRICING IMPLICATIONS OF REMOTE WORK

3.1 Overview

Remote working may have very different forms, so it makes sense to look at the different transfer price implications of each of them. Naturally, such an analysis is highly factual, and each fact pattern has to be analysed on its own merit. However, to identify practical and analytical priorities, an overview of the spectrum of possible transfer price consequences is useful. The following table gives an overview of the potential transfer price implications of cross-border remote working. The table is based on the OECD Model Tax Convention and the UN Model Tax Convention principles as well as general international transfer pricing principles. The overview table intends to show technical/analytical connections between remote working and tax/transfer price

3. Cf. Cambridge Dictionary 'remote work'; for a more detailed definition cf. *Picker* NZA-Beilage 2021, 4; *Schuster/Verleger* IWB 2020, 861.
4. Exceptions are interstate transfer pricing in the United States or specific intercontinental profit allocation situations in Switzerland.

consequences. Empirically, these connections may or may not represent frequent patterns of the likelihood of actual transfer price implications. For example, the entry in column 'home office', the row 'PE risk' does not intend to state that cross-border home office work per se and necessarily creates a PE. Rather, this entry seeks to point out the technically possible creation of a PE of the enterprise by home office work as well as frequent corresponding concerns of taxpayers and tax administrations.

The top rows of the overview table look at the fundamental transfer price questions of whether and how remote working creates any consequences for ongoing transfer pricing and the allocation of functions. The table then addresses the international enterprise tax question probably most widely discussed, specifically whether and in what circumstances remote working could possibly give rise to a PE in the home office country. Subsequent rows then draw the logical consequence from the assumed existence of a PE. Thus, these rows address questions of profit allocation between the headquarters and a PE, gain realization in particular through a transfer of functions, relocation of a place of management, and implications of an exit from the assumed PE structure.

	Business Trips	*Home Office*	*Secondment*	*Employer's Service/Project Service*	*Virtual Teams/Virtual Organization*
Ongoing Transfer Pricing	Per se no implication	Per se no implications	Cost flat compensation All costs = arm's length principle? (extra salary, extra hours, schooling allowance, higher base salary)	Transfer price methods, primarily cost plus method	Per se no implications Inter-entity allocation (Article 9 OECD-MC)
Allocation of functions changed?	If PE arises	– Yes, in case of PE – Substance (of principal companies, etc.) – Either- or versus split allocation	May be/depends on number and impact of secondees	If PE arises	Significant impact: – Much harder to allocate functions, assets, risks to entities – Unintended reallocations if people move or roles pass

	Business Trips	*Home Office*	*Secondment*	*Employer's Service/Project Service*	*Virtual Teams/Virtual Organization*
PE risk	Agency establishment (sales, etc.)/service PE	– Highly factual – Fixed place of business PE – Agency establishment – Service PE	No/low unless secondee carries on business of formal employer	– Supervisor example (Article 5 section 15 OECD-MC Comm.) – Construction and assembly	Highly factual: – Fixed place of business PE – Agency establishment
Profit allocation Head Quarters (HQ) – PE	Authorised OECD Approach (AOA) – Income versus expenses = zero sum? – Control over risk? – Assets – Comparable uncontrolled transaction (CUT) for (sales) activity	– Cost plus – High value added and non-routine functions	(Only if PE)	– AOA – Special regimes for construction and assembly	Intra-entity; same as home office PE

	Business Trips	*Home Office*	*Secondment*	*Employer's Service/Project Service*	*Virtual Teams/Virtual Organization*
Gain realization? – Assets/intangibles – Functions, transfer package, business opportunities, platform technology opportunity	Customer relations? Markets? Business opportunities? Only if buy/sell? Development, Enhancement, Maintenance, Protection and Exploitation (DEMPE) functions	Spectrum of intangibles potentially affected	Know-how transfer to receiving entity (temporary) transfer of functions	Business opportunities	Spectrum of intangibles potentially affected
Relocation of place of management		Possibly dual residence?			Possibly dual residence
Implication of exit?	– Re-transfer of assets – Self-created intangibles of PE – Loss utilization	Same			Same as home office PE

3.2 Focus on Transfer Pricing Implications of PEs

The table in the preceding section has illustrated and made clear that transfer pricing implications arise in particular where remote work leads to the assumption of a PE of the employer enterprise in the home office jurisdiction. The spectrum of transfer pricing implications of virtual teams and virtual organizations run by remote workers may even be more complex than those of a home office PE. Virtual teams and virtual organizations lead not only to questions of allocation of functions, assets, and risks but also possible transfers of functions and other restructuring questions. In addition, they also complicate inter-entity profit allocation according to Article 9 OECD-MC. Virtual organizations have the potential to create not only significant Articles 5 and 7 OECD-MC issues but also Article 9 OECD-MC. At the same time, the specific issues of remote working as defined in this chapter potentially generated by virtual organizations also have to do with the complexities and issues of a home office as a PE. In that sense, the issue of PEs potentially created by home office work is at the centre of this paper's transfer price analysis.

Out of the multitude of transfer price issues, this chapter, therefore, focuses on the questions in which circumstances of remote work from the home office could conceivably give rise to a PE and what transfer price implications ensue. Primarily, it is the establishment of a PE by a cross-border remote working activity that triggers transfer price complexities.[5]

In general, as with other business activities, there are four different categories of PEs which might be triggered by remote work:

(1) fixed place of business PE;
(2) agency PE;
(3) service PE; and
(4) management PE.

3.2.1 Fixed Place of Business PE[6]

A 'fixed place of business' PE requires a geographically more or less fixed place of business, facility, or installation over which the enterprise has the power of disposal and through which the business of the enterprise is carried out. Such a PE presupposes a certain (intended) duration of the enterprise's activities. Duration may come about when employees work from home (classical 'home office' situation). The employees would ordinarily also be expected to carry out business activities for the enterprise (as

5. *Rasch/Rosenberger/Brülisauer* IStR-Beiheft 2021, 1; *Schuster/Verleger* IWB 2020, 861; Rödl&Partner Homeoffice: Eignung zur künftigen Begründung einer Betriebsstätte, 14 October 2020, https://www.roedl.de/themen/home-office-betriebsstaette-arbeitszimmer, last accessed on 20 January 2023.
6. Article 5 section 1 OECD-Model Convention 2017; Article 5(1) UN Model Double Taxation Convention 2021.

part of their dependent work). The home office is 'fixed' within the meaning of Article 5, paragraph 1 OECD-MC as it is usually stationary and the activity is intended to be exercised for a certain duration. In such cases, the employer may possibly have or may be deemed to have a certain degree of control over the home office. Depending on the facts of the individual case, the establishment of a PE by remote working activity is conceivable.[7]

3.2.2 *Agency PE/Dependent Agent PE*

If the employee resident abroad has the authority (during his remote work) to conclude (sales or other) contracts for the employer and if the employee habitually concludes these, an agency PE in the employee's country of residence may be established. Under Article 12 Multilateral Instrument and to the extent the article has been implemented, the same applies when the employee working remotely habitually plays the principal role leading to the conclusion of contracts concluded by the enterprise whether they are:

(a) in the name of the enterprise; or
(b) for the transfer of the ownership of or for the granting of the right to use property owned by the enterprise or that the enterprise has the right to use; or
(c) for the provision of services by that enterprise.

In such a case, the establishment of a PE does not depend on a fixed business facility. Thus, a power of disposal of the employer over the home office will be dispensable.[8]

3.2.3 *Service PE*[9]

In addition, the work of an employee that is exercised in a home office or other remote location could, when the relevant tax treaty provides such a clause, give rise to a 'service PE'. This could primarily be the case when the employee's work represents a service rendered by the employer/foreign enterprise to a third party and such in-country work is exercised over a period of more than 183 days of presence in the source country.[10]

The concept of a service PE primarily captures technical and commercial services even though it might also apply itself to advisory or consulting services. In tax treaties,

7. *Schuster/Verleger* IWB 2020, 861; *Rasch/Rosenberger/Brülisauer* IStR-Beiheft 2021, 1.
8. OECD, Multilateral Convention to implement tax treaty related measures to prevent base erosion and profit shifting, Article 12; *Schuster/Verleger* IWB 21/2020, 861; *Rasch/Rosenberger /Brülisauer* IStR Beiheft 2021, 1.
9. Article 5 section 3 UN-MC; no explicit provision in the OECD-MC, but the commentary to the OECD-MC contains suggested formulations for the definition of service PEs, as they could be included by the contracting states in DTAs, cf. Article 5 OECD-MC Commentary para. 144.
10. Article 5 OECD-MC Commentary paras 144 ff., 156, 166; UN-MC Article 5 (3) lit. b); *Rasch/Rosenberger/Brülisauer* IStR-Beiheft 2021, 1 (4). *See, e.g.*, Germany – Turkey Double Taxation Agreement Article 5 section 3 lit. b).

specific clauses for service PEs do not seem to be really widespread. For these reasons, a discussion of service PEs resulting from remote work is not further pursued in this chapter.

A service PE has to be distinguished from a conceivable PE triggered by the activity of an employee seconded to or regularly working at an affiliate entity's premises under a service contract. When the employer (sending entity) has contracted to provide a service to the receiving entity and the employee executes the sending entity's business at the receiving entity, this may give rise to a PE. This may arise primarily when the sending entity obtains a power of disposal of a business establishment of the receiving entity.[11] Such a scenario can therefore be subsumed under the case of the fixed place of business PE.

3.2.4 Management PE[12]

Finally, the income from the work of an employee could constitute (the) management of the foreign enterprise. Thus, assuming other preconditions are present, the location where the employee exercises the management work could qualify as a place of management PE.

A place of management will only constitute a PE if the requirements of the foundational PE definition of Article 5, paragraph 1 OECD-MC or UN-MC, respectively, are met.[13] Thus, a place of management PE is a specific variant of a fixed place of business PE. A place of management PE potentially raises specific tax implications such as a relocation of management functions, a dual residence of the enterprise or issues with the tax recognition of a tax consolidation group.[14] Yet, the place of management PE, first of all, represents a specific case in point of the general concept of a fixed place of business PE and is not as widespread as the latter. Therefore, it is not further discussed.

The analysis in this chapter consequently focuses on fixed place of business PEs, agency establishments, and the transfer price implications for ongoing profit allocation between the HQ and PE. The requirements of duration or permanence of a PE that are generally affirmed when the in-country presence of the enterprise substantially exceeds six months[15] are presumed to be present.

11. *Beduhn/Staudler* IStR 2015, 937 (940); Article 5 OECD-MC; Article 5 UN-MC Commentary, para. 15 i.c.w. Article 5 OECD-MC Commentary, para. 39; Vogel/Lehner OECD-MA 2017 Article 5 (1) para. 49.
12. Article 5 section 2 lit. a) OECD-MC; Article 5 section 2 lit. a) UN-MC.
13. Article 5 OECD-MC Commentary, para. 45.
14. *Schuster/Verleger* IWB 2020, 861; Rödl&Partner Internationale Matrixorganisationen – Herausforderungen für die steuerliche Compliance, 6 August 2019, https://www.roedl.de/themen/entrepreneur/familienunternehmen-trends/matrixorganisation-unternehmen-international-compliance-internationales-steuerrecht, last called on 20 January 2023; for a detailed look on the possibility of management PEs, cf. *Müth/Simon* DStR 2022, 744.
15. OECD Updated Guidance 21 January 2021, section 23.

4 HOW FAR DOES HOME OFFICE WORK GIVE RISE TO A FIXED PLACE OF BUSINESS PE?

During and since the time of the COVID-19 pandemic, the OECD and several tax administrations have taken efforts to remove unnecessary PE risks. On 3 April 2020, the OECD Secretariat published its position on the impact of the COVID-19 pandemic and resulting public health measures on the issue of PEs potentially created by employees working remotely. Some tax administrations stated that they would follow the OECD guidance, and there was a large degree of consensus among them. The activities of employees who temporarily worked in a home office due to governmental COVID-19 restrictions should generally not result in a PE for the employer. Some administrative guidelines specified additional requirements such as the company not having a PE prior to COVID-19 travel restrictions or that there were no changes to the company's economic circumstances.

COVID-19-related administrative reliefs from PE taxation were generally tied to an employee's home office being exclusively caused by COVID-19-related public health measures and were limited in time for the duration of such measures. Consequently, home office work continued subsequent to publicly imposed contact and travel restrictions and raised particular challenges for delineating COVID-19-related home office work from other such work.

The main focus of the discussion is on the rather more permanent legal context for home office work subsequent to the pandemic. For post-COVID-19 times, not so much of the administrative consensus seems left.[16] For the post-COVID-19 situation, the analysis structures the administrative, juridical, and literary discussion with the main practical features of home office fact patterns. These are analysed to determine how much they represent a valid taxation nexus.

4.1 Practical Features of Home Office Work as Relevant for a Fixed Place of Business PE

4.1.1 Frequency and Duration of Home Office Work

Administrative directives issued during the COVID-19 crisis regularly justified not establishing a home office PE on the basis of temporary residency due to travel restrictions. A comparable case is the Irish Revenue rules applicable for the tax year 2022 according to which refugees from Ukraine working remotely in Ireland do not create a PE.[17]

16. In COVID-19 guidelines, statements can be found that, if the home office activity continues, the establishment of a permanent establishment 'may be considered', the 'conclusion [that there is no permanent establishment] could change', or that 'further examination of the facts and circumstances would be required to determine whether a permanent establishment exists'. Only a few administrative instructions go into more detail.
17. Revenue Irish Tax and Customs 14 April 2022, Revenue eBrief No. 090/22.

Regarding the frequency and duration of home office work, situations of occasional or a maximum of 25% of the work time at the home office are discussed and are classified as non-PE situations by the Austrian Tax Administration.[18] According to the Danish Tax Council, the important factor in determining a PE is whether the employee's home office activity is incidental and sporadic or whether the home office activity is planned or can be scheduled.[19]

A slightly different and less explicitly discussed situation is present when the remote worker uses his home office on one or two or a maximum of two to three days per week (use between 25% and 50%) but does not use it for the majority of the work time. In this case, a review of the individual case will (probably) be inevitable.[20]

Finally, this situation may be contrasted with a fact pattern where the employee works at home every day and far more than 50% of the time; only occasionally he may physically enter the enterprise establishment whether it is for exceptional meetings, employee reunions, etc.[21]

It seems far from clear that this quite practical criterion should technically be relevant for the deeming of a PE, at least under the OECD Model Convention and comparable treaties. Different from an agency establishment, there is no requirement that the fixed place of business is used permanently for the exercise of the business itself.[22] True, the place of business must be fixed in the sense that it has a constant or definable connection with the territory and that it is of a sustained, non-temporary nature.[23] In addition, the OECD Model Convention Commentary 2017 denies a place of business for the enterprise 'where the enterprise's presence at a location is so intermittent or incidental that the location cannot be considered a place of business of the enterprise'.[24] This criterion, however, is not the same as the question of how often the fixed place of business is used for work and whether it is used 100% of the working hours or less than, say, 25% of the working hours. Even a one-day-per-week home office frequency does not seem to be 'so intermittent or incidental' as necessary to reject a fixed place of business. There is a connection with the technical requirement of a fixed place of business through which the enterprise's business is run insofar as a certain regularity or recurrence ('a certain degree of permanency'[25]) of use going along with the non-temporary nature of the fixed place of business itself would have to be expected.

18. Austrian Transfer Pricing Guidelines 2021, para. 262; Austrian Federal Ministry of Finance, EAS 3415; Austrian Federal Ministry of Finance, EAS 3323.
19. Danish Tax Council 12 May 2022, SKM-number: SKM2022.250.SR.
20. Cf. *Massoner* (EY) Homeoffice als Betriebsstätte, https://www.ey.com/de_at/tax/homeoffice-als-steuerliche-betriebsstaette-es-wird-ernst, last called on 20 January 2023.
21. According to the Austrian Tax Administration, in this case, it is no longer possible to classify the home office activity as 'occasionally', cf. Austrian Transfer Pricing Guidelines 2021, para. 262; Austrian Federal Ministry of Finance, EAS 3415.
22. Article 5 OECD-MC Commentary, para. 32.
23. Cf. Article 5 OECD-MC Commentary, para. 28.
24. Article 5 OECD-MC Commentary, para. 12. *See also ibid.*, para. 18; UN-MC Commentary para. 3.
25. OECD, Updated guidance on tax treaties and the impact of the COVID-19 pandemic, 21 January 2021, para. 14.

In the authors' views, to the extent that the number of days per week or proportion of work time spent at the home office does at all play a part in assuming or denying a PE, this should rather be seen as a pragmatic materiality threshold to appropriately limit and focus the use of fiscal and business resources.

4.1.2 Initiative for Home Office: Who Has Initiated or Driven the Home Office Work?

In the context of the COVID-19 pandemic, lockdowns, and travel and contact prohibitions issued by public authorities forced employees around the globe to work from home and to discharge their work as efficiently and productively as possible under the circumstances. For this situation, there seems to have been an international consensus that a home office due to more or less absolute government coercion should not be taken as an occasion to assume a PE.[26]

The other end of the spectrum is voluntary home office work by employees at their own request. In this scenario, employers may more or less readily support, tolerate, or even promote such voluntary home office work. As far as what has been seen, there are only a few statements on whether this scenario in and of itself would give rise to a PE. According to the Swedish Tax Agency, no power of disposal of the company can be assumed if the home office activity takes place due to the employee's own wishes and the company has no business interest in or any advantage of the employee working from home (e.g., when the company is not active in the Swedish market).[27] The Spanish General Directorate of Taxes considers that, once all COVID-19 travel restrictions are lifted, it also depends on whether the employee unilaterally decides to remain in Spain.[28] According to the Danish Tax Council, it is relevant whether the activity carried out from the home office is advantageously performed from Denmark whereby the employer has an interest in the work being performed from Denmark.[29] Looking at administrative and international organizations' comments, the (in-)voluntary nature of home office work does not seem to be a critical aspect of the PE question. Considering the rather objective, factual concept of fixed place of business PEs in model conventions and tax treaties, this generally seems appropriate.

The question does take another turn where the employer expects or requires the employee to discharge his work from home and does not offer any workplace at the enterprise establishment. The Austrian tax administration has taken this scenario as a

26. *Rasch/Rosenberger/Brülisauer* IStR-Beiheft 2021, 1 (9 f.); also cf. Hong Kong: Inland Revenue Department, Tax Issues arising from the COVID-19 Pandemic; Greece: Independent Authority for Public Revenue 22 July 2020, E. 2113 pp. 9 ff.; Austria: Federal Ministry of Finance 22 May 2020, 2020-0.271.800; New Zealand: Inland Revenue Covid-19 Tax residency; Swedish Tax Agency 13 May 2022, dnr: 8-1677220; OECD, Analysis of Tax Treaties and the Impact of the COVID-19 Crisis, 3.4.2020, para. 9; OECD, Updated guidance on tax treaties and the impact of the COVID-19 pandemic, para. 10.
27. Swedish Tax Agency 13 May 2022, dnr: 8-1677220, para. 4.1.
28. Spanish General Directorate of Taxes 18 January 2022, consultation number: V0066-22.
29. Danish Tax Council 12 May 2022, SKM-number: SKM2022.250.SR.

reason to assume a PE.[30] In this line of thinking, what matters less is the (in-)voluntary nature of home office work itself but rather the inferences that this suggests for the power of disposal over the employee's home.

In practical cases, it may well be challenging to factually discern whether an employer expects or requires home office work. This is illustrated by the example of a workspace booking software. Consider, for example, a consulting or software development business that has reduced the number of available offices or workspaces in its building. The employer knows from experience that usually only perhaps 40%-50% of employees will show up physically at the office building; most will prefer to work from home. After having reduced the number of available offices, employees who wish to work at the building are required to book their office space in advance through an office space management software. Of course, the employer expects a certain portion of its employees to work from home on any given day. Yet, any given employee could book an office 100% of the time. The employer would not have any specific expectation or requirement of home work specifically 'directed against' any individual employee, whether that individual has a home in the headquarter country or abroad. Additionally, in many other fact patterns, it should be far from clear whether the question of expected or required home office work can be answered in a satisfactory manner.

4.1.3 Disposal over Home Office: Who Can Decide on Whether and Which Home Office Is Used?

This feature of the various forms of home office activity is probably the most critical.

The situation is relatively clear when the employee owns or rents a house or apartment and lends it to the employer on a contractual basis. All other requirements present, a PE should be assumed.[31]

As a more widespread base case, a situation may be considered where the employee owns or rents his own apartment or home and uses it for home office activity. In principle, it seems evident that the enterprise does not have a legal or de facto right or position to have the home office location at its disposal. However, the overlap with the preceding discussion on whose initiative the home office is used must also be considered. As mentioned, the Austrian tax administration has declared that a home office used at the request of the employer may be regarded as a PE of the employer's enterprise.[32] This finds support in the OECD Model Convention Commentary 2017 on Article 5, section 12 where the commentary notes that according to the OECD's view 'no formal legal right to use a particular place is required' and instead states that the enterprise will have to have 'the effective power to use that location'. Specifically addressing a home office situation, the commentary states that:

30. Austrian Federal Ministry of Finance, EAS 3415; also cf. Article 5 OECD-MC Commentary, para. 18.
31. *Rasch/Rosenberger/Brülisauer* IStR 2021, 1 (8 f.).
32. Austrian Federal Ministry of Finance, EAS 3415.

> where, however, a home office is used on a continuous basis for carrying on business activities for an enterprise and it is clear from the facts and circumstances that the enterprise has required the individual to use that location to carry on the enterprises business (e.g. by not providing an office to an employee in circumstances where the nature of the employment clearly requires an office), the home office may be considered to be at the disposal of the enterprise.[33]

Quite apparently, the OECD Model Convention Commentary 2017 has a situation in mind where the employer not only initiates and drives the discharge of work tasks from home but at least de facto has the economic power to require the employee to use his own living space for dependent work. The authors argue that the OECD performs a conceptual shift without making it fully explicit. Assume that the employee is expected or required to execute his work tasks in his home office in Country A and is not offered a workplace at the employer's enterprise establishment in Country B. Additionally assume that the home office work is carried out on a continuous basis and is, of course, not auxiliary or preparatory. After some months, the employee leaves his first apartment and moves into another newly rented apartment. In the logic of section 18, the PE has moved along. The employer has had no say and may have gained only *ex post* knowledge of the employee's new home office. Clearly, the employer did not have any legal or de facto right or position to influence or decide which of the two apartments is used for home office. Now assume further that the employee rents a second apartment in Country A so that he may choose which apartment to use for home office work and which not. Assume the second apartment is considerably farther away from the enterprise establishment in Country B. The employee considers the first apartment as his working home and the second apartment as his family home. So, he may claim personal income deductions based on the concept of a professionally induced dual household. Again, the employer has no say over which of the two apartments is used for the employment work. Again, in the logic of section 18, a PE would be assumed to be present. Now, consider another variation where the employee considers that the shorter distance between his first apartment in Country A and the enterprise establishment in Country B is still too long and too burdensome to make even occasional trips for necessary stays at the enterprise establishment in Country B. He therefore decides to relocate his working home to Country B but keeps his family home in Country A. Presumably, there is consensus that under, section 18 of the commentary, the PE would be situated in Country B rather than in Country A. Again, the employer has no say or influence on which of the two apartments is used for home office purposes.

These examples point to the fact that the OECD Model Convention Commentary 2017, section 18, seems to give up the idea that power of disposal has to relate to a specific location that is fixed, i.e., has a defined, continuous special relation with the territory of Country A. The use of some unspecified location there is enough to assume a PE. Such undefined, unspecified identity of the location in question seems to be inconsistent with the analytical approach taken in section 12 of the commentary where it speaks of 'a particular place', 'that place', or 'that location'.

33. Article 5 OECD-MC Commentary, para. 18; also cf. Article 5 UN-MC Commentary, para. 6.

The conceptual shift can also be seen when considering the nature or extent of the employer's influence over the employee's home office. Evidently and also illustrated by the examples above, the employer has no formal or de facto right to dispose of the use of the employee's apartments in Country A. The employer rather has the de facto power to expect the employee to use some unspecified and suitable location for the discharge of his work obligations. The criterion in section 18 seems to be that an employer refuses to allow the employee to use the enterprise office building or makes it practically too laborious to do so. There is no doubt that, thereby, the employer exerts some influence on the choice of the employee's work location and restricts the choices to non-enterprise locations. This raises the question of how far the negative influence or power to exclude the use of enterprise offices should be equivalent to a positive power of disposal over the place of actual work execution.

Incidentally, it is not clear that the conceptual shift (no legal or factual power to actively decide on the use of the location) has a parallel in the well-known 'painter example'.[34] It affirms a PE at the office building of a painter's main client where the painter spends the better part of each work week over a time span of two years. At least under German law, based on the painting contract, the client will be obligated to put the office building at the disposal of the painter in order to enable him to fulfil his painting obligation. Of course, this is not an active legal right to have disposal over the use of the office building. However, if the client does not make it possible for the painter to enter the office building and exercise his painting task, the painter, after requisite notification to the client, may subsequently abstain from doing his work and may even be entitled to claim damage. This situation is different from the home office examples that were discussed. In these, the employer has no right to access, make use of, or instruct the employee to use a specific, individual location for the enterprise.

For the sake of completeness, such a dependent work home office situation has to be contrasted with 'true home workers' who are self-employed. The Austrian tax administration has recognized this difference and has denied a PE of the enterprise retaining such self-employed home workers.[35]

4.1.4 *Ownership of Equipment Used at Home Office: Who Can Dispose of a Notebook, Desk, Etc.?*

The conceivable assumption of a PE due to an employee's home-based remote work has been discussed. The use of digital work devices (notebooks, smartphones, etc.) at home, however, gives rise to questions not answered by the previous discussion.

This question becomes interesting if considering the typical home office situation where an employee is active with digital company devices at his private premises.[36] In such a case, the tendency (of, e.g., the Austrian Tax Administration) so far has been that even the provision of a laptop or a mobile phone by the employer should lead to

34. Article 5 OECD-MC Commentary, para. 5.3.
35. Austrian Federal Ministry of Finance, EAS 3415.
36. This does not address the situation of a 'tele-workplace' (Tele-Arbeitsplatz) fully equipped by the employer.

a fixed place of business.[37] Bearing in mind that the employer will have the power of disposal over digital work devices, the operational use by the employee would cause the likelihood of a PE.[38]

In the recent past, however, there was a notable development in case law. Thus, the Austrian Administrative Court ruled on the limits of power of disposal in home office cases.[39] The Administrative Court ruled that shared use of a desk in another taxpayer's office was not sufficient to constitute a PE. Rather, an *entire* room, including other furnishings and equipment, must be made available for carrying out the activity. This is particularly interesting since this statement contradicts previous Austrian administrative practice.[40] Parts of literature see an end to the home office PE in Austria. If the shared use of a desk in the office of another taxpayer is not sufficient for granting a power of disposal, an employer a fortiori cannot have power of disposal over the employee's *private* premises.[41] So, a right of joint use of the employee working at the kitchen table, in the living room, in a workroom, or in another private room cannot be sufficient to constitute the employer's power of disposal.[42] Such a limitation for assuming power of disposal by the enterprise could also contribute to clarifying things on an international level. Other authors caution that the judgement does not expressly speak of excluding PEs in home office activities so the implications of the court decision for assuming a home office PE are not clear.[43] Recently, the Tax Court Stuttgart has ruled that the use of an office based on shared rights of use in a cooperative did represent a PE of the enterprise since the power of disposal manifested itself through exclusive possession of a floor-standing container.[44]

Unfortunately, these decisions on the PE implications of a shared office (desk) use cannot be transferred to an employee home office situation. In this type of scenario, the existence of a fixed place of business is likely; the employer's power of disposal, however, is much less so. In contrast, there should be no doubt about an employer's power of disposal over digital devices used by a home-working employee. Instead, it is much less clear whether the devices represent a fixed place of business or a fixed

37. Cf. Austrian Federal Ministry of Finance, EAS 3415; Austrian Transfer Pricing Guidelines 2021, para. 262; Article 5 OECD-MC Commentary, para. 18 f.
38. Austrian Federal Ministry of Finance, EAS 3415.
39. VwGH (Austrian Higher Administrative Court) 22 June 2022 – Ro 2020/13/0004.
40. Austrian Transfer Pricing Guidelines 2021, para. 261; Austrian Federal Ministry of Finance, EAS 1969; also cf. Austrian Federal Ministry of Finance, EAS 3415.
41. *Bendlinger/Bendlinger* SWI 2022, 436 (451); cf., *Gottholmseder/Hahn* KPMG Tax News 07-09/2022, https://home.kpmg/at/de/home/insights/2022/09/tn-vwgh-urteil-zu-betriebsstaettenbegruendung.html, last called on 27 January 2023.
42. *Bendlinger/Bendlinger* SWI 2022, 436 (451); cf., *Gottholmseder/Hahn* KPMG Tax News 07-09/2022, https://home.kpmg/at/de/home/insights/2022/09/tn-vwgh-urteil-zu-betriebsstaettenbegruendung.html, last called on 27 January 2023; cf. also Article 5 OECD-MC Commentary, para. 18 f.
43. *Bendlinger/Bendlinger* SWI 2022, 436 (451); *Plansky* EY Tax News Austria 4.12.2022, https://www.ey.com/de_at/tax/aktuelle-entwicklungen-bei-betriebsstaetten, last called on 3 February 2023; cf., Gottholmseder/Hahn KPMG Tax News 07-09/2022, https://home.kpmg/at/de/home/insights/2022/09/tn-vwgh-urteil-zu-betriebsstaettenbegruendung.html, last called on 27.1.2023.
44. Tax Court Stuttgart 14/10/2021 3 K 589/19.

business facility.[45] Of course, the digital devices are portable and mobile by nature. Nevertheless, it might be argued that their ongoing use at the employee's home, which is undoubtedly a fixed place, puts the devices stationary in relation to a particular point on the surface of the earth and thus makes them fixed business facilities. However, in today's work environment, digital devices such as smartphones, laptops, etc. are probably work utensils as basic as a pen and paper used to be in former times. It is assumed that, in those times, probably nobody would have deemed a fixed place of business had a clerical or commercial employee that used his employer's pen and paper at home. It is not clear why, today, this should be different for a smartphone and laptop. These devices rather appear to be everyday work utensils carried around by the employee wherever he goes. The authors assume that there is a consensus that a stationary spatial relation would not be attributed to a particular point on the surface of the earth to any human individual, so the same should be relevant for basic work devices handled by humans. In addition, value is created by the employee's human activity rather than by the presence of the digital devices themselves. Thus, there is also an economic argument to not attribute a quintessential role to digital devices used at the home office.

4.1.5 Nature of Home Office Work: Does the Employee's Activity Qualify as Auxiliary or Preparatory?

The question of whether an employee's activity qualifies as auxiliary or preparatory has to be considered dynamically. What is an auxiliary or preparatory activity in one company may be the main activity in another. However, there are clearly administrative, clerical, or internal support or peripheral work activities, such as finance, HR administration, etc. that will often be regarded as auxiliary and preparatory and therefore do not qualify as PEs.[46]

However, when the employee's activity is part of the core business activity of the employer, such as doing telephone and video conference services out of a shared service centre or IT development services, this would regularly not be auxiliary or preparatory.[47]

It is again the Austrian tax administration that has explicitly taken up this situation where the employee meets customers at his home office.[48] In many cases, this will go beyond the scope of an auxiliary or preparatory activity. At the same time, affirming a core, non-auxiliary activity in this fact pattern triggers a follow-up question. What tax consequences should ensue if the employee does not have physical but instead virtual

45. Cf. Austrian Federal Ministry of Finance, EAS 3415; Austrian Transfer Pricing Guidelines 2021, para. 262; BFH (German Federal Fiscal Court) 17 September 2003 – I R 12/02. BStBl. II 2004, 396, a notebook is sufficient for a place of business, but the question whether it's 'fixed' remains unanswered; different view Tipke/Kruse/*Drüen* AO § 12 para. 8; Mössner/*Lang* Steuerrecht international tätiger Unternehmen, para. 2.103.
46. Cf. *Schuster/Verleger* IWB 2020, 861.
47. *Ibid.*
48. Austrian Transfer Pricing Guidelines 2021, para. 262; Austrian Federal Ministry of Finance, EAS 3323.

meetings with customers from his home office? That said, the relevance of the (non-) auxiliary or preparatory nature of the home office work activities is self-evident.

4.2 Practical Importance of Agency Establishments for Home Office Situations

The previous fact pattern of an employee physically or virtually meeting customers at the home office points to the practical importance of sales and marketing activities for the assumption of a PE at the home office. As known, an agency establishment does not require a power of disposal of the enterprise over a fixed place of business such as the employee's home. For purposes of this analysis, the authors consider the spectrum and business importance of activities of customer development, customer acquisition, pre-sales customer care, contract negotiation, sales contract conclusion, etc.[49] In many cases and many industries, it will be possible to exercise such activities while working remotely.

5 ALLOCATION OF FUNCTIONS AND TRANSFER PRICE METHODS FOR A FIXED PLACE OF BUSINESS PE

Going beyond general principles, the actual, down-to-earth transfer pricing consequences of a home office PE are not well established and are not often discussed. The most popular practical transfer pricing approach in a home office PE set-up is to more or less assume a low value-added service that the home office PE renders towards the headquarters and has to be remunerated at cost-plus,[50] adding a profit markup of 5% to 10%.

The authors will therefore attempt to formulate some economic and conceptual principles that could be a basis for practical transfer pricing. This should also help to analyse how far the popular cost-plus service approach has theoretical and economic validity.

Both the OECD-MC and the UN-MC recognize that the arm's length principle is decisive for the profit differentiation between a PE and a parent company. For the most part, Article 7 OECD-MC and Article 7 UN-MC converge, but the latter explicitly rejects the AOA introduced in the former in 2010. Therefore, the commentary on the UN-MC 2021 refers to the OECD-MC Commentaries of 2008 and 2005, respectively. According to this approach, the principle of causation is decisive according to which the source state may only tax the profits of a non-resident company to the extent that they are attributable to the PE located in the source state.

In proceeding, it is assumed that, in the case of a home office PE, the allocation of functions between entities (inter-entity allocation) should generally remain unaffected.

49. On the possibility of a dependent agent permanent establishment in procurement (rather than sales and marketing), cf. *Schoppe/Leuwer* BB 2016, 1623 (1625). The OECD does not mention any examples in which this scenario occurs.

50. United Kingdom Office of Tax Simplification Hybrid and distance working report, December 2022, paras 4.30 ff.

The focus is on the allocation of functions within the same entity. Probably, the universal approach for the allocation of functions is to look at the physical location at which the relevant people exercise the respective function.[51] This approach appears to rest on the premise that, in the overwhelming majority of cases, looking at the physical exercise by people of a certain function leads to a clear and workable allocation of the function. Unfortunately, this premise of the criterion of physical exercise of function is put into question in a remote working situation. Consider a situation in which the employee uses his home office for about 50% or more of the work time but still exercises a significant portion of work at the main enterprise establishment. A similar situation may be present when the home office is regularly used for concluding contracts with customers while the enterprise establishment is still largely used for the same activity. Examples like these raise the question of whether a function can be allocated simultaneously/in parallel both to the main enterprise establishment/headquarters and to the home office or whether a function can only be allocated to either of them. The German tax administration has taken the position that a people function can only be allocated either to the headquarters or to the PE.[52] Other than that, the question does not seem to have been addressed.

The either-or approach seems appropriate when a (clear) majority of work activity is exercised either at the headquarters or at the home office PE. Assume that the either-or approach is adopted but, in a practical situation, the minority of some work activity exercised at the home office still gives rise to the enterprise's PE. Then, the minor quantitative scope of exercise of function at the home office PE should necessarily be seen as a routine or low value-added service rendered by the home office PE to the headquarters. Given the functional allocation premise that the people function can only be allocated to that entity in total, the characterization of the dealing as a low value-added or routine service seems appropriate also when the people function itself should be of a non-routine, entrepreneurial, or high value-added nature. The authors argue that such a functional allocation is economically appropriate, especially for a significant value-added function and for the - often unrealistic - scenario that an individual's work activity circumscribes the totality of a function.

Still assuming the either-or approach is adopted, the question comes up of how to deal with situations when a work activity representing a significant people function or significant value-adding function is split about 50:50 between the home office and the headquarters. In such a situation, it would appear to be appropriate to leave the

51. OECD Report on the Attribution of Profits to Permanent Establishments 2010, Part I paras 15 and 60, '[...] the determination of which activities and responsibilities of the enterprise are associated with the PE should be determined from an analysis of the "fixed place" that constitutes the permanent establishment and the functions performed *at that "fixed place"*'; *Rasch/Rosenberger/Brülisauer* IStR Beiheft 2021, 1 (10); Oestreicher/Schnitger/Wellens /*Wellens/van der Ham* Gewinnabgrenzung nach dem Authorised OECD Approach (AOA), para. 7.77; Wassermeyer/Andresen/Ditz/*Andresen* Betriebsstätten Handbuch, para. 5.19.
52. Betriebsstättengewinnaufteilungsverordnung ('BsGaV', German Directive on the Distribution of Profits of Permanent Establishments) Article 4; Verwaltungsgrundsätze Betriebsstättengewinnaufteilung ('VWG-BsGa', German administrative principles on Profit Allocation to Permanent Establishments), para. 71.

allocation of the function and its rationale to the enterprise unless the exercise of that assessment proves to be abusive.[53]

When the work activity is predominantly exercised at the home office PE, the either-or approach necessitates the exhaustive and exclusive allocation of the respective function to the PE. It is not clear whether and which dealing should be appropriately hypothesized between the home office PE and the headquarters. Assume, for example, a situation where the parent company in Country A instructs and exercises control over the development of software rendered as a service by the subsidiary in Country B. Now assume the manager exercising the actual management and control over the software development mostly works from his home office in Country C and thereby gives rise to a PE. In this situation, under the either-or approach, the function represented by the work activity of the individual manager will be fully and exhaustively allocated to the home office PE in Country C. Assume there is no other individual at the parent company in Country A exercising real control or monitoring over the software development, then the principal function of the parent company in respect of the software development service contract should be allocated to the parent company's PE in Country C. As a consequence, it may be wondered whether the inception or shift of the work activity of the controlling manager in Country C represents a transfer of functions from the parent company in Country A to its PE in Country C. Apart from this one-off initial transaction, it is not apparent that any ongoing dealing between the parent company headquarters and its PE in Country C could appropriately be hypothesized.

Now assume, probably more realistically, that the work of instructing and supervising the software development is exercised by a whole team of (software development) managers employed by the parent company in Country A. Some of these managers work at the enterprise establishment/headquarters while others do so from home. Such a setup and, more generally, any locationally split exercise of significant value-adding functions, seem to suggest a consideration of a profit split approach. The residual profit of the parent company (principal of the software development under contract) would be allocated to the headquarters and home office PEs based on proportionate inputs that are contributed such as work time or salary shares. To illustrate the highly factual nature of such an analysis, consider a variation of the previous example where the parent company has established an international executive development management committee that meets once a month at the headquarters location. Those parent company managers who are members of the committee or who, from time to time, report to the committee, are expected to be physically present at these meetings at the parent company location. Additionally, the most important aspects of software development management and control are exercised in and on the basis of these committee meetings at the headquarters. Such activities can be for approving the strategic and product planning for software development, milestone/stage-gate decisions, budget management, etc. In contrast, the management and control of software development by the subsidiary are rather limited to day-to-day

53. *See also* BSGaV, para. 4; VWG-BSGa, para. 71.

operational aspects when parent company managers work between committee meetings at their homes (or at the enterprise establishment). In such a scenario, a simple time- or salary-based profit split will not appropriately reflect the contributions of the headquarters and home office PEsto the residual profit generated out of the software development principal function.

The example illustrates that, in many cases, a function as a unit of a transfer price analysis will encompass the work of a whole group or a multitude of people. If a function is conceptualized as a meaningful step of value creation in the enterprise's value chain or, alternatively, as a 'cash-generating unit', it will regularly be much larger than one individual's work scope.

The example also shows the practical and administrative superiority of the either-or approach. In the setup of the software development principle, it should ordinarily be possible to identify the 'centre of gravity' of management and control activities. Assume the centre of gravity is at the headquarters. This will vastly simplify the understanding of any hypothesized dealings between home office PEs and the headquarters but also the economic profit delineation under a non-AOA. As a result, scenarios calling for a profit split will be restricted to situations where value contributions are close to a 50:50 split between the headquarters and home office PEs.

Thus, from the perspective of simplification and administrative ease, an either-or approach seems vastly superior. First, all technical requirements in tax treaties (such as power of disposal) have to be analysed and confirmed before a home office PE can be assumed. Then, a relatively simple cost-plus service approach seems to be a workable trade-off between legitimate fiscal interests in home office states and the need to support flexible wealth creation by international businesses. Hence, a safe harbour regulation based on the principles described above could be a suitable option to increase tax certainty.

6 ALLOCATION OF FUNCTIONS AND TRANSFER PRICE METHODS FOR A HOME OFFICE AGENCY ESTABLISHMENT

6.1 Practical Importance and Common Forms of Home Office Agency Establishments

The previous section worked out some basic transfer price implications of a fixed price of business PE if one is created by a remote or home office worker. At the same time, the creation of a PE of the foreign enterprise in the form of a (dependent) agent should be much more of a practical concern. This is because the creation of an agency establishment does not require any sort of disposal of the enterprise over the home office residence. In addition, the Multilateral Instrument (MLI) has provided an extension of the concept of agency establishment in Article 12 MLI, and this provision has given rise to more expansive agency establishment concepts being pursued in practice or being passed into law.[54] For businesses, identifying critical sales and/or

54. *See, e.g.*, Japanese domestic legislation on agency establishments or Double Taxation Agreement Australia-Germany Article 5 (8).

marketing activities and (re-)structuring business processes in order to avoid triggering an agency establishment is a considerable practical, organizational, and informational challenge. Likewise, tax administrations are faced with the task of distinguishing between innocuous marketing and sales support activities, on the one hand, and critical contract conclusions or critical contributions to such, on the other hand. As known, a home office worker's activity has to be such that he concludes contracts 'repeatedly and not merely in isolated cases',[55] or the authority to conclude contracts has to be habitually exercised.[56] OECD Article 12 MLI provides for an extension of such an agency establishment when the home office worker 'plays a critical role' in the conclusion of sales contracts.[57]

However, a contract conclusion and the playing of a critical role in such has to be distinguished from mere participation in negotiations.[58] In this context, 'messenger' type situations are practically quite relevant when the home office employee has no or minimal negotiation room and merely communicates offers for sale receiving customer responses in return. Such fact patterns harbour significant factual and legal ambiguities and present challenges for both tax administrations and businesses.

In practice, the conclusion of contracts or playing a critical role out of a fixed residence by an employee may well induce tax administrations to assume the habitual recurrence or the minimum duration of such critical agency activity more easily.[59] Since digitalized work relations and cross-border organizational work processes including sales and marketing will be more and more widespread which also underlines the practical importance of an agency establishment in this context. If an agency establishment is to be assumed, then the PE encompasses the total scope of activity of the home office employee for the enterprise and not merely the activity that gives rise to the assumption of an agency establishment.[60]

In practice, the scenario must also be considered in which a number of employees work out of multiple home offices in the same country and habitually conclude contracts or play a critical role in the conclusion of such. This fact pattern is not addressed by the Multilateral Instrument. Here, even though not directly applicable, the anti-abuse provision of Article 14 MLI comes to mind. The article deals particularly with the execution of construction or installation projects that represent one coherent operation but have been split up artificially. There seem to be good reasons to restrict this anti-abuse provision to specific projects. An application by analogy of the concept of splitting up contracts to multiple home offices would run counter to the practicality and feasibility of tax compliance both for taxpayers and for tax administrations.

Questions of dependent agency may also arise when one manager in a groupwide matrix organization works out of his home office for a number of affiliated group

55. Article 5 OECD-MC Commentary, para. 83.
56. Article 5 OECD-MC Commentary, para. 98.
57. Conceptually, a dependent agency can also relate to the input (procurement) side of the business while this chapter focuses on the more widespread dependent agency on the output (sales) side.
58. Article 5 OECD-MC Commentary, para. 97.
59. *See also ibid.*, para. 180.
60. *Ibid.*, para. 99.

entities. To the extent that the preconditions of a dependent agent are fulfilled, this can, in practice, lead to a multitude of possible PEs.

6.2 Functional Analysis, Transfer Price Methods, and Profit Allocation for a Home Office Agency Establishment

When analysing the transfer pricing implications of a home office agency establishment, the natural starting point for the functional analysis is to assume the agency establishment represents a sales agent. Stated in a different manner, the agency establishment itself is not regarded as buying and selling goods or services but rather as concluding or critically catalysing contracts for the sales of goods and services. Further, those functions would be intuitively imputed to the agency establishment that a typical sales agent would also exercise. Consequently, a sales agent's commission would appear to be an arm's length remuneration for the agency activity itself.

Calculating the profit of a dependent agency PE is one of the least clear and unequivocal determined areas of international tax law. Thus, the following discussion sets out a reasonable, proposed approach on the basis of the AOA. In a simple example, assume the enterprise concludes a contract for the sale of a product with an in-country customer at a price of 100 units. The fair sales agent's commission allocated to the agency establishment shall be 10 units. Accounting for an income of 10 in the agency P&L (credit commission income 10) raises the question of any economically related deductions in the P&L. Clearly, the (proportionate) salary and ancillary costs of the home office worker, from a tax perspective, are deductions for the PE rather than, as the contractual perspective suggests, for the headquarters. Assume that the amount of the sales agent's commission has been determined by means of a comparable uncontrolled price or by stripping down the comparable financials of an independent buy-sell distributor. Then, it is most unlikely that the amount of commission is identical to the salary and ancillary cost earned by the home office employee. Depending on the amount of relevant sales, the absolute amount of commission could be higher or lower. Assume the salary of the home office employee increased by ancillary costs (social security contributions, etc.) is 8. This results in an agency establishment profit of 2 and is taxable in the home office country in the hands of the foreign enterprise.

Economically and empirically, the commission of 10 relates to an independent, entrepreneurial sales agent.[61] Unlike the home office employee, an independent sales agent bears a risk of loss and enjoys full opportunities from a successful sales brokerage. The home office worker, in contrast, by virtue of its dependent employee status, is shielded from the risk of loss and bankruptcy. As a consequence, there is no reason to assume a priori that the expense in the PE P&L should equal the income. For clarity's sake, the salary cost addressed here is that which is attributable to the agency establishment, most intuitively on the basis of proportionate time spent by the employee at the headquarters and at the home office. It may be argued that, in a

61. *Niehaves* IStR 2011, 373 (377 f.), has pointed out the conceptual inconsistency with the concept of a dependent agent under Article 5(4) OECD-MC.

working labour market, the marginal utility of labour should equal the salary. This argument, however, overlooks the entrepreneurial risk premium. Since the employee is shielded from the risk of loss and bankruptcy, retaining the employee does not create any utility for the enterprise in absorbing such risk. Consequently, such risk absorption cannot be part of the marginal utility of the business, and remuneration for risk absorption will ordinarily not be part of the employee's salary.

Of course, transfer pricing principles mandate not only to allocate functions but also risks. Thus, the question is whether and which risks should be allocated to the agency establishment. Legal contracts are unlikely to be helpful since they relate to the legal entity as a whole. Quite reasonably, the OECD Report on the Attribution of Profits to PEs 2010 recommends a case-by-case analysis of facts and business processes.[62] In the OECD categories, activities that influence, control, manage, or decide on assuming risks have to be diligently analysed. Assume the home office worker exercises the risk-taking and risk-controlling activities in relation to products sold. Then, the inventory risk and the 'economic ownership' of a stock of inventory are allocated to the agency establishment.[63] In the example, this leads to the booking of sales revenue of 100 crediting the PE P&L. By implication, the cost of goods sold has to be recorded for the acquisition and use/distribution of products by the PE. Assume an appropriate gross margin at this level of trade is 15%; then, the debit entries at the agency PE P&L add up to 93 (85 cost of goods sold plus 8 salary, etc.) resulting in a profit of 7. As known in transfer price practice, for a lack of comparable information on product-related gross margins, the (aggregate) gross margin is regularly calculated backwards from an appropriate level of the net margin (return on sales).[64] This usually results in a more stable and more appropriate PE result.

Incidentally, if on the basis of the detailed factual analysis, no risks whatsoever were to be allocated to the agency PE, then the marginal utility of labour would be equal to the salary cost. This presupposes that the agent/home office employee does not take *any* decisions and exercise *any* activity that has a bearing on enterprise risks in the sales process. It is hard to imagine such a scenario in real life. The more of a difference that the home office worker's sales (brokerage) activity makes in the marketplace, the more impact it will naturally have on risks incurred in and as a result of sales. However, if, as discussed here, the agent is an employee, approximations to a no-risk control-sales activity are conceivable. Against this background, a widespread view that regards profit allocation to an agency establishment as a zero-sum game can now be more clearly considered. The income attributable to the agency PE is matched by a corresponding expense, and this match is seen as coming about from necessity. For example, the German administrative regulations on profit allocation to PEs state that, when the agent does not manage risks, no profit allocation to the agency establishment should ensue.[65] Quite similarly, the Austrian-German Double Taxation Agreement

62. OECD Report on the Attribution of Profits to Permanent Establishments 2010, Part I para. 245.
63. *Ibid.*, Part I para. 243.
64. Characterizing the dependent agent permanent establishment as a quasi – buy-sell distributor also calls for the allocation of sufficient capital to the agency permanent establishment balance sheet as a buffer for absorbing the effects of risks materializing.
65. VWG-BsGa, para. 422.

explicitly provides that, when functions and risks are appropriately rewarded, the assumption of a PE does not lead to an incremental profit being taxable at the level of the PE, and this is agreed by both contracting parties.[66]

In both of the above agency establishment scenarios, i.e., a sales agency and buy-sell distribution, the home office worker exercises a greater or lesser degree of risk control. Affected risks may be, in particular, general pricing or sales risk, accounts receivable risk, and inventory risk. Therefore, an independent sales agent's commission or, as the case may be, a full buy-sell distribution margin will have to be captured in the PE P&L. According to the 'zero-sum theory' reported, a corresponding expense in the PE P&L would have to be booked as debit entry. Again, this view overlooks that, when there is a level of risk control at the PE, the commission or buy-sell margin will include a premium for the likelihood of the respective risks materializing. In any given year, these risks may or may not materialize. Additionally, from this angle, it is economically implausible that proper remuneration of functions and risks of the agency establishment as exercised and borne in the home office country should lead to a net zero profit for the PE.

6.3 A Proposal for Simplification of Home Office Agency Establishment Transfer Pricing

The above examples oversimplify the complexities of international business organizations and the interplay between large numbers of cooperating employees in various group entities as well as between home office and enterprise headquarters activities of one and the same individual. The scenario of one matrix manager working remotely at home and possibly creating agency establishments for a dozen or more entities is just one illustration of this point. In addition, the examples have been static whereas modern organizations are probably adapting to a volatile, uncertain, complex, and ambiguous (VUCA) environment more than ever. The notion of a functional analysis valid for a year or some years altogether repeatedly resembles wishful thinking.

In the authors' views, even among those countries that have adopted the AOA for the determination of PE profits, it is far from clear that there is consensus about the conceptual and empirical foundations of agency establishment profit determination.[67] Much less consensus can be expected when looking at all jurisdictions including those that have not adopted the AOA.[68] Taking the extremely factual nature of the analysis into the equation, attempting to tax profits of home office agency establishments correctly appears like a large-scale work programme for all parties involved, i.e., tax administrations, businesses, and advisors.

In this situation, the authors would like to recall the overall purpose of taxation, specifically to support or at least not excessively disturb the creation of human wealth,

66. Double Taxation Agreement Germany-Austria Protocol, para. 2.
67. Cf. illustration in Oestreicher/Schnitger/Wellens/*Wellens/Hillmann*, Gewinnabgrenzung nach dem Authorised OECD Approach (AOA), Chapters 17-22; cf. *Frotscher* Internationales Steuerrecht, para. 427.
68. For example, under the UN-MC, cf. Article 7 UN-MC Commentary, para. 1.

in this instance, through flexible, remote working. Taking into account the very significant complexities posed by wage tax, social security, immigration law, and other areas, it seems like a good idea to reduce or remove transfer pricing obstacles for flexible working and resulting wealth creation.

The question then is how far profit allocation to home office agency establishments can be simplified without unduly violating profit attribution (transfer pricing) principles. Of course, a robust application of the postulates of the zero-sum theory to home office agency establishments would lead to a simple result. Yet, this neither seems to be economically justifiable nor promising in tax policy and practice. Instead of transferring concepts of the discussion of fixed place of business PEs, the authors propose the following principles.

A function should be understood as a meaningful step of value creation in the enterprise's value chain or as a cash-generating unit. In practice, this often implies that a significant value-adding function comprises the work of a whole number of people and not just one person.

This big picture or holistic approach to a functional analysis more often suggests that a function should be allocated either in total and preferably by default to the headquarters or to the PE as a whole. The either-or approach will simplify profit allocation even in situations when non-routine or significant value-adding functions are under scrutiny. As long as the minority of contributions to such a function will be rendered out of the agency establishment, a cost plus reward for the limited and partial country-sales (value) contribution should still be appropriate.

When, as a matter of exception, functional contributions are split about 50:50 between a dependent agent PE and the headquarters, a business-wise justified allocation of non-routine or entrepreneurial profits to either the headquarters or the agency establishment should be recognized.

Only when the majority of non-routine or entrepreneurial functions are allocated to a dependent agent PE, a sophisticated transfer price analysis and profit allocation, potentially requiring a profit split, be in place. It is submitted that based on the above principles, such situations should be a rare exception.

These principles again could be used as a basis for safe harbour regulations, simplifying the handling of home office agency establishments.

7 SUMMARY OF FINDINGS

Some of the most important findings of this chapter may be summarized as follows.

Remote work in all of its forms (work while travelling on business trips, home office work, secondments, service arrangements or projects of the employer, virtual teams/virtual organizations) is here to stay and will spread.

Remote work gives rise to very significant complexities and risks in the area of personal income tax, employer's wage tax obligations, social security contributions, immigration and visa rules as well as corporate income tax and transfer pricing. The chapter focuses on corporate tax and transfer pricing. The wide spectrum of expectable and possible transfer price implications is presented in a generic overview table.

Particularly noteworthy are agency establishment PEs, fixed place of business PEs, transfers of functions, reallocations of places of management, and transfers of intangibles.

Post-COVID-19, there does not seem to be widespread administrative consensus about when to assume a PE in the case of home office or remote work. The chapter provides a discussion of practical features of home office situations as they relate to the tax technical preconditions for assuming a PE.

The analysis of some important current administrative statements and court decisions suggests that fixed place of business PEs should be much less of a concern than agency establishment PEs. This is primarily due to the unlikely existence of the employer's power of disposal over the employee's home. The concept of 'expected home office work' is critically discussed. The chapter then looks at the role of digital devices used for home office work and examines how far they might give rise to a PE.

Rather than fixed place of business PEs, agency establishment PEs (dependent agent PEs) could be more of a concern for tax administrations and taxpayers. Nevertheless, in terms of tax policy, the criteria for assuming a PE either as a fixed place of business or as a dependent agent should be restrictively harmonized.

The discussion also deals with the basic issue of transfer pricing in the ongoing PE-headquarters business. The analysis focuses on the allocation of functions, transfer price methods, and profit allocation for fixed place of business PEs and agency establishment PEs. Common practical scenarios for both types of PEs are used to reflect on foundational questions of transfer price analysis. Questions considered are:

- the organizational scope of a function as a basic unit of transfer price analysis; and
- whether a function can be allocated in parts to a home office PE and headquarters or whether a function should be allocated in its totality to either.

The discussion shows that a 'micro-level approach' that focuses closely on (parts of) an individual's work activity as a function multiplies the complexities. Such a micro-level approach creates a need for a sophisticated transfer price analysis for minor a 'value at risk' and, in particular, quite often seems to invite a profit split methodology with its inherent assessment uncertainties. Such an approach also seems unsuitable considering the pace of volatility and change in current business environments. For the situation of a dependent agent PE, the chapter sets out a reasonable approach for a functional analysis and profit calculation on the basis of the AOA. This example illustrates the considerable factual, conceptual, and economic challenges of agency PE profit determination, especially in a remote work context.

The chapter finally proposes some applications of generally accepted transfer price principles to simplify PE profit determination and make administrative enforcement and taxpayer compliance more workable. The purpose should not be to obstruct but rather to support the creation of wealth through flexible, remote working.

CHAPTER 6
Transfer Pricing in Times of High Inflation

Rutger P.F.M. Hafkenscheid

1 A WORLD OF HIGH INFLATION

After more than twenty years of low inflation, the world is again suddenly facing high inflation. Several events have fuelled inflation. The lockdowns during the COVID-pandemic distorted global supply chains while, at the same time, the pandemic led to a wave of early retirements leading to ultra-tide labour markets and driving up salaries and thus production costs. Another culprit was excessive stimulus provided by governments to support those who became unemployed that translated into over-heated demand. Meanwhile, droughts and heatwaves contributed to disappointing harvests of crops such as coffee and wheat. Further, the long-lasting Suez Channel's blockage due to a vessel accident added to the supply chain distortion and resulted in surging container prices and transportation costs (and demonstrated the vulnerability of global supply chains). Then, in 2022, Russia invaded Ukraine, resulting in a surge in energy and food prices. with Russia being a major crude producer subjected to Western countries' sanctions and Ukraine as one of the world's largest granaries whose harvest was disrupted, and transportation lines distorted. Where in 2021 the Economist[1] expected that inflation would be short-lived, the paper said in 2022 that it believed that a new era of high inflation had begun.[2] Public-debt loads have soared over the past two decades, and markets have begun to fear that central banks will eventually have to help finance governments' obligations, for example, by creating new money to buy bonds. The COVID pandemic may also have made governments more open to the continuous use of stimuli to fight recession. Food and fuel price increases do not only translate directly into the rise of consumer prices but also have an indirect effect through the increase of production costs.

Like in any crisis, there are winners and losers. Energy companies, for example, have reported record profits such that, in September 2022, the European Union agreed to implement a windfall tax as an emergency measure.[3] The council regulation on an emergency intervention to address high prices of 6 October 2022 laid down the

1. *What Will Happen to Inflation in 2022? It's Back – But Not for Long*, The Economist, 8 November 2021.
2. *Central Bankers Worry That a New Era of High Inflation Is Beginning: There Are Three Reasons to Believe That May Be Case*, The Economist, 30 August 2022.
3. BBC News: EU Agrees Windfall Tax on Energy Firms, 30 September 2022, last accessed 6 December 2022.

temporary rules for taxing 'surplus profits generated by Union companies and permanent establishments with activities in the crude petroleum, natural gas, coal and refinery sectors'.[4] A similar Energy Profit Tax was introduced in the United Kingdom in May 2022.[5] Also, the food and agriculture industry usually benefits from higher consumer prices. Although consumers may opt out of expensive food alternatives, food and beverage manufacturers are usually resistant to inflation because their products are always in demand. However, even in the luxury segment of the alcoholic beverage industry, suppliers can take advantage of inflation. For example, a luxury vodka brand's consumer price comprises only a small part of production costs and a very large part of excise meaning that their profit margins are only slightly affected by commodity price increases such as grain. If such a luxury brand increases its retail prices according to the general consumer price indices (which consumers will mostly only slightly notice), it will boost its revenue and profits.[6]

High inflation also generates losers. Businesses with slim margins and high energy costs or those selling products with a high price elasticity suffer, struggle to survive, and sometimes even close their doors. Highly leveraged companies fear the increased cost of their debt now that interest rates are increasing. Businesses with long-term commitments, such as property development companies, may see their budgeted profits evaporate due to increased energy prices, costs of building materials, and higher salaries. At the same time, property investment companies may see their finance expenses increase and the value of their assets dampen because property investment becomes less attractive compared to alternative investments such as governments and corporate bonds.

Inflation will also change the dynamics of doing business internationally. Governments will try to protect their local economies and will become prone to protective measures. Production will become relatively more attractive in some countries while, in others, it will become less attractive. With the increase in energy prices, production close to the end market may save significant amounts of costs as it may reduce transportation costs and, in the case of perishable goods, costs of storage and cooling. Additionally, inflation will also affect currency rates. Countries with higher inflation will likely have weaker currencies which will drive up the relative prices of import and

4. Article 14(1), Council Regulation (EU) 2022/1854 of 6 October 2022 on an emergency intervention to address high energy prices.
5. UK: HM Treasury, Policy paper, Energy Profits Levy Factsheet – 26 May 2022, Updated 15 June 2022, last accessed 12 December 2022.
6. Suppose that the retail price of a bottle of luxury vodka used to be EUR 40 before inflation, comprising EUR 6.67 VAT, EUR 12.5 excise and EUR 2.50 of ingredients. Now suppose that the ingredient prices increase by 10% (in line with the consumer price index) and that firm would be able to piggyback on the consumer price index by increasing the retail prices with 10%, then the firm would boost its (nominal) revenue along with its profit with approximately 14%. This can be calculated as follows. The pre-inflation net revenue per bottle was EUR 20.83 (EUR 40 minus EUR 6.67 VAT and EUR 12.50 excise) and the gross margin per bottle was EUR 18.33 (EUR 20.83 minus production costs EUR 2.50). The post-inflation net revenue per bottle would be EUR 24.17 (EUR 44 minus EUR 7.33 VAT and EUR 12.50 excise), an increase of 16% (or pre-inflation euros 5.5%), and the gross margin per bottle EUR 21.42 (EUR 24.17 minus production cost EUR 2.75), an increase of 16.8% (or in pre-inflation euros 6.2%).

financing costs while, at the same time, decrease the purchasing power of its consumers.

All of these events will have a significant impact on how international businesses will operate and will, therefore, also affect the dynamics of profit allocations between countries. Add to this the higher need for governments to finance their expected stimulus packages through taxes, and it may be expected that the world will experience more attention from tax authorities for transfer pricing.

This chapter will discuss some transfer pricing challenges that may arise from high inflation. As the introductory comments demonstrate, it is a phenomenon with many macro and microeconomic facets, meaning that any article on the transfer pricing aspects of high inflation will lack completeness.

2 SOME GENERAL REMARKS ON INFLATION AND TAXATION

2.1 Inflation Is the General Increase in Prices and Fall in Purchase Power

Inflation can be defined as 'a general increase in prices and fall in the purchasing value of money'.[7] Note that it concerns the *general* price level in an economy or country and not the price increase in a specific transaction or commercial relation. The definition also relates inflation to the *overall* purchasing power of money. When analysing (the effects of) inflation, it is important to realize that the term may have various meanings in different contexts.

2.2 Inflation Indicates the Average Price Increase

First, inflation is a metric to indicate the *average* price increase of a certain set of goods and services. Its most well-known indicator is the Consumer Price Index (CPI) which measures the percentage change in the price of a basket of goods and services consumed by households over a certain period of time. The overall inflation will never reflect the purchasing power of an individual consumer because different consumers have distinct spending habits. For example, if the CPI increases due to a hefty increase in meat prices, the actual purchasing power of a vegetarian may not be affected at all. Instead, if this vegetarian's salary is adjusted with the CPI, his purchasing power will have increased.

2.3 Inflation Is Measured in an Index

Second, price increases of goods or services that are not a component of the CPI will have little or no impact on the official CPI number but may nevertheless heftily affect an individual's purchasing power. For example, over the past fifteen years, property

7. Oxford University Press 2022.

prices in most countries have increased significantly, but this is only partly reflected in the CPI as this metric does not measure asset inflation. Low inflation leading to low-interest rates was partly responsible for this asset inflation, but high inflation leading to higher interest rates may have the reverse effect, depressing housing prices that may eventually reduce a person's wealth (and real-term spending power) more significantly than the CPI.

2.4 Inflation Is Bound to a Currency

Third, inflation refers to the purchasing value of money for a certain currency. A currency, like the euro and the dollar, may cover a large territory in which there may be extreme differences in price movements between the various locations within that territory.

2.5 Inflation Is Not Always Rational

Fourth, it must be realized that humans are not the rational *homo economici* that economic science assumes them to be. People make decisions on heuristics[8] and bounded rationality[9] and, for example, notice frequent 'out-of-pocket' purchases more than sudden price shocks of incidental purchases which leads to different consumer behavioural reactions. Indeed, people in the Western world have become used to low inflation and have started to believe that it was effectively eradicated. High inflation, according to them, had become a 'Black Swan' not because the risk of it was actually gone, but because it could not be imagined that the risk existed.[10] Reversely, people in countries with a more structural high inflation cannot imagine a world where prices are relatively stable.

2.6 Taxable Profits Are in Nominal Currency

It is further important to note that the taxation of profits in all industrialized countries is based on the *nominal* value of money and not on its purchasing power.[11] This means that the effects of inflation inherently form part of the (consolidated) income of the multinational group, even though the taxable profit of a group may include inflationary elements and may thus excavate the profits in real terms, taxation includes the inflationary part. This also means that, for the distribution of taxing rights between

8. D. Kahneman *Thinking, Fast and Slow* (2010).
9. Guillermo Campitelli & Fernand Gobet, *Herbert Simon's Decision-Making Approach: Investigation of Cognitive Processes in Experts*, 14(4) Review of General Psychology 354-364 (2010).
10. N. Taleb, *The Black Swan* (2010).
11. In the past, some countries, including the Netherlands, allowed certain tax allowances (in the form of deductions) that should mitigate the inflationary elements in an enterprise's taxation of profits, but these allowances typically deferred the tax effects of inflation rather than providing permanent exemptions of the inflationary part of an enterprise's profit.

countries, the effects of inflation must somehow be allocated between the various parts of a multinational group.

3 THE REGULATORY FRAMEWORK: THE OECD TRANSFER PRICING GUIDELINES

Most Western countries apply the OECD Transfer Pricing Guidelines for Multinational Enterprises and Tax Administrations[12] (hereafter to be referred to as the TPG) for the interpretation of the arm's length principle and the evaluation of transfer prices. The latest version of the TPG was published in 2022 and, even though the first version dates back from 1979 in an era when inflation was still widespread in the industrialized world, the word 'inflation' can be found only two times in the text.[13] Therefore, the TPG does not provide specific guidance for the transfer pricing aspects of inflation nor for that of high inflation. Therefore, inflation and its effect on transfer prices must be analysed as part of the usual transfer pricing analysis for which the TPG give guidance.

In the context of inflation, two types of analyses must be performed. First, it must be analysed how inflation may affect the commercial relations between independent parties acting at arm's length with each other to compare that with the commercial relations between the related parties (*see* section 4). Second, it must be analysed how inflation may affect benchmark data that are being used in comparability studies (*see* section 5).

4 THE COMMERCIAL RELATIONS BETWEEN PARTIES

Chapter I of the TPG gives guidance for the performance of an adequate transfer pricing analysis and, more specifically, the analysis of commercial relations. According to section D, an adequate transfer pricing analysis comprises an analysis of:

- the contractual terms (section D.1.1.);
- the functions performed (section D.1.2.);
- the characteristics of property and services (section D.1.3.);
- the economic circumstances (section D.1.4.); and
- the business strategies (section D.1.5.)

As inflation refers to the *general* price level in an economy or market territory but not to the price charged in a specific transaction between two specific parties, it is one of the economic circumstances under which an enterprise operates. It is therefore necessary to analyse the *reaction* of market parties to the risk and effects of inflation that is relevant for the analysis of inflation in a transfer pricing context. Inflation inherently does not imply any direct impact on transfer prices but rather affects or

12. OECD *Transfer Pricing Guidelines for Multinational Enterprises and Tax Administrations 2022* (2022).
13. In 1979, global inflation averaged 13.29%; *see* https://www.macrotrends.net/2497/historical-inflation-rate-by-year.

generates an attitude, a reaction, or a business decision by the transacting parties that are confronted with its economic circumstances. How commercially behaving parties would react to it and how they would make their business decisions to benefit from or mitigate the effects of inflation will bc analysed below. The most important considerations are those about contractual terms (section 4.1) and functional analysis (section 4.2).

4.1 The Contractual Terms

4.1.1 Contractual Index Clauses

Although inflation is an economic phenomenon that usually does not directly translate into the pricing between parties, there are situations in which it indeed has a direct effect on transfer prices, e.g., when contractual terms between related parties in a transaction include arrangements about the effects of inflation. Such arrangements will come to the forefront in the analysis of contractual terms referred to in section D.1.1. Contractual arrangements around inflation are often made in long-term agreements such as lease agreements, service contracts, maintenance contracts, and management agreements that comprise an indexation clause that automatically indexes the price; even certain bonds include clauses that link the interest rate to a CPI.

When analysing the consequences of a price index clause, it must first be analysed to what extent the arrangements were concluded under arm's length conditions. Inflation is a macroeconomic phenomenon and is a risk factor towards which commercially behaving parties must take a position. How the parties in a transaction will try to manage and control these risks in an arm's length manner is a question to be answered in the functional analysis that precedes any pricing analysis as discussed in section 4.2.

4.1.2 Applying an Index Clause in Practice

Once it has been established that entering a price index clause was at arm's length, it should be analysed whether parties that are acting commercially would be willing to hold each other to the contractual terms once unexpected high inflation occurs. Indeed, high inflation may have been unforeseen at the time in which the contract was entered but may work out very negatively for the recipient of a good or service and, therefore, it may be that there are reasons to deviate from the contract. First, it may be that applying the contractual terms becomes so onerous that it would be *legally* difficult to hold the other party to those contractual terms. Whether that is the case will depend on the jurisdiction in which the transaction takes place. In some jurisdictions, such as the Netherlands, contractual relations are to be interpreted against the background of whether their effect is reasonable and equitable which allows courts under certain circumstances to apply the contract different from its literal wording. Other jurisdictions do not provide such a possibility. Analysing the contractual terms must therefore be performed in the context of the applicable law. Second, it may be that the changed economic circumstance of inflation is a (commercial) reason for contract renegotiations. Doing business is a two-sided relationship from which both parties should benefit. High inflation may change the dynamic of this process and the benefits that both parties can and may expect from their commercial relation, particularly in the long term. Additionally, in unrelated transactions, parties may see more commercial benefits in renegotiating their contractual terms than in adhering to them for the sake of it. Whether and to what extent the renegotiation of the contractual terms is at arm's length will also depend on the relative bargaining power of each of the contracting parties.

4.1.3 *Burden of Proof for Deviation from an Existing Index Clause*

Evidently, the existence of a consumer price indexation clause forms the starting point of the analysis of the commercial relations between related parties. If either the taxpayer or the tax administration claims that parties in commercial relations would have deviated from the contractual term or renegotiated them, the burden of proof for that claim lies, in principle, with the party invoking such a deviation or assumed renegotiation. The author believes, however, that independent parties in commercial relations would not lightly renegotiate or deviate from explicit price index clauses. After all, these aim to prospectively allocate the effects of inflation between transacting parties and therefore inherently lend themselves less for deviations on the mere basis that the effect that the clause aims to allocate has materialized differently from the expectations. The uncertainty about materialization was the reason for entering the price index arrangement.

4.1.4 *Indirect Contractual Effects of Inflation*

Apart from price index clauses that directly trigger price increases under a contract, there are many other contracts in which the contractual terms may effectuate indirect effects from inflation, such as loan agreements with floating interest rates. Inflation usually drives up interest rates as central banks use the interest instrument to counter inflation so contracts with floating interest rate clauses will be indirectly affected by inflation. By entering into floating interest debt, the borrower explicitly accepted the risk of interest volatility, and it will therefore be unusual for unrelated parties to deviate from the agreed interest clause on the mere basis that inflation was unforeseen.

The recent occurrence of high inflation will change people's idea of its risks, meaning that parties will start to consider price index clauses more actively in their contracts. How they will do that should be analysed in a functional and risk analysis.

4.2 Functional Analysis

4.2.1 *Inflation Is a Market Risk Factor to Be Allocated Based on Functionality*

Inflation is a macroeconomic circumstance under which businesses operate and generally invokes economic reactions and business decisions from market parties rather than having direct and imperative effects on the commercial relations between parties (except for the situation discussed in section 4.1.1). For market participants, it is the (materialization of a) market risk to which a business is exposed. Indeed, the analysis of high inflation starts before the actual inflation occurs, i.e., at the time when inflation was just a possibility or an expectation but not yet a reality. However, also, if the risk of inflation has materialized, the reaction of a business to its actuality largely instigates an analysis of risks: The occurrence of inflation requires businesses to make decisions about how to respond to it and such decisions, like any, are made under uncertainty and requires the business to take a position towards the future. The analysis of the effects of (high) inflation should therefore focus on how, in arm's length situations, market parties allocate the risks of inflation between them.

In its report on Actions 8-10 of the Base Erosion and Profit Shifting Project, the OECD has extensively addressed the subject of risk allocation as part of the functional analysis.[14] The report has found its way into section D.1.2.1 TPG. The essence of the OECD approach is that risks are to be allocated between related parties in a transaction based on the question of which party has the functionality to manage and control the risks. *See* the six-step plan discussed in paragraph 1.60 TPG (hereafter: the Risk Allocation Framework) of which steps 3 and 4 are pivotal.[15] In step 3, it must be analysed how the associated enterprises operate in relation to the assumption and management of the specific, economically significant risks and in particular: (i) which enterprise or enterprises perform control functions and risk mitigation functions; (ii) which encounter upside or downside consequences of risk outcomes; and (iii) which have the financial capacity to assume the risk. As per step 4, the analysis in step 3 takes precedence over the contractual allocation of risk, meaning that the functional analysis should be decisive if the allocation of risk determined from it deviates from the contractual allocation.

The OECD approach has been criticized both with fundamental and practical arguments. The fundamental question is whether it is the decision-making about risks or the legal assumption of risk that should form the basis of distribution of taxing rights. The argument against the OECD approach is that the taxation of income earned by corporate entities is fundamentally based on the legal allocation of risk to that entity which is distinct from the humans who represent the entity; a functionality approach collides with this fundamental feature of corporate taxation.[16] The practical argument revolves around the ambiguous ways in which a multinational enterprise group's risk management is organized.[17] Nevertheless, this article will discuss the management of inflation-related risks using the OECD approach. This is because this approach has become the standard in the market despite the fundamental and practical drawbacks.

14. OECD *Aligning Transfer Pricing Outcomes with Value Creation, Actions 8-10, 2015 Final Reports*, OECD/G20 Base Erosion and Profits Shifting Project (2015).
15. R.P.F.M. Hafkenscheid, *The BEPS Report on Risk Allocation: No So Functional*, International Transfer Pricing Journal (January/February 2017).
16. Hafkenscheid (2017), *infra*.
17. R.S. Collier & I.A. Dykes, *On the Apparent Widespread Misapplication of the OECD Transfer Pricing Guidelines, Risk and Post-BEPS Problems for the Arm's Length Principle*, 76(1) Bulletin for International Taxation (2022).

These are most pronounced for tax haven companies where corporate risk assumption and functionality are mostly segregated. The aim of this chapter is to discuss the effects of inflation on the commercial relations between operating companies rather than to focus on the potential contractual profit shifting to tax haven companies. For the purposes of the article, the author, therefore, focuses on non-Base Erosion and Profit Shifting (BEPS) situations, i.e., assumes that every party in the related transaction has sufficient functionality and financial capacity to manage, control, and assume the risks that are contractually allocated to it. Many dilemmas arise even in non-BEPS situations when it comes to inflation-related risk allocation.

4.2.2 Definition of Risk for the Purposes of This Article

The term 'risk' has various definitions many of which focus on the negative connotation of the term, i.e., the possibility of running into danger. In this article, the term is applied more neutrally, i.e., as 'the deviation from the expected outcome'. This definition not only treats risk both as a danger and an opportunity but also allows us to approach risk in quantitative terms. This is important when discussing the effects of inflation as contracting parties will consider it in terms of how their business results are being affected by its occurrence. The deviation from the expected allows for measuring the sensitivity to inflation of each party in a contract and thus to review to what extent the sensitivity aligns with the risk profile of each party. A party with a low-risk profile is expected to be less sensitive to deviations from the expected than the party with a high-risk profile. A quantitative analysis will reveal the relative sensitivity, and this can best be approached in a case study as discussed in the next section. The author emphasizes that it intends to highlight the process of functionally analysing the effects of inflation in an arm's length situation; the study neither intends to be exhaustive nor does it mean to be decisive.

4.2.3 Case Study on Allocation of Inflation Risk

4.2.3.1 Case Description: Central Entrepreneur Model

Consider the division of a multinational group that manufactures widgets that it sells to the market for EUR 25. The division has a principal company in Country X (PrincipalCo) and a manufacturing company in Country Y (ManufacturingCo) that operates as a contract manufacturer for PrincipalCo and is remunerated with a benchmarked transactional net margin of 3% on all-in budgeted costs (Transactional Net Margin Method (TNMM) Cost). For 2022, the market demand was budgeted at one million widgets. The fixed manufacturing costs were budgeted at EUR 5 million while the raw material costs were budgeted at EUR 12 per widget assuming a 100% production efficiency ratio (i.e., no fall-out). Based on these assumptions, the budgeted transfer price per widget that ManufacturingCo would charge to PrincipalCo is EUR 17.51 (EUR 5 million + 1 million widgets × EUR 12) × 1.03/1 million widgets). PrincipalCo is budgeted to incur 10 euro cents per widget in variable costs and EUR 5.5 million in fixed costs.

The budgeted profit and loss accounts are as follows:

ManufacturingCo (Budget)			
	#	€	€000
Revenue	1 m	17.51	17,510
Raw material	1 m	12.00	-12,000
Fixed cost			-5,000
Net margin	3 %		**510**

PrincipalCo (Budget)			
	#	€	€000
Revenue	1 m	25.00	25,000
COGS	1 m	17.51	-17,510
Gross Margin			7,490
Variable sales	1 m	0.10	-100
Fixed Cost			-5,500
Net Margin			**1,890**

Consolidated (Budget)			
	#	€	€000
Revenue	1 m	25.00	25,000
Raw material	1 m	12.00	-12,000
Variable sales	1 m	0.10	-100
Fixed Cost			-10,500
Net Margin			**2,400**

4.2.3.2 Effect of Price Increase on Consolidated Net Margin

Suppose that the prices of raw materials increase by 10% on average in 2023 due to disrupted supply chains of raw material suppliers. The consolidated profit would be highly sensitive to this price increase as the table below shows; the actual net margin would deviate 50% from the budgeted net margin.

Consolidated (Actual)			
	#	€	€000
Revenue	1 m	25.00	25,000
Raw material	1 m	13.20	-13,200
Variable sales	1 m	0.10	-100
Fixed Cost			-10,500
Net Margin			**1,200**

The question arises of which entity should bear the risk of this price increase. One of the aspects that will contribute to answering that question is an analysis of how the sensitivity of each party to the price increase relates to that of the consolidated margin to that increase.

4.2.3.3 Price Increase Maintained by ManufacturingCo

Suppose that, according to the contract, ManufacturingCo bears the price risk of raw material procurement. It would then still charge only the budgeted price of EUR 17.51 to PrincipalCo. The effect of the price increase would be as shown in the schedule below:

ManufacturingCo (Actual)			
	#	€	€000
Revenue	1 m	17.51	17,510
Raw material	1 m	13.20	-13,200
Fixed cost			-5,000
Net margin			**-690**

Compared with the budgeted margin of EUR 510,000, the net margin would decrease by 235%,[18] meaning that the margin is significantly more sensitive to the price increase of the consolidated net margin.

Note that this loss can be entirely traced back to the increase in raw material prices and that ManufacturingCo did what it was expected to do, i.e., efficiently manufacture a million widgets. It did not waste raw materials (no fall-out), and it managed to control its fixed cost in accordance with the budget. In short, it kept its commercial promises but was confronted by an external event, i.e., price increases. ManufacturingCo's tax authorities may therefore disapprove of the loss, claiming that it does not align with the entity's status as a low-risk entrepreneur. However, is it true that, in arm's length situations, a low-risk entrepreneur should always be insulated from the risk of high inflation? It is likely that the contract between ManufacturingCo and PrincipalCo was concluded during the long historic era of low inflation, that the annual budget was

18. -EUR 1.2 million / EUR 510,000 × 100% = -235%.

based on historic stable prices (even annually increased with a small historic inflation rate), and that the 3 % margin benchmark was found in databases with data stemming from times of low inflation. Now that the inflation risk materialized, it appears that it is a non-arm's length decision of ManufacturingCo to accept inflation risk but, like Rosa Luxemburg used to say, 'before a revolution happens, it is perceived as impossible; after it happens, it is seen as having been inevitable'.[19] Behavioural economics suggests that humans tend to base decisions on recallable events and so, in the long era of low inflation, had come to believe that inflation had been eradicated.[20] In the past era of low inflation, many market parties have not considered the risk of high inflation and are taken by surprise by its sudden occurrence. This may have been irrational but true. The interesting question is how the TPG approaches the lack of rationality in human behaviour and business decision-making. The TPG does not explicitly address the issue of economic rationality but often refers to the concept of 'options realistically available', suggesting that the TPG assumes fully rational behaviour.[21] However, the author believes this to be an unrealistic approach in situations when unrelated parties also do not consider the risk of sudden high inflation even if it had been rational to do so.

It should nevertheless be established, in accordance with the Risk Allocation Framework, whether ManufacturingCo had the functionality to manage, control, and assume the risks of sudden raw material price shocks. If it did but - conforming to the perhaps irrational market practice - did not secure itself against the risk, it appears that the risk of such price shock indeed remains with ManufacturingCo. If it did not have such functionality, it may be concluded that the inflation risk should not be borne by ManufacturingCo and that, under arm's length conditions, the entity should have been able to pass on the inflated raw material prices to PrincipalCo.

4.2.3.4 Price Increase of Raw Materials Passed on to PrincipalCo

Now, assume that, indeed, ManufacturingCo was allowed to pass on the new prices to PrincipalCo. This would result in an adjusted transfer price charged to PrincipalCo of EUR 18.75 ((EUR 5 million + 1 million widgets × EUR 12 × 1.10) × 1.03/ 1 million widgets). The effect of this passing-on of PrincipalCo's net margin would be as follows:

	PrincipalCo (Actual)		
	#	*€*	*€000*
Revenue	1 m	25.00	25,000
COGS	1 m	18.75	-18,746
Gross Margin			6,254
Variable sales	1 m	0.10	-100

19. https://en.wikipedia.org/wiki/Rosa_Luxemburg.
20. J.S. Hammond, R.L. Keeney & H. Raiffa, *The Hidden Traps in Decision-Making*, Harvard Business Review (September-October 1998).
21. The term 'options realistically available' is used seventy-two times in the TPG.

	PrincipalCo (Actual)		
	#	€	€000
Fixed Cost			-5,500
Net Margin			**654**

Compared to the budgeted net margin, PrincipalCo's actual net margin would decrease by 65%.

After the price adjustment, ManufacturingCo's net margin would be as follows:

	ManufacturingCo (Actual)		
	#	€	€000
Revenue	1 m	18.75	18,746
Raw material	1 m	13.20	-13,200
Fixed cost			-5,000
Net margin			**546**

Note that PrincipalCo has been hit harder than that consolidated decline, i.e., EUR 1.890 million minus EUR 654,000 = EUR 1.236 million. The reason is that ManufacturingCo would have benefited from the raw material price increase because it charges a 3% mark-up on the increase, i.e., 3% × EUR 1.2 million = EUR 36,000, which equals the difference between the consolidated profit decline of EUR 1.2 million and PrincipalCo's profit decline of EUR 1.236 million.[22] The remarkable outcome of this passing-on would be that ManufacturingCo would have benefited from the inflation as it would have increased its net margin by 7%.[23] Whether that would be at arm's length can also be questioned. Maybe the exercise would reveal that, if ManufacturingCo may fully pass on a price increase to PrincipalCo, it would not be at arm's length to include the raw materials in the basis for calculating the markup of 3%. Alternatively, the exercise could also reveal that only a part of the price increase should be passed on to PrincipalCo, for example, only the part that exceeds the *expected* inflation.

4.2.3.5 Multiple Scenario Sensitivity Analysis

This article defines risk as the deviation from the expected and can be tested by comparing the sensitivity of each party to a price deviation. So far, the relative sensitivity was analysed for a single price scenario, i.e., the scenario with a 10% raw material price increase. A multiple-scenario analysis would make the analysis even more insightful as the impact of one factor (here, raw material prices) on another factor (here, net margin) is analysed under multiple economic scenarios, i.e., using a range of values for the influencing factor (here, a percentage range of price increases). Such an

22. ManufacturingCo's profit would be EUR 546,000 after the passing-on against EUR 510,000 that is budgeted.
23. (EUR 546,000 – EUR 510,000)/EUR 510,000 × 100% = 7%.

analysis helps to get a deeper insight into the fundamental relation between two factors and thus allows establishing whether that fundamental relation makes sense from an economic perspective.

The graphs represent the relation between net margin and price change of raw material and thus demonstrate how, in general, the net margin of each entity responds to a price change depending on how its risk is allocated.

Figure 6.1 Sensitivity to Price Changes: No-Passing onto PrincipalCo

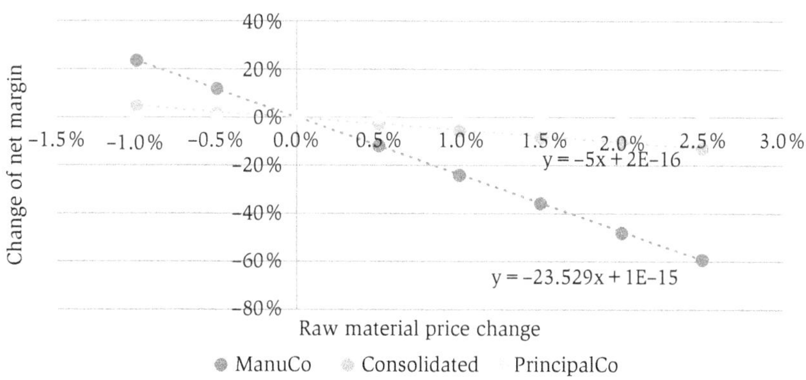

Figure 6.2 Sensitivity to Price Changes: Passing onto PrincipalCo

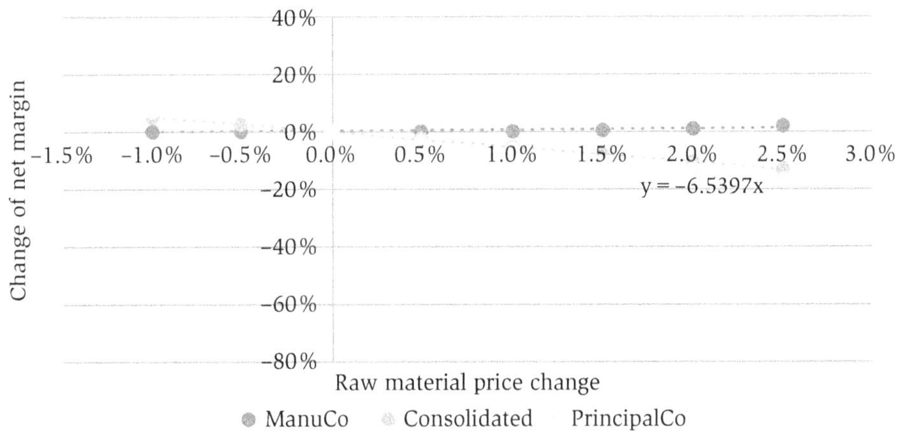

The graphs illustrate the correlations between the raw materials price change and the net margins of the groups, ManufacturingCo and PrincipalCo. Graph 1 shows that, in the example, every per cent of raw material price increase translates into almost a 5%[24] decrease of the consolidated net margin and a 23.529% decrease in ManufacturingCo's net margin if, indeed, it assumes the raw material price risk. Graph 2 depicts that, if PrincipalCo assumes the raw material price risk, every per cent of price change translates into a net margin change of 6.539% for that company. Comparing Graph 1 and Graph 2 reveals that, if ManufacturingCo assumes the raw material price risks, its net margin is *structurally* more exposed to changes in raw materials than if PrincipalCo assumes these risks which raises the question of whether such a structural higher exposure aligns with ManufacturingCo's assumed lower risk profile. Whether that should be considered at arm's length in this specific case is dependent on its merits, i.e., what the contractual arrangements were and whether third parties would have taken the inflation risk into account; it also considers the mental trap that humans tend to ignore risks that have not recently materialized. By making a multiple-scenario sensitivity analysis, the differences in sensitivities between the two allocation alternatives become more pronounced. Over the past twenty years, inflation was low, and thus the risk profile of the alternative in which ManufacturingCo was assumed to be allocated the raw materials price risk almost equalled the risk profile where that risk was assumed to be with PrincipalCo. The graph, however, demonstrates the effective huge differences in the risk profiles. The argument that the author means to make is

24. The algebraic formula for the relation between the raw material price increase x and net margin y is $y = -5x + 0.0000000000000002$. As the constant in this formula is neglectable, one percent of raw material price change translates into a five times higher inverse change of the net margin.

that only a thorough sensitivity analysis will reveal the exposure to risks by each party in a transaction. It is thereby important to note that a sensitivity analysis should preferably include not just one risk factor but the most important risk factors to which the group and each of the entities in that group are exposed. Which factors are the most important can, again, be analysed by a sensitivity analysis.

4.2.3.6 *Effect of External Price Strategy*

The example can be taken a bit further. Suppose that PrincipalCo decides to increase the external price in line with the general CPI, i.e., with 10% to EUR 27.50. The decision to do so clearly may have an effect on the market demand for widgets. Therefore, PrincipalCo would only do so if it expects to repair the profit decline as a result of the increased raw material prices. Assume that a sales price increase would reduce market demand by 10% to 900,000 widgets. The consolidated profit would then be as follows:

	Consolidated (After price increase)		
	#	*€*	*€000*
Revenue	0.9 m	27.50	24,750
Raw material	0.9 m	13.20	-11,880
Variable sales	0.9 m	0.10	-90
Fixed Cost			-10,500
Net Margin			**2,280**

Before the external price increase, the consolidated profit was budgeted to be EUR 2.4 million and, therefore, the increased profitability from the external price increase almost outweighs the loss of market demand. The profit would change by -5% compared to the budget. How does this price strategy influence the allocation of risks between ManufacturingCo and PrincipalCo? Assume that ManufacturingCo indeed was able to pass on the increased raw material price to PrincipalCo through an increase of the transfer price from the original budgeted price of EUR 17.51 to EUR 18.75. The impact on ManufacturingCo's net margin would be as follows:

	ManufacturingCo (Actual)		
	#	*€*	*€000*
Revenue	0.9 m	18.75	16,875
Raw material	0.9 m	13.20	-13,200
Fixed cost			-5,000
Net margin			**-5**

Recall that, in the situation before PrincipalCo increased the external prices, ManufacturingCo's budgeted profit was EUR 546,000, so the decision by PrincipalCo would result in a -101% change in profit compared with the budget. In the supply chain, ManufacturingCo is unlikely to have the role or power to set or influence external prices. Its function is to manufacture efficiently and effectively and not to market or sell. Therefore, the risk of price adjustments should, in arm's length situations, be borne by PrincipalCo and not ManufacturingCo. This would require that the budgeted transfer price between the two be adjusted based on the new expected volume of 900,000 widgets, i.e., that the total manufacturing costs are spread over 900,000 items instead of over one million items. The budgeted net margin after the adjustment would look like this, resulting in an adjusted transfer price of EUR 19.32:

	ManufacturingCo (Budget)		
	#	*€*	*€000*
Revenue	0.9 m	19.32	17,386
Raw material	0.9 m	13.20	-11,880
Fixed cost			-5,000
Net margin	3%		**506**

This means that ManufacturingCo, in line with its functional profile, is largely insulated against the effects of inflation. Note that it is not entirely insulated from inflation, albeit only indirectly; before inflation arose, its budgeted profit was EUR 510,000 while, after it, it would be EUR 506,000, i.e., a -0.71% decrease, which again would be more in line with ManufacturingCo's functional profile.

The effect of the price increase decision for PrincipalCo would be as follows:

	PrincipalCo (Actual)		
	#	*€*	*€000*
Revenue	0.9 m	27.50	24,750
COGS	0.9 m	19.32	-17,386
Gross Margin			7,363
Variable sales	0.9 m	0.10	-90
Fixed Cost			-5,500
Net Margin			**1,774**

Compared to the initial budget, the profit would change by -6.14%[25] which, against the -5% decrease in the group profit, appears to better align with its functional and risk profiles.

Again, a sensitivity analysis could reveal the relative sensitivity of each party's net margin to a change in volume as a result of the price-increase decision by PrincipalCo. The chart below depicts the correlation between net margin (y-axis) and change in sales volume (×-axis) as a result of the external price increase, assuming that

25. (EUR 1,774,000 - EUR 1,890,000)/EUR 1,890,000 × 100% = -6.14%.

ManufacturingCo can adjust its transfer prices to the adjusted external price decision. As the graph demonstrates, the price decision does have an effect on the net margin of ManufacturingCo but that net margin is less sensitive to volume changes than PrincipalCo's net margin.

Figure 6.3 Sensitivity of Net Margin to Change of Volume

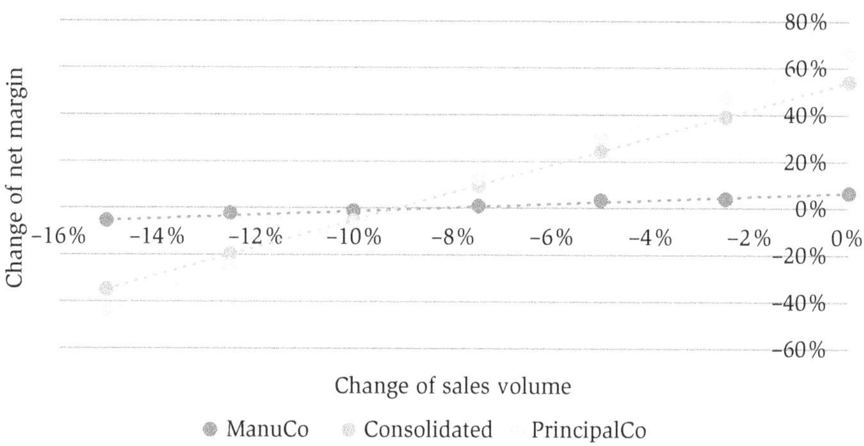

4.2.3.7 Response of Parties to New Era of Inflation

Another question to consider is how ManufacturingCo and PrincipalCo, behaving at arm's length, would respond to the occurrence of high inflation in their future commercial relations. Now that this is a new reality, market participants would try to mitigate the risks of further inflation and should allocate these risks at arm's length. It is thereby noted that inflation is an external risk, meaning that it is impossible for either of the parties to take measures that would influence the occurrence of inflation. When, for example, operational risks such as the fall-out of raw materials in a production process can be influenced by improving production procedures, no such measures can be taken to influence inflation. This also means that risk management mainly culminates in taking measures of how each party in the transaction responds to the event of inflation in their commercial relations. Therefore, inflation risk management is largely a matter of making contractual arrangements between parties on how to allocate the effects of inflation between them. These arrangements should clearly reflect each party's functionality in accordance with the Risk Allocation Framework, but parties eventually have a certain degree of discretion to allocate the risks between them the way they deem appropriate. The level of individual discretion is dependent on the relative bargaining power of that party. Such contractual allocation should also be at arm's length in the sense that the risks assumed should be remunerated with an arm's length (expected) return, but the choice of how risks are being allocated is no longer subject to scrutiny. In the case study discussed here, it would be necessary to analyse whether it would be arm's length for either party to accept inflation risks for years after the first year in which high inflation occurred. Again, the Risk Allocation Framework should reveal which party has the functionality to manage, control, and assume the risks. If ManufacturingCo indeed has that functionality, it should be analysed how both parties make their arrangements about the next year's budget. It would be expected that budgets, particularly the raw material price, should account for higher inflation expectations than was the case before, meaning that part of the expected higher inflation would be included in the budgeted raw material price. This would automatically reduce ManufacturingCo's risk that further high inflation hits its bottom line. Alternatively, ManufacturingCo could protect itself against future deviations from the expected inflation through an arrangement with PrincipalCo that caps the risk that the inflation exceeds the average of the preceding years. Finally, it should be considered whether the historic benchmark rate of 3 % would still be a reliable comparable for the future TNMM cost markup. ManufacturingCo could also try to seek remuneration for the inflation risks by negotiating a higher margin.

In situations when high inflation is expected to be more structural, contracting parties may have different strategies to deal with its effect, particularly if one party is established in a country with more stable prices and the contracting party is established in a country with high inflation. Economically, the differences in inflation rates will be reflected in the (expected) foreign exchange rate development of the currencies. For example, if a supplier in a stable-price country sells to a customer in a high-inflation country, the exchange rate of the high-inflation country will expectedly decline towards the currency of the stable-inflation country. Arrangements must then be made between the two parties to deal with the foreign exchange risks that will influence the commercial relations, such as terms of payment and the currency in which the transactions take place. The supplier, for example, will likely be inclined to transact in its own stable currency to avoid foreign exchange losses on its trade receivables. The customer, however, must include the foreign exchange losses that it is expected to incur in its forecasts to make up for them. Indeed, these are questions of risk allocation.

4.2.3.8 Lessons from the Case Study

The allocation of inflation risks should follow the Risk Allocation Framework as described in the TPG. However, as this is an external risk that can only be managed by responding to it rather than by influencing its occurrence, a significant part of the analysis will cover the (expected) financial effects of inflation for each party in the contract. It will reveal how each party is directly and indirectly affected by the risk and/or the actual occurrence of inflation. It will also reveal to which extent the allocation of inflation risk to a party in the transaction is aligned with the role of that party in the supply chain. In arm's length situations, parties would generally be more inclined to accept the consequences of their own decisions and are less inclined to be confronted with decisions on which they have no influence. A financial analysis can reveal the relationship between cause and effect and thus help to establish the influence of each party's decision-making.

As inflation is an external risk, it lends itself more to contractual allocation within the boundaries of the Risk Allocation Framework. In their existing contracts, parties in a supply chain may have given less attention to the (consequences of) inflation than would have been justified by the actual risk of it due to the long era of low inflation and the common mental trap to underestimate events that have not occurred for a longer period of time. The lack of such arrangements should not too easily be considered as non-arm's length. Now that inflation has occurred, parties should again consider its consequences in their commercial relations.

The author notes that the case study discussed here represents a thought experiment rather than a real-life case. In practice, most taxpayers reconcile the actual numbers of a routine entity with the budget through true-ups rather than by adjusting transfer prices through adjustments of budgets. The aim of the thought experiment is to demonstrate the mechanics and relations between risk and return and how a quantitative analysis generates much more insightful results than a purely qualitative analysis that is the market practice.[26]

5 COMPARABILITY STUDIES

5.1 General

In addition to the analysis of how inflation may affect the commercial relations between independent parties, it must be analysed how it may impact benchmark data that are being used in comparability studies. Benchmark data are inherently historic which makes them vulnerable in periods when economic circumstances change drastically, such as the transition from an era of low inflation to a time of (sudden) high inflation. Therefore, in a comparability analysis, if a transfer price for a period in which there is high inflation is established by reference to historic data from a period in which there was low inflation, the data may turn out to be unreliable. Although the arm's length principle aims to establish transfer prices between related parties that are comparable to prices used between unrelated parties, it is very rarely the case that true benchmarks for transfer prices can be found in publicly available databases in the form of comparable uncontrolled prices (CUPs). The CUP method is mostly used for financial transactions such as loan agreements and guarantees. The effect of inflation on benchmarks in financial transactions is discussed in section 5.2. In practice, most other transactions priced with benchmark data comprise the application of the transactional net margin method (hereafter TNMM) which is not actually a method that prices the transaction as such but rather the net profit margin for a (set of similar)

26. The author believes that this market practice can be justified for its practicality but that it also puts the theory behind arm's length pricing in perspective. It feels ridiculous that, after all of the negativity in the TPG about the risk allocation framework, the profit of a significant part of multinationals' activities are effectively remunerated with a predetermined profit that is insulated from the risks that were analysed in the functional and risk analysis.

transaction(s) executed by one party. The net margin is then 'translated back' to the price for that specific transaction between the related parties. The effect of inflation on net margins when applying the TNMM is discussed in section 5.3.

5.2 The Effect of Inflation on Benchmarks in Financial Transactions

As discussed in section 2, central banks often try to fight high inflation with the increase of interest rates that influence benchmarks used as comparable data for intra-group loans. Such interest rate increases may affect intra group transactions in multiple ways. Existing intra-group loan agreements may refer to interest benchmarks, such as EURIBOR, and intra-group interest will automatically change with the change of these benchmarks in such situations. Alternatively, existing intra-group loans may comprise fixed interest rates that were set in the period before inflation started to rise and the interest period that continues in the time of high inflation. Absent special clauses for inflation, there is no need to reset the fixed interest rate during the interest term. The effect of a fixed interest rate is that the risk of interest rate changes (be it as a result of inflation or other causes) is allocated to the lender and not to the borrower. Rising interest rates will therefore likely deprive the economic value of a fixed-rate intra-group loan in the hands of the lender, but this should, as such, not be a reason to adjust the agreed interest rate. The question arises, however, of how a comparability study is affected by rising rates in cases where new intra-group loans are being agreed upon. The comparability study of intra-group loans starts with the analysis of the loan's credit risk which is determined by the ability of the borrower to meet its debt service obligations. High inflation may indeed have a significant impact on the borrower's ability to meet them. The borrower's earning capacity may have changed, and its cost efficiency may have declined. For example, in situations when intra-group loans are provided on top of external senior debt carrying a floating interest rate, the increase of base rates may have a significant impact on the borrower's debt service capacity simply because the debt service obligations towards the senior lender have increased. Inflation may also have an indirect effect on the borrower's balance sheet. Consider the situation in which a property investment company has borrowed externally and internally to finance its properties. The increase in market interest usually has a negative effect on the property value, triggering covenants of the senior loan agreements. For example, the decline in property value may cause the senior loan-to-value to exceed the maximum, triggering cash sweep events and causing the default risks of the junior intra-group to rise. However, as rents are generally indexed with inflation, the annual cash inflow of a property investment company may also increase. All of these changes have an effect on the borrower's credit risk profile after inflation has started to rise and must be considered when analysing it. It is thereby important to realize that, in most available rating tools, the credit rating is simulated based on historic data input and, thus, it may be necessary to input the required data on a forward-looking rather than a backward-looking basis.

A second consideration when applying commercial databases for the pricing of intra-group loans is how inflation may have affected the default rates of the various credit rating categories. Between 2002 and 2021, the default rates of Standard & Poors' rated investment grade debt ranged between 0% and 0.42%, while those of the speculative grade debt ranged between 0.91% and 9.91%.[27] Thus, rating categories indicate a relative credit risk and not an absolute, meaning that, over time, a certain rating category may have different default rates and, therefore, also different expected loss numbers for which a metric forms the basis of credit margins.

A third question is whether the credit margins benchmark data from commercial databases are also inherently historic and if they are still reliable comparables for the evaluation of loan agreements concluded in times of high inflation if these data are based on pre-inflation transactions. Credit margins vary not only with the 'objective' criteria, such as expected default rates and expected losses but also with the perceived risk and the price that the markets demand for those perceived risks. Times of high inflation are generally perceived as times of high uncertainty in which the market tends to demand higher prices for risk assumption.

All in all, significant adjustments may be required when rating tools and benchmarks are being used to price interest rates for intra-group loans in times of high inflation. This is even more so in cases when the intra-group loan is a junior loan to external debt. These types of loans have lower credit ratings and, as follows from the Standard & Poor's default rate data mentioned above, the default rate data of lower-rated debt vary wildly between the different years, making a default rate analysis prone to statistical noise. Further caution is required because only little data are available for subordinated debt which further increases the influence of statistical noise. In cases of the subordination of intra-group loans towards external debt that is obtained on or around the same time that the external debt was obtained, the author, therefore, advocates that the external debt interest rate be used as an internal CUP. Adequate adjustments can be made based on the relation between leverage and reward according to corporate finance theory.[28]

5.3 The Effect of High Inflation on Benchmarks Used for the TNMM

The TNMM examines the net profit relative to an appropriate base (e.g., costs, sales, and assets) that a taxpayer realizes from a controlled transaction (or transactions that are appropriate to aggregate) according to paragraph 2.64 TPG. The one-sided method only considers the supplier side of a transaction and therefore lacks the inherent tension between two parties in a transaction that results in an arm's length price and that will result in price increases in times of high inflation. Benchmark data that are used in the TNMM are based on profit margins of unrelated companies that have the same functional profile as the supplier in the related transaction and therefore have no direct relationship with the price of the transaction. Indeed, the TNMM establishes the presumed value added by the supplier when performing the (routine) function that is

27. RatingDirect®, (2022), *Default, Transition and Recovery, 2021 Annual Global Corporate Default and Rating, Transition Study*, 13 April 2022, Standard & Poor's.
28. *See*, for a description of such method, Hafkenscheid, *Van de zakelijke, onzakelijke en de onmogelijke lening*, section 4, NL Fiscaal Weekblad, NLF-W 2021/24.

to be remunerated rather than that it refers to the price of a transaction. Situations of high inflation are beneficial in that the benchmark data derived from databases that provide net margins rather than prices may be less affected by inflation than those providing prices. However, as the case study in section 4.2.3 demonstrates, the arrangements between related parties about how the risks of inflation are allocated and whether the supplier has the possibility to pass on price increases to the buyer may have a significant impact on the supplier's profitability. The same may be true for the unrelated suppliers that are used as a benchmark. Databases rarely provide any information about the assumption of risk by the entities used as comparables. The TPG acknowledges these weaknesses (*see* paragraphs 2.71-2.72) but lacks specific guidance on how to overcome them. The author believes that, when the TNMM is applied, the comparable net profit margin found as a benchmark should be considered as an *expected* margin rather than as a *fixed* or target margin to be applied in an uncontrolled transaction. The case study exemplifies that differences may occur between the expectations of parties when they enter a transaction and the materialization of the risks that are included in the expectations. A thorough analysis of the underlying transaction applying economic logic may add more rigour when trying to understand the mechanics and dynamics of the commercial relations between the related parties than trying to find 'better' benchmark data when they are unlikely to be available. For example, as in the case study, if the analysis of the transaction reveals that the supplier cannot pass on the risks of increased raw materials, then a thorough scenario analysis including those of continued high inflation may help to make appropriate adjustments to historic net profit margins such that the supplier, assuming the risks of high inflation, can be expected to achieve the benchmark margin. Assume that ManufacturingCo expects two inflation scenarios for the raw material prices in 2023, e.g., an increase of 6% with a likelihood of 60% and an increase of 12% with a likelihood of 40%. As unlikely data are available that account for the inflation effect on the historic benchmark data, the inflation scenarios could be used to allocate the inflation risk between ManufacturingCo and PrincipalCo. An arm's length manner to do so would be to use the expected inflation rate, i.e., the probability-weighted average, rather than a single scenario rate. Using the 3% historic TNMM margin, the budgeted transfer price for the widget would be set at a price using that expected inflation rate which would be calculated as 60% × 6% + 40% × 10% = 7.6%. This would result in a transfer price of [(1 million × EUR 13.20 × 1.076 + EUR 2.5 million) × 1.03]/1 million = EUR 17.20. If the lower inflation scenario occurs, ManufacturingCo would benefit from a higher-than-expected actual margin while it will suffer from a lower-than-expected actual margin if the higher scenario occurs.[29] As the transfer price already accounts for the inflation risk scenarios, there would be no need to adjust the TNMM margin for its

29. In the lower inflation scenario, ManufacturingCo's actual margin would be [1 million × EUR 17.20 – (1 million × EUR 13.20 × 1.06 + EUR 2.5 million)] = 4.32% of the cost base while, in the higher scenario, it would be [1 million × EUR 17.20 – (1 million x EUR 13.20 × 1.10 + EUR 2.5 million)] = 1.08%.

influence.[30] The question arises of what happens if the parties do not account for the inflation scenarios in their transfer prices. Assume, for example, that the transfer price between ManufacturingCo and PrincipalCo was determined based on the 6% inflation rate scenario. It would then be calculated as [(1 million × EUR 13.20 × (1 + 6%) + EUR 2.5 million) × 1.03]/1 million = EUR 16.99. This would clearly affect ManufacturingCo's expected profitability. In the lower inflation scenario, ManufacturingCo would earn its 3% margin[31] but, if the high inflation scenario occurs, it would earn [1 million × EUR 16.99 minus (1 million × EUR 13.20 × (1 + 10%) + EUR 2.5 million)] = -0.20% meaning that it would bear the risk of high inflation without being remunerated for it. Therefore, if the benchmark data stem from a period of low inflation, an adjustment should be made to that benchmark to make up for the increased inflation risk compared to the historic inflation risk. Logically, the adjustment should be such that the transfer price between them would be EUR 17.20. This would mean that the inflation-adjusted margin should be 4.29% instead of 3%: [(1 million × EUR 13.20 × 1.06 + EUR 2.5 million) × 1.0429]/1 million = EUR 17.20.

6 SUMMARY AND CONCLUSIONS

After more than twenty years of low inflation, the world is suddenly facing high inflation again. It will change the dynamic of doing business which will have a significant impact on how international businesses operate. It will therefore also affect the dynamics of profit allocations between countries. This is likely to be reflected in increased attention to transfer pricing. The OECD TPG do not provide specific guidance for the transfer pricing aspects of inflation let alone for high inflation. Therefore, inflation and its effect on transfer prices must be analysed as part of the usual transfer pricing analysis described in the guidelines. In the context of inflation, two types of analyses must be performed, i.e., how inflation may affect the commercial relations between independent parties and how it may impact benchmark data that are being used in comparability studies.

Contracts may have previously had direct arrangements for inflation (such as index clauses) and indirect arrangements (such as floating interest rates that are affected by inflation). When contractual terms between related parties in a transaction included arrangements about the effects of inflation, whether those arrangements were made at arm's length and whether there may have been reasons to deviate from them would have been considered. When arm's length contractual arrangements were made, the parties apparently wanted to prearrange the allocation of inflation risk as it could not easily be retracted. However, there is now little room for deviation when inflation indeed occurs.

The allocation of inflation risks should follow the Risk Allocation Framework as described in the TPG. As it is an external risk that can only be managed by responding

30. The author is abstracting here from the question of whether the margin may need to be increased because of the greater volatility that ManufacturingCo has accepted. Higher volatility means greater risk, and this is often reflected in a higher risk premium.
31. [1 million × EUR 16.99 minus (1 million × EUR 13.20 × 1.06 + EUR 2.5 million)] = 3%.

to it rather than by influencing its occurrence, a significant part of the analysis will cover the (expected) financial effects of inflation for each party in the contract. It will reveal how each party is directly and indirectly affected by the risk and/or the actual occurrence of inflation. It will also reveal to what extent the allocation of inflation risk to a party in the transaction is aligned with the role of that party in the supply chain. In arm's length situations, parties would generally be more inclined to accept the consequences of their own decisions and less disposed to be confronted with decisions on which they have no influence. Inflation is an external risk and thus lends itself more to contractual allocation within the boundaries of the Risk Allocation Framework.

Benchmark data are inherently historic which makes comparability studies vulnerable in periods in which economic circumstances change drastically, such as the transition from an era of low inflation to a time of (sudden) high inflation. For financial transactions, significant adjustments may be required when rating tools and benchmarks are being used to price interest rates for intra-group loans in times of high inflation as historic data are highly influenced by the level of inflation. Benchmark data that are used in the TNMM are based on profit margins of unrelated companies that have the same functional profile as the supplier in the related transaction and may therefore have a less direct relationship with the price of the transaction. However, the arrangements between related parties about how the risks of inflation are allocated and whether the supplier has the possibility to pass on price increases to the buyer may have a significant impact on the supplier's profitability. A thorough analysis of the underlying transaction applying economic logic may add more rigour when trying to understand the mechanics and dynamics of the commercial relations between the related parties than trying to find 'better' benchmark data when they are unlikely to be available.

CHAPTER 7

Transfer Pricing and Crypto Assets

Vincent Ooi & Ilka Ritter *

* The analysis and opinion expressed in this chapter are those of the writer and do not necessarily reflect the views or position of the United Nations. The writers would like to thank Thomas Hülster for his insightful comments and Chloe Lee for her excellent research assistance.

1 INTRODUCTION

The advent of blockchain and distributed ledger technology (DLT) enables the creation of assets that only exist in digital form and are issued and transferred digitally. Those assets are oftentimes referred to as 'crypto assets'.[1] It is difficult for tax authorities to ignore them due to their increasingly widespread use in (e-)commerce and as investment vehicles. Due to several characteristics, their use may result in tax and transfer pricing issues.[2] In November 2021, the total market capitalization of the global cryptocurrency market alone peaked at over USD 2.9 trillion. While this fell to just USD 798 billion at the end of 2022, it remains a huge market.[3] Despite this, there is no dedicated guidance on the application of transfer pricing principles to transactions involving crypto assets.

It is important to note that crypto assets can be used in a considerable variety of ways while serving different functions in a range of business models. The mere fact that they are used does not inherently mean that it will be difficult to apply transfer pricing rules. Ultimately, it will depend on the precise business model and the specific intercompany transaction. Of course, issues and/or their gravity will differ between companies that deal with crypto assets as their main business (e.g., crypto exchanges) versus companies that have some (limited) investments in them. However, crypto assets generally exhibit three characteristics that complicate their taxation and may, in turn, have an impact on cross-border intercompany transactions.[4]

The first is the fact that the majority of crypto assets have very little market activity, making it difficult to determine their open market value. It is important to note that they are not a homogenous class but are extremely varied in their characteristics, popularity, and functions. For every well-known digital token like Bitcoin, there are hundreds, if not thousands, of virtually completely unknown tokens held by a mere handful of people. This may create considerable difficulties in establishing an arm's length price.

Second, even the most established crypto assets tend to be subject to extreme volatility in terms of their market values. Some of them, such as stablecoins, are expressly designed to counter this volatility but, unless they are backed by underlying

1. Cambridge Centre for Alternative Finance, *Global Cryptoasset Regulatory Landscape Study* (2019). Available from 2019-04-ccaf-global-cryptoasset-regulatory-landscape-study.pdf (cam.ac.uk).
2. Anecdotal evidence regarding the use of crypto assets as investment vehicles can for example be found in Luke Conway, *Public Companies with the Most Bitcoin*, The Street (2021) (available at Public Companies With the Most Bitcoin – The Street Crypto: Bitcoin and cryptocurrency news, advice, analysis and more).
3. Wayne Duggan, *January Crypto Market Outlook*, Forbes (2 January 2023) (available at https://www.forbes.com/advisor/investing/cryptocurrency/crypto-market-outlook-forecast).
4. Please refer to section 2 for a more detailed discussion on what constitutes a 'crypto asset' and the different types of such assets.

real-world assets on a one-to-one matching basis, there are limits to how much stability can be achieved. This volatility has to be factored in when determining an arm's length price as, depending on the type of transaction and its contractual terms, at least one party will have to bear the risk (and potential upside) of the fluctuating value of the crypto assets. The fact that market values change rapidly also complicates the comparability analysis that taxpayers have to undertake to arrive at an arm's length price.

Third, the inherent structure of the distributed ledger blockchain technologies that generally underpins crypto assets lends itself particularly well to pseudonymity.[5] Global regulatory frameworks are currently still in their infancy and are not yet ready to overcome this issue.[6] While transactions on most blockchains are public, it is often difficult to identify the ultimate beneficial owners of specific accounts (or wallets) between which the transactions are taking place. Tax authorities may be unable to match taxpayer identities to them which makes it difficult to determine the parties of a transaction and, ultimately, if the transacting parties are related enterprises as defined by the respective domestic law.

This chapter will begin with a brief introduction to crypto assets, explaining the underlying technology, and providing a basic overview of their classification. It will then examine a range of common tax and transfer pricing issues that may arise over the course of the 'life-cycle' of a crypto asset. One of the key points that will be established is the need to identify a tax differential before transfer pricing considerations become relevant. Stated otherwise, what kind of transactions involving crypto assets will result in a taxable gain or deductible loss that can have an impact on the overall tax liability of a taxpayer? In the absence of this tax differential, there are limited incentives for taxpayers to engage in transactions with non-arm's length transfer pricing.

Following that, the chapter will address each of the three issues listed above in turn: (1) limited market activity; (2) extreme volatility; and (3) pseudonymity and discuss how they pose difficulties in a transfer pricing context and offer potential solutions. While crypto assets are a relatively new asset class, the transfer pricing challenges that they raise are certainly not novel. Existing solutions that have been employed in the past to deal with transactions that exhibit similar characteristics may be productively revisited and adapted for use in these new contexts. Throughout, this chapter will stress the potential of crypto assets to be used for tax avoidance and the need for transfer pricing practices to keep pace with the evolution of technologies and business practices involving them.

5. The difference between anonymity and pseudonymity will be discussed below.
6. There is a range of reporting and exchange of information initiatives currently in force around the world, most of them modelled on the OECD's Common Reporting Standard (CRS). Examples include the European Commission's DACs and the United States' Foreign Account Tax Compliance Act (FATCA) regime. Additionally, running in parallel to these initiatives but in the area of anti-money laundering and terrorism financing rather than tax is the Finance Action Task Force (FATF) Recommendations. Until fairly recently, none of these initiatives specifically dealt with crypto assets.

2 CRYPTO ASSETS AND THE UNDERLYING TECHNOLOGY

2.1 Definition of Crypto Assets

The term crypto assets is generally used to refer to digital financial assets (also known as digital tokens) that are based on DLT,[7] though there is no universally accepted definition. Three leading international exchange of information initiatives define crypto assets as follows. The Financial Action Taskforce (FATF) is an intergovernmental organization founded in 1989 on the initiative of the G7 to develop policies to combat money laundering. It uses the term 'virtual assets' instead and defines them as 'a digital representation of value that can be digitally traded, or transferred, and can be used for payment or investment purposes'.[8] The European Commission's Directive on Administrative Cooperation (DAC8) defines them as 'a digital representation of a value or of a right, which is able to be transferred and stored electronically, using distributed ledger technology or similar technology'.[9] The Crypto-Asset Reporting Framework (CARF) of the OECD defines them as 'a digital representation of value that relies on a cryptographically secured distributed ledger or a similar technology to validate and secure transactions'.[10] All three definitions are broadly framed and not restricted to representations of value using DLT specifically. The CARF and DAC8 definitions refer to 'similar technology' while the FATF Recommendations do not mention any specific technology at all.

2.2 The Underlying Technology Behind Crypto Assets

DLT, typically implemented through blockchains, involves a network of computers that are connected to each other that all partake in establishing the current state of the network. Records of transactions are stored across the network in these computers rather than being centralized in a single main computer.[11] A 'crypto asset' is basically a 'chain of digital signatures' that carry information about previous transactions relating to the asset, the digital identity of the present owner, and a cryptographic lock tied to the present owner. The lock ensures that only the present owner who holds the matching key may have access to the asset and transfer/spend it.[12] When there is a 'transfer' of a crypto asset, the transaction is included in a 'block' of records that is added to the decentralized ledger. Despite being no more than a 'chain of digital

7. Jean Bacon et al., *Blockchain Demystified: A Technical and Legal Introduction to Distributed and Centralised Ledgers*, 25(1) Richmond Journal Law & Technology 1 (2018).
8. Glossary of the FATF Recommendations. *See* FATF, *Updated Guidance for a Risk-Based Approach to Virtual Assets and Virtual Asset Service Providers* 109 (2021).
9. Recital 5 of the proposed DAC8. *See* European Commission, Proposal for a Council Directive Amending Directive 2011/16/EU on Administrative Cooperation in the Field of Taxation (2022), 16-17.
10. Section IV (A)(1) of the CARF rules. *See* OECD, *Crypto-Asset Reporting Framework and Amendments to the Common Reporting Standard* 73 (2022).
11. Vincent Ooi, Kian Peng Soh & Jerrold Soh, *Blockchain Land Transfers: Technology, Promises, Perils*, 45 Computer Law & Security Review 1, 3 (2022) DOI: 10.1016/j.clsr.2022.105672.
12. Ooi et al. (*supra* n. 11), 3.

signatures', courts in numerous jurisdictions have expressed a willingness to recognize crypto assets as property capable of legal protection.[13]

2.3 Classification of Crypto Assets

Crypto assets can take on a wide range of different forms but are generally classified into three main categories - payment, utility, and security tokens. Payment tokens are generally intended to be used as a medium of exchange; utility tokens for the purchase of goods or services; and security tokens to confer rights to physical or financial assets. This classification was based on the model used by the Swiss Financial Market Supervisory Authority (FINMA)[14] for securities regulation and, as one of the first comprehensive classification schemes, has received widespread adoption.[15] Since then, blockchain technology and its use have developed significantly, and it has become increasingly common to see crypto assets that do not fall within these three categories. There are especially non-fungible tokens (NFTs) that have become quite popular lately. They are a form of crypto asset that certifies digital files such as photos or sound files to be unique. As each NFT has a unique identifier, they are distinct from most crypto assets that are mutually interchangeable with each other.[16]

The understanding of security tokens has changed with finer distinctions being drawn between those that are exogenous and endogenous (i.e., those representing value outside themselves and those that do not).[17] Endogenous security tokens typically play similar roles to traditional securities and are commonly just known as 'security tokens'. Exogenous security tokens are generally backed by some kind of asset such as precious metals or other currencies. Thus, they are also known as 'asset-backed tokens'.[18] Some of these are known as 'stablecoins' with the idea being that the assets backing the token will ensure that fluctuations in its value will be limited. Stablecoins have been defined as tokens that aim 'to maintain a stable value relative to a specified asset, or a pool or basket of assets'.[19]

Further distinctions have been drawn between the various categories of stablecoins. 'The most "stable" are those that are backed by real-world assets of the same value on a 1-1 basis while others are only partially backed by real-world assets. There are stablecoins backed by other crypto assets (not necessarily on a 1-1 basis) as well as

---

13. For example: The UK (*Elena Vorotyntseva v. Money-4 limited* [2018] EWHC 2596); Canada (*Copytrack Pte Ltd v. Wall*, 2018 BCSC 1709); New Zealand (*MB Technology v. Ecomi Technology* [2020] NZCA 371); and Singapore (*Quoine Pte Ltd v. B2C2 Ltd* [2020] SGCA(I) 02).
14. FINMA, *FINMA Publishes ICO Guidelines* (Press Release, 16 February 2018), 2.
15. *See* Vincent Ooi, *A Framework for Understanding the Taxation of Digital Tokens*, 50(4) Australian Tax Review 260, 261-262 (2021) for a discussion of the origins of such a classification and whether it continues to be fit for purpose.
16. *See* Wendy Lim, *Taxation of Non-fungible Tokens*, 50(4) Australian Tax Review 270, 270 (2021).
17. Jason Allen, *Cryptoassets and Property Law: Singapore Edition* (Ver 1.0b1), (Asian Business Law Institute and Singapore Academy of Law), 8-10 (2022).
18. *See* Rosa Garcia-Teruel & Hector Simon-Moreno, *The Digital Tokenization of Property Rights: A Comparative Perspective*, 41(105543) Computer Law & Security Review 1, 4 (2021).
19. *See* Douglas Arner, Raphael Auer & Jon Frost, *Stablecoins: Risks, Potential and Regulation*, BIS Working Papers No. 905 (2020), 3.

'algorithmic stablecoins' that instead attempt to maintain their peg through the use of a combination of financial engineering, algorithms, and market incentives.[20]

It is important to note that the FINMA classification of crypto assets is neither mutually exhaustive nor mutually exclusive. As shown above, there could be other categories of crypto assets that do not fall neatly within that classification scheme. Further, they may fall into more than one category. For example, a coin that is intended to be freely used as a medium of exchange may also confer voting rights on the holder for decisions relating to it. This may make that asset both a payment and a security token.

Different types of crypto assets may each raise different kinds of tax and transfer pricing issues. Transactions involving asset-backed tokens backed by real-world assets on a 1-1 basis will typically pose transfer pricing issues comparable to transactions involving fiat currency or commodities. Whereas NFTs are inherently designed to be unique and can be particularly difficult to accurately value.

Payment tokens (also known as cryptocurrencies) could generally have similar, though not analogous, transfer pricing issues compared to highly volatile fiat currencies.[21] Utility tokens can be considered analogous to vouchers for the future redemption of goods or services. Security tokens are likely to most closely resemble the traditional forms of securities after which they are modelled.[22] However, the type of crypto asset in question only provides a first indication regarding its tax treatment and the kind of transfer pricing issues that might arise. The fact that something is this type of asset does not necessarily change its tax treatment in and of itself. Domestic tax law in most countries overwhelmingly looks more at the surrounding circumstances of a transaction or arrangement rather than the nature of the asset, and orthodox tax principles will typically have to be applied.[23]

However, there are some notable cases where the nature of the asset might make a difference. Several jurisdictions around the world are considering implementing or have implemented tax rules that are specific to crypto assets. For example, India taxes gains or income derived from certain crypto assets at the rate of 30%.[24] Australia and Singapore have enacted legislation to exclude digital payment tokens (cryptocurrencies) from their goods and services tax (VAT) regimes when they are used as a medium

20. *See* Ryan Clements, *Built to Fail: The Inherent Fragility of Algorithmic Stablecoins*, 11 Wake Forest Law Review Online 131 (2021) DOI: 10.2139/ssrn.3952045; and US Treasury, *Report on Stablecoins* 4 (2021).
21. However, most jurisdictions do not recognize them as such. As of 1 January 2023, Bitcoin has been recognized as legal tender in El Salvador and the Central African Republic, though these remain the only two countries at the present moment to do so.
22. Christophe Waerzeggers & Irving Aw, *Difficulties in Achieving Neutrality and Other Challenges in Taxing Cryptoassets*, in *Cryptoassets: Legal, Regulatory, and Monetary Perspectives* 220, 220 (Chris Brummer ed., 2019).
23. Ooi (*supra* n. 15), 260.
24. Justin Bharucha & Aashika Jain, *How Cryptocurrencies are Taxed in India* (Forbes) (2022) (available at https://www.forbes.com/advisor/in/investing/cryptocurrency/cryptocurrency-tax-in-india/).

of exchange.[25] Perhaps the example of crypto assets being subject to special rules with the most wide-ranging impact is that of exchange of information where, as noted above, three of the leading initiatives have expressly defined them and instituted specific rules to deal with them.[26]

2.4 Are Crypto Assets Intangibles?

At first glance, it would seem that crypto assets are intangibles as they do not have a physical form. However, the term 'intangibles' in transfer pricing practice does not include financial assets[27] which, in turn, are defined as 'any asset that is cash, an equity instrument, a contractual right or obligation to receive cash or another financial asset or to exchange financial assets or liabilities, or a derivative'.[28] Some countries classify crypto assets as commodities that would not only influence their tax treatment but also other regulatory aspects. Given how broad the range of crypto assets can be, it would be expected that some would be classified as 'financial assets' and therefore not intangibles while others could constitute intangibles for transfer pricing purposes.

Of the various categories of tokens, security tokens would generally be likely to be classified as equity instruments or derivatives. Asset-backed tokens and stablecoins would very likely be characterized as derivatives. Payment tokens are hard to categorize as they serve a similar function as that of cash (or money), however, they are not generally recognized as legal tender (with the exception of two countries).[29] Utility tokens and NFTs could potentially be classified as intangibles.

It is important to note that the classification of crypto into asset types is also a matter of the applicable accounting rules. These differ between countries and standard-setting bodies, for example, between the International Financial Reporting Standards (IFRS) and US Generally Accepted Accounting Principles (US GAAP). While the tax treatment can differ from accounting principles, they often provide a first starting point for analysis.

---

25. Australia: Treasury Laws Amendment (2017 Measures No. 6) Act 2017 (Cth) Sch. 1; Singapore: Inland Revenue Authority of Singapore (IRAS), IRAS e-Tax Guide: GST: Digital Payment Tokens (19 November 2019).
26. The OECD's CARF, European Commission's DAC8 and FATF's Recommendations.
27. *See* United Nations Department of Economic & Social Affairs, *United Nations Practical Manual on Transfer Pricing for Developing Countries* (2021) ('UN Manual'), 6.2.1.3; and OECD, *OECD Transfer Pricing Guidelines for Multinational Enterprises and Tax Administrations* (2022) ('TP Guidelines'), Chapter VI and Annex II to Chapter VI.
28. TP Guidelines (*supra* n. 27), 6.6. The definition in the UN Manual (*supra* n. 27), 6.2.1.3, references the OECD/G20 BEPS Action Plan 8 Report as follows: 'something which is neither a physical nor a financial asset, which is capable of being owned or controlled for commercial purposes, whose use or transfer would be compensated had it occurred between independent enterprises in comparable circumstances'.
29. *See supra* n. 21.

3 THE TAXATION OF CRYPTO ASSETS

3.1 The Need for a Tax Differential

It should be noted that, before transfer pricing will be important to consider, there must be a tax differential and/or another tax reason present. This could be domestic tax incentives or loss carryforward that may be used to lower the overall tax payment of a particular multinational enterprise (MNE) through non-arm's length transactions. They also depend on a country's rules for the realization and deductibility of losses stemming from crypto assets that may also depend on the asset category in which a particular crypto asset is characterized and where it appears in a company's balance sheet. In the absence of a tax differential or other tax reasons, there are limited incentives for taxpayers to engage in conduct that would require transfer pricing scrutiny. A tax differential could be achieved through the minimization of gains or the maximization of losses. Generally speaking, most jurisdictions are more ready to tax gains than they are to allow the deduction of losses. This means that most types of gains will be taxable as income or capital gains while most jurisdictions will have rules restricting or delaying the deduction of losses.

3.2 Common Tax Events Involving Gains from Crypto Assets

While the ways in which transactions involving crypto assets can be structured are extremely broad and varied, there are a number of common taxable events. Throughout its 'life cycle', depending on the nature of the token, the following is likely to take place: (1) creation – through mining and forging or issuing and purchasing; (2) transfer – through exchange for goods and services, other tokens, or fiat currency; and (3) disposal – through redemption or token burning.[30]

Creation

Mining and forging are the processes through which transactions of crypto assets are verified in some distributed ledger protocols. Such a mechanism must exist to ensure that the record of transactions is accurate. Miners and forgers are compensated for their efforts by being issued fresh tokens by the system. Issue and purchase is the straightforward process of a crypto venture creating tokens and selling them to purchasers. The kind of issues that may arise here largely depends on the type of token in question. For payment tokens that are generally classified as income from the carrying on of a business or trade, income tax will generally be payable on the receipts. For utility tokens, their issuance is likely to be seen as akin to vouchers and, thus, any resultant receipts are likely to be taxable as income. For security tokens, since they are similar to debt or equity securities, proceeds from their issuance are likely to be non-taxable for income tax purposes.

30. Ooi (*supra* n. 15), 264.

Transfer

A transfer involves the exchange of crypto assets for goods and services, other tokens, or fiat currency. In many jurisdictions, a transfer would constitute a realization event where any gains or losses would be taken into account for tax purposes.

Disposal

Redemption typically involves utility tokens, and it is distinguished from transfer in that, once redemption occurs, the crypto assets are taken out of circulation. Token burning is a practice that shares many similarities with share buybacks. Token issuers may acquire their tokens and permanently take them out of circulation for similar reasons as to why a company would buy back its own shares. Typically, this is done to allow the token price to increase as there would be fewer remaining tokens in the market.

3.3 Deductibility of Losses from Crypto Asset Transactions

The crypto market suffered quite a few setbacks in 2022 with the current 'crypto winter' arguably starting in May 2022 when TerraUSD (UST), a 'stablecoin', failed to maintain its 1:1 peg with the US dollar. This resulted in a loss of confidence in the stablecoin and a massive sell-off by investors.[31] The effects were not limited to UST, but shockwaves occurred throughout most of the crypto world resulting in large drops in value for several cryptocurrencies[32] and the bankruptcies of several crypto-related businesses such as funds, lending platforms, and exchanges.[33] In November 2022, FTX Trading Ltd, once the third-largest cryptocurrency exchange by volume, started bankruptcy proceedings with several criminal proceedings currently underway.[34] The collapse of FTX is the largest crypto-related bankruptcy by far and is likely to have resulted in millions of investors losing their funds.[35]

With this unprecedented amount of losses spread among taxpayers, there will naturally be attempts to set off these losses against other income for tax purposes. However, generally, most tax authorities will carefully scrutinize tax losses to protect their tax base. It would appear that, given the considerable publicity of the 'crypto winter', tax authorities have given and will continue to give crypto losses particular scrutiny.

31. S. Ehrlich *Unstable Stablecoin: How Crypto's Crash Broke the Buck for TerraUSD*, Forbes (10 May 2022). Retrieved from https://www.forbes.com/sites/stevenehrlich/2022/05/10/unstable-stablecoin-how-cryptos-crash-broke-the-buck-for-terrausd/?sh=3aa95b976ff4.
32. K. Bettes, *Crypto Crash: Why Has Cryptocurrency Dropped? Newsroom of the University of New South Wales* (29 June 2022). Retrieved from https://newsroom.unsw.edu.au/news/business-law/crypto-crash-why-has-cryptocurrency-dropped.
33. Notably, Three Arrows Capital, Celsius Network and Zipmex.
34. Thomas Conlon, Shaen Corbet & Yang Hu, *The Collapse of FTX: The End of Cryptocurrency's Age of Innocence* (2022) (available at https://papers.ssrn.com/sol3/papers.cfm?abstract_id=4283333).
35. Mindy Herzfeld, *Who Will Pay for FTX's Losses?*, 108 Tax Notes International 921 (2022).

Most tax systems will allow for losses to be set off against future income in some way. However, it is not uncommon for there to be specific rules that prevent losses from certain sources from being used to set off income from other sources. For example, losses incurred from non-commercial 'hobby' activities cannot generally be set off against employment income. Some tax systems will prescribe that only trade or business losses can be set off against other sources of income. Yet, other systems will have source matching meaning that losses from one source can only be set off against gains from that exact same source.[36]

3.4 Transfer Pricing Considerations over the Lifecycle of Crypto Assets

Based on the above discussion, the following section will explore related party transactions that would typically occur over the lifecycle of a crypto asset.

Creation

Typical transactions with relevancy for transfer pricing during the creation of a crypto asset would be the provision of mining and forging services, i.e., the verification of transactions using a DLT by one related party for another related party across borders. There are several commercial reasons why using a service provider for this activity could make sense from a business perspective, including but not limited to the availability of equipment/machinery, employees, and the price and availability of electricity. Any crypto asset generated would typically be attributable to the service recipient with the service provider receiving an arm's length remuneration for the services performed though this may be further complicated when several related parties work on various parts of the process simultaneously.

Other typical transactions could be either the sale of crypto assets by a related party to another related party for resale (involving the transfer of ownership from a related party to another) or the provision of sales and marketing functions by one related party for another.

Transfer

During the transfer of crypto assets for goods and services, other tokens or fiat currency from one related enterprise to another, potential arising transfer pricing issues would revolve around difficulties establishing market values of what both parties are exchanging. Loans provided by a related party to another denominated in crypto assets will also fall under the category of 'transfer' and will necessitate establishing an arm's length interest rate accounting for the inherent value fluctuations of crypto assets.

Disposal

In the case of redemption, the exchange of utility tokens for previously promised goods or services generally does not give rise to transfer pricing issues.

36. *See, e.g.*, Lee Burns & Richard Krever, *Taxation of Income from Business and Investment, Tax Law Design and Drafting: Volume 2* 590-591 and 631 (Victor Thuronyi ed., 1998).

Analysis

Based on the discussion of typical related party transactions that could occur over the lifecycle of a crypto asset, the section below outlines transfer pricing considerations.

The first step in undertaking a transfer pricing analysis always involves the accurate delineation of the transaction, i.e., establishing the facts of the transactions based on evidence and the conduct of the parties. This includes an analysis of the contractual terms that govern the transactions followed by an evaluation of the functions, assets, and risks of each participant and how these relate to the business' value generation.[37] For crypto assets, depending on the type of transaction, this analysis can be guided by the parties' conduct on the blockchain.

Based on this analysis, the most appropriate transfer pricing method would be selected taking into account the existence of the data necessary to establish an arm's length (range) of prices. The market for crypto assets is defined by limited market activity and extreme volatility that will make pragmatic approaches that use the best available comparables a necessity for both taxpayers and tax administrations. Adjustments may need to be considered and made when they improve the reliability of the comparables.

It should be noted that most general transfer pricing principles apply to crypto assets. For example, the general expectation would be for a related party that merely carries out routine sales functions to earn a small but stable margin while the principal gain or loss would be attributable to the entrepreneur of the transaction, i.e., the one who bears the risk of the transaction generating a loss. Likewise, for loan transactions denominated in crypto assets, the interest rate would need to reflect the credit risk of the borrower and the volatility of the 'currency'. In transfer pricing, however, it is often challenging to translate these general principles into concrete arm's length conditions. Please refer to sections D and E for a discussion on two specific challenges, i.e., the limited market activity of crypto assets and the extreme volatility of markets.

Losses

The existence of a large amount of losses may give rise to transfer pricing issues as associated enterprises attempt to either make losses 'usable' for tax purposes and/or shift gains from other profitable businesses to use their crypto losses. For example, a related party that owns them may have incurred losses that are entered in their balance sheets during the 'crypto winter'. Hence, assuming these are not tax deductible in that tax jurisdiction or in the absence of profitable business, related parties may consider transferring said crypto assets to a related party in order to realize a taxable transfer loss. Alternatively, a related party may decide to undergo a business restructuring, i.e., structure an inbound transfer of functions and assets and, hence, the potential for profits to may make the losses usable. From a transfer pricing standpoint, the 'crypto winter' creates plenty of incentive for related enterprises to misuse the arm's length principle, especially in relying on the difficulties in valuing crypto assets (as in the case of less popular tokens and NFTs).

37. UN Manual (*supra* n. 27), 3.1.8ff.; and TP Guidelines (*supra* n. 27), 1.33ff.

4 TRANSFER PRICING ISSUE 1: LIMITED MARKET ACTIVITY

4.1 Overview of Crypto Market Activity

A wide range of different kinds of crypto assets (tokens) currently exist that are actively traded and an even larger number of those that have practically no trading activity. Only tokens with sufficient liquidity are traded on the more mainstream crypto exchanges, leaving a large number of 'insignificant crypto-currencies'.[38] However, even tokens that are actively traded may not be particularly liquid. Hence, some of them rely on 'liquidity pool tokens' that function like traditional market makers.[39] Highly liquid crypto assets such as Bitcoin will probably not raise transfer pricing issues with regards to their valuation since there will be a readily ascertainable market value derived from the quoted prices on leading crypto exchanges, and liquid crypto assets are a perfectly substitutable good. In fact, several tax authorities have indicated that they will generally accept valuations of tokens based on an exchange rate that is verifiable (i.e., listed on an established crypto exchange) and consistently applied.[40] However, it has been noted that the prices of tokens can differ widely from one exchange to another, and there are difficulties in establishing from which exchange the rate should be taken.[41] A practical suggestion has been made to take an average of rates which militates the challenge somewhat but does not solve it.[42]

The difficulty with regard to valuation is more prevalent for less popular tokens that may be concentrated in the hands of a few and do not have the same volume and frequency of transactions as the leading coins. There is also the additional issue of the potentially extreme volatility of token values which is something that will be discussed in detail in the following subchapter.

4.2 Transfer Pricing Issues with Less Popular Tokens

For transactions involving less popular tokens, there are likely to be issues in arriving at an arm's length price, especially when applying the comparable uncontrolled price (CUP) method.[43]

For the purposes of the CUP method, a comparable uncontrolled transaction must meet one of two conditions. Either it is the case that none of the differences (if any) between the transactions being compared of the transacting parties could materially affect the price in the open market, or reasonably accurate adjustments can be made to

38. Hermann Elender et al., *The Cross-Section of Crypto-Currencies as Financial Assets* in *Handbook of Blockchain, Digital Finance, and Inclusion, Volume 1* 148 (David Lee & Robert Deng eds, 2018).
39. *See* Ooi (*supra* n. 15), 267.
40. *See* IRS Valuation Guidance for Cryptocurrencies Notice 2014-21, 2014-16 IRB 938; and IRAS, IRAS e-Tax Guide: Income Tax Treatment of Digital Tokens (9 October 2020), 5.4-5.5.
41. Stevie Conlon, Anna Vayser & Robert Schwaba, *Valuation of Cryptocurrencies and ICO Tokens for Tax Purposes*, 12 Estate Planning and Community Property Law Journal 25, 35 (2019).
42. IRAS, IRAS e-Tax Guide: Income Tax Treatment of Digital Tokens (9 October 2020), 5.4-5.5.
43. UN Manual (*supra* n. 27), 3.5.2.4; and TP Guidelines (*supra* n. 27), 3.38.

eliminate the material effects of such differences.[44] It is fairly clear that, in the case of less popular tokens, the first condition will very rarely be satisfied which leads to the need for some adjustments .[45] Tokens vary widely in their characteristics and market value, making it difficult to say that their differences will be unlikely to affect their market price. The paucity of transactions involving the same token or even similar tokens will mean that it will be rare to find data on materially similar transactions. The extreme volatility of crypto assets in general also means that market conditions are likely to change significantly from one transaction to the next, meaning that even historical transaction data relating to the same token in question may be of limited utility in determining the CUP.

The question then arises as to whether it would be possible to make reasonably accurate adjustments such that the CUP method could be used.[46] Alternatively, the use of crypto indices for benchmarking purposes could be contemplated.

4.3 Transfer Pricing Issues with NFTs

Many of the transfer pricing issues that apply to less popular tokens similarly apply to NFTs and vice versa. NFTs also typically do not have the transaction volume and frequency to reliably establish comparable uncontrolled transactions and are also subject to the same volatility in prices as those that complicate comparability adjustments. However, as they might reasonably be considered to be intangibles in some cases, there are additional transfer pricing conditions that are applicable. The UN Manual and the OECD TP Guidelines state that intangibles often have unique characteristics and, as a result, have the potential for generating returns and creating future benefits that differ widely.[47] This would appear to be an apt description of NFTs in general. In fact, it might be worth exploring the argument that this applies to crypto assets in general and that they should be subject to additional considerations for intangibles regardless of whether they could be classified as financial assets.

The differences between intangibles can have significant economic consequences that may be difficult to account for in a reliable manner.[48] One of the risks that needs to be carefully adjusted for in the case of crypto assets is that of token obsolescence and depreciation in value[49] since the crypto field moves quickly and new tokens can rapidly replace older ones. It is also possible to have situations where large comparability adjustments are necessary to the point that the intangibles that are compared are not sufficiently similar to support a valid transfer pricing analysis.[50] In such a case, it may be necessary to use another transfer pricing method that is less dependent on the identification of comparable intangibles or comparable transactions.[51] However, the

44. UN Manual (*supra* n. 27), 4.2.2.1; and TP Guidelines (*supra* n. 27), 2.15.
45. UN Manual (*supra* n. 27), 4.2.2.4; and TP Guidelines (*supra* n. 27), 2.16.
46. UN Manual (*supra* n. 27), 4.2.2.5-4.2.2.6; and TP Guidelines (*supra* n. 27), 3.47.
47. UN Manual (*supra* n. 27), 6.1.5; and TP Guidelines (*supra* n. 27), 6.116.
48. UN Manual (*supra* n. 27), 6.4.1; and TP Guidelines (*supra* n. 27), 6.129.
49. UN Manual (*supra* n. 27), 3.5.3.12; and TP Guidelines (*supra* n. 27), 6.128.
50. UN Manual (*supra* n. 27), 3.6.3.2; and TP Guidelines (*supra* n. 27), 6.129.
51. UN Manual (*supra* n. 27), 3.6.3.2; and TP Guidelines (*supra* n. 27), 6.129 and 6.139.

transfer pricing methods most likely to be suitable for transactions involving transfers of intangibles are the CUP method and the transactional profit split method.[52] One-sided methods like the resale price method and the transactional net margin method are generally not reliable for directly valuing intangibles.[53]

One potential solution to the difficulties in finding comparable uncontrolled transactions and appropriate transfer pricing methods is to use valuation techniques to estimate the arm's length price for intangibles that are transferred.[54] This generally involves using valuation methods that appropriately consider the validity of assumptions underlying the valuation and are in line with the arm's length principle.[55] At this point, it might be useful to consider how valuations are done in the art world. After all, NFTs have several features that make them somewhat similar to artwork, in particular, the uniqueness of each piece and generally low transaction volumes and frequency.

Professional valuers in the art market have had to deal with these issues for centuries and have developed frameworks for valuation. One of the most important factors influencing the value of artwork is the accumulated reputation of an artist with his awards and media recognition having the most impact.[56] Values of artworks are affected by a range of factors such as objective and subjective appraisals, rational and irrational forces, and quantitative and qualitative factors.[57] While past auction prices can help understand and forecast trends in the art market, assessing the value of an artwork requires a degree of human expertise and subjectivity.[58] That said, valuation is a field with sophisticated techniques that are constantly developing with improvements in technology and methodology.[59] Valuing artwork (and NFTs) may be difficult and subjective to some extent, but professional valuation assessing the value of an NFT over time may be able to assist in the transfer pricing assessment. Tax authorities may want to consider allowing for professional expert opinions to form part of transfer pricing documentation.

Crypto assets such as NFTs and less popular tokens may be considered to be hard-to-value intangibles. The starting point in such cases would be to refer to what independent enterprises would have done in comparable circumstances to take account of the valuation uncertainty. In some situations, this might involve the use of

52. UN Manual (*supra* n. 27), 6.5.1.2; and TP Guidelines (*supra* n. 27), 6.145.
53. UN Manual (*supra* n. 27), 6.5.1.2; and TP Guidelines (*supra* n. 27), 6.141.
54. UN Manual (*supra* n. 27), 6.5.4; and TP Guidelines (*supra* n. 27), 6.153.
55. UN Manual (*supra* n. 27), 6.5.4; and TP Guidelines (*supra* n. 27), 6.156.
56. Jens Beckert & Jörg Rössel, *The Price of Art: Uncertainty and Reputation in the Art Field*, 15(2) European Societies 178, 191 (2013) DOI: 10.1080/14616696.2013.767923.
57. Elizabeth von Habsburg et al., *Art Appraisals, Prices, and Valuations*, in *Fine Art and High Finance: Expert Advice on the Economics of Ownership* 31 (Clare McAndrew ed., 2010).
58. von Habsburg et al. (*supra* n. 57), 31.
59. Leandra Lederman, *Valuation as a Challenge for Tax Administration*, 96 Notre Dame Law Review 1495, 1498-1499 (2021), citing George Gau, Tsong-Yue Lai and Ko Wang, *Optimal Comparable Selection and Weighting in Real Property Valuation: An Extension*, 20(1) Real Estate Economics, American Real Estate and Urban Economics Association 107, 107 (1992) (stating 'Vandell (1991) develops a rigorous minimum variance approach for modelling the selection and weighting of comparables. His technique, together with [others] .... represent [sic] significant progress toward transforming the traditional sales comparison approach into a more scientific method').

anticipated benefits from the intangibles as a means of determining their value by working on the basis of projections.[60] In other situations, it might be useful to consider *ex post* outcomes[61] though, given the unpredictability of the values of crypto assets, this has the potential to be rather inaccurate and unfair.

Ultimately, it has to be acknowledged for some categories of crypto assets that applying any form of transfer pricing methodology will be difficult and apt to produce results that may be inaccurate. Tax authorities should therefore focus less on determining what an arm's length price might be and instead devote their attention to the reasonable effort undertaken by the taxpayer at the time of the transaction. In line with the accepted principle that there can be a range of acceptable arm's length prices within which no transfer pricing adjustments should be made, with crypto assets, especially NFTs, the levels of uncertainty may be such that this principle may become even more important. With the focus very much on demonstrating reasonable efforts, it would perhaps be apt to consider lowering the threshold above which contemporaneous transfer pricing documentation must be maintained. This, of course, will have to be balanced against the increased administrative burden on taxpayers.

5 TRANSFER PRICING ISSUE 2: EXTREME VOLATILITY

5.1 Overview of Volatility in Crypto Markets

Despite the best efforts of financial and software engineers as well as the development of stablecoins, crypto markets remain overwhelmingly volatile with extreme swings in the values of tokens on average.[62] Compared to standard financial assets, crypto assets display a much higher dispersion in their returns,[63] and there is a much greater divergence in the gains and losses between the various tokens. As such, they have been described as a high-risk investment.[64] While there is definitely a difference in the volatility of crypto asset values between tokens that are well-established like Bitcoin and less popular tokens, it is worth noting that, even for established tokens, the volatility can still be considerable. The situations where extreme volatility is likely to make a major difference include business models where a party has to purchase or hold onto crypto assets either due to them being the party's stock-in-trade or capital assets or cases where they are used for financing purposes. In the latter case, the issue will be something analogous to currency risk.

60. UN Manual (*supra* n. 27), 6.5.4; and TP Guidelines (*supra* n. 27), 6.182.
61. UN Manual (*supra* n. 27), 6.5.4.19; and TP Guidelines (*supra* n. 27), Annex II to Chapter VI: Hard-to-Value-Intangibles, para. 17.
62. D. Baur & T. Dimpfl, *The Volatility of Bitcoin and Its Role as a Medium of Exchange and a Store of Value*, Empirical Economic (2021). Retrieved from https://doi.org/10.1007/s00181-020-01990-5.
63. Elender et al. (*supra* n. 38), 148.
64. Elender et al. (*supra* n. 38), 164.

5.2 General Business Use of Crypto Assets

Much of the analysis in the previous subchapter is similarly applicable to the discussion of the extreme volatility of crypto asset values. The large amount of risk makes it difficult to find comparable uncontrolled transactions and raises issues on how to conduct a comparability analysis while accurately making comparability adjustments to account for the differences in the risk of price volatility. Risk is something that needs to be carefully considered in determining transfer prices as a functional analysis would be incomplete otherwise. The assumption of risks typically influences the prices and other conditions of transactions.[65]

The key question to consider is whether the party assuming the risk exercises control over the risk and has the financial capacity to assume the risk.[66] If that party does not fulfil either condition, then the risk should be allocated to the party that actually fulfils both conditions or, if there is more than one, then the party exercising the most control.[67] When two or more parties assume a specific risk, control it together, and individually have the financial capacity to assume their share of it, that assumption of risk should be respected.[68] Once the allocation of the assumption of risk has been assessed, the next step is to factor in the consequences, mitigation, and remuneration of risk allocation[69] as all three can have an impact on the arm's length price between the parties to the controlled transaction.

5.3 Borrowing and Lending of Crypto Assets

Special considerations apply when applying a transfer pricing analysis to orthodox borrowing and lending transactions. Generally, there is an abundance of readily available data on interest rates and a wide selection of comparable uncontrolled transactions from which to choose for the comparability analysis. This means that taxpayers typically apply the CUP method in determining arm's length interest rates.[70] It has also been noted that lending markets are typically very competitive and will tend to arrive at a rather narrow range around the 'market rate' for a loan of a similar nature to similar borrowers.[71]

When determining potential comparables for a loan transaction, common relevant factors that should be taken into account often have to do with the risk assumed by the lender and sometimes by the borrower. Factors such as long maturity dates, absence of security, subordination, or application of the loan to a risky project will increase the risk for the lender and tend to increase the interest rate. On the other hand, factors such as strong collateral, a high-quality guarantee, or restrictions on the borrower's future

65. UN Manual (*supra* n. 27), 9.9; and TP Guidelines (*supra* n. 27), 1.56-1.58.
66. UN Manual (*supra* n. 27), 3.4.4.30; and TP Guidelines (*supra* n. 27), 1.60.
67. UN Manual (*supra* n. 27), 3.4.4.41; and TP Guidelines (*supra* n. 27), 1.98.
68. UN Manual (*supra* n. 27), 3.4.4.40; and TP Guidelines (*supra* n. 27), 1.95.
69. UN Manual (*supra* n. 27), 3.4.4.41; and TP Guidelines (*supra* n. 27), 1.100.
70. UN Manual (*supra* n. 27), 9.10.1; and TP Guidelines (*supra* n. 27), 10.90.
71. UN Manual (*supra* n. 27), 9.23.3.5; and TP Guidelines (*supra* n. 27), 10.91.

behaviour will reduce the risk for the lender and tend to result in a lower interest rate.[72] Of course, other factors also matter such as the general availability of funds in the market, interest rates set by central banks, and the currency in which the loan is taken.

When crypto assets are borrowed and lent, some considerations will be the same as those for orthodox loan transactions. However, two main factors may differ. First, it is likely that crypto assets will be loaned to a borrower engaged in some kind of crypto-related business. Given the current turmoil in the crypto world,[73] lenders are likely to consider these 'risky projects' that will increase the interest rate. Second, if the repayment obligation is denominated in crypto assets, there will be a risk similar to a currency risk that will be borne by both the borrower and lender. The former will face the risk of value appreciation while the latter will face the risk of value depreciation of the crypto assets. Given that crypto values can be extremely volatile, it is likely that interest rates will have to be adjusted accordingly to reflect this. Alternatively, the parties may already agree to interest adjustment clauses in their initial loan contracts depending on either the particular crypto asset's performance or, in cases of rare crypto assets, with reference to more frequently traded crypto assets or crypto indices. Particularly in cases when it may be difficult to prove the market values of crypto assets at any given time due to the token not being listed on any crypto exchange, it would be crucial for taxpayers to maintain contemporaneous transfer pricing documentation.

6 TRANSFER PRICING ISSUE 3: PSEUDONYMITY

6.1 Technical Reasons for the Pseudonymity Issue

It may initially appear counterintuitive that crypto assets can give rise to the challenge of identifying taxpayers. The use of DLT, much touted as ensuring maximum transparency, ensures that transaction records of crypto assets are generally replicated in a large number of ledgers on many different nodes. How, then, can there be a challenge with identifying taxpayers if the transaction history of crypto assets is practically in the public domain? The blockchain technology that underlies crypto assets involves 'wallets' that are used to 'hold' crypto assets. While each 'wallet' is unique and identifiable, the identification issue arises when trying to determine who owns the 'wallets' as they do not contain any information that could identify their owners.

This creates a challenge of pseudonymity as opposed to anonymity. In the case of the latter, a party acts in a way that makes it unidentifiable. The same party could perform the same action multiple times, and there would be no way of knowing that it was the same person. In the case of the former, however, a party acts in a way in which they can be identified, but there is a 'mask' or 'shield' that conceals their identity outside the system in which they are acting. Thus, everyone might know that the same person performed the same act thrice, but they have no information about who that person might be.

72. UN Manual (*supra* n. 27), 9.13.1; and TP Guidelines (*supra* n. 27), 10.90.
73. *See* section 3.3, above.

6.2 Pseudonymity as a Challenge for Transfer Pricing

Pseudonymity is a challenge for tax authorities in general. Most obviously, it offers considerable opportunities for tax avoidance and evasion since attributing the 'wallets' to real-world individuals/companies is a difficult task. Without being able to identify those behind the 'wallets', the fact that the record of crypto asset transactions is available in the public domain does not help tax authorities to identify if taxpayers are avoiding or evading tax. This is a familiar challenge in the world of exchange of information where tax (and other) authorities have difficulties identifying the actors. This leads to the development of the concepts of the 'controlling person', 'beneficial owner', and 'ultimate beneficial owner' as well as a range of international initiatives. The main way that the pseudonymity issue raises challenges for transfer pricing is that associated enterprises may be able to conduct transactions not applying an arm's length price and escape scrutiny due to the inability of tax authorities to identify them as the parties holding the 'wallets' with which the transfers of crypto assets are made. It should be noted though that, in most jurisdictions and depending on the value of the underlying transactions/taxes not reported, doing so would not be considered tax avoidance but tax evasion and open to scrutiny under a country's criminal tax law.

6.3 International Responses

As noted above, this is not a new challenge. There are a range of international initiatives[74] in place to facilitate exchange of information that aid tax authorities in getting a clearer picture of the natural persons behind structures and transactions. The OECD's CRS is currently one of the most influential models with other initiatives adopting their standard of reporting and exchanging information.[75] Until relatively recently, most of these initiatives were not prepared to deal with the sudden increase in popularity of crypto assets and did not include these types of assets in their framework.

However, in order for the exchange of information initiatives to work, tax authorities must first have the relevant information to exchange. For tax purposes in general, much information is obtained from the intermediaries that facilitate access to financial markets such as banks, stockbrokers, or investment professionals. All of these professionals are required to collect and report information on their clients to the tax authorities in the jurisdiction in which they operate. It is shared using the international exchange of information framework with other tax authorities. This framework, as extended to crypto assets, would appear to be able to resolve the pseudonymity issue. It would finally be possible to match 'wallets' to their owners because such information would be collected by the crypto exchanges and other intermediaries used by taxpayers.

74. *See supra* n. 6.
75. For example, the European Commission's DACs refer to the CRS.

However, one of the main selling points of crypto assets is that it is technically not necessary to go to any intermediary to access the crypto market. Tokens can be freely transferred between individuals without having to involve any banks, for example. As such, there could be some 'wallets' that were never registered with intermediaries which makes it impossible to identify their owners. At the present moment, at least, the proportion of people who are technologically savvy enough to navigate the holding and transfer of crypto assets themselves without the need for intermediaries is rather low. The vast majority of people holding or using them will still need to use intermediaries and can thus be identified by the international exchange of information systems. Further, crypto assets are fundamentally useless if they cannot be traded for something tangible or real-world financial assets. At some point, they must interface with the traditional banking system to be worth anything. Authorities will be on the lookout for and carefully monitor sudden inexplicable inflows of funds that could suggest that crypto assets have been exchanged for fiat currency.

The inability of the international exchange of information initiatives to effectively deal with crypto assets was recognized fairly early, prompting international organizations to rethink how the exchange of information could be done. Three leading international exchange of information initiatives that define crypto assets were listed above, i.e., the FATF recommendations, the European Commission's DAC8, and the OECD's CRS. Here, the focus will be on the latter two initiatives because information exchange under the FATF typically does not extend to tax matters (unless issues such as tax fraud are concerned).

The OECD's CARF is a separate framework from its existing CRS. The CARF is specifically designed to deal with the collection and automatic exchange of information on crypto-asset transactions.[76] It lays out extensive rules in four main areas including: (1) scope of crypto assets to be covered; (2) entities and individuals subject to data collection and reporting requirements; (3) transactions subject to reporting and the information to be reported in respect of such transactions; and (4) the due diligence procedures to identify crypto asset users and the relevant tax jurisdictions for reporting and exchange purposes.[77] While the CARF was most clearly developed from the CRS, it does depart from the latter in several ways. Under this framework, three transactions are reportable: (1) exchanges between relevant crypto assets and fiat currencies; (2) exchanges between one or more forms of relevant crypto assets; and (3) transfers (including reportable retail payment transactions) of relevant crypto assets.[78]

There are also due diligence procedures that allow reporting crypto asset service providers (RCASPs) to determine the identity and tax residence of their individual and entity crypto asset users as well as the natural persons controlling certain entity crypto asset users.[79] These build on the self-certification-based process of the CRS and existing anti-money laundering (AML) obligations in the 2012 FATF Recommendations, including updates in June 2019 with respect to obligations applicable to virtual asset service

76. CARF (*supra* n. 10), Introduction at [7].
77. CARF (*supra* n. 10), Introduction at [12].
78. CARF (*supra* n. 10), Introduction at [20].
79. CARF (*supra* n. 10), Introduction at [25].

providers.[80] The reporting requirement under the CARF would only be relevant for transactions that involve 'high-value transactions' targeted in terms of retail payments that exceed USD 50,000. As with the CRS, the CARF is intended to be implemented through bilateral or multilateral tax treaties, tax information exchange agreements, or the Convention on Mutual Administrative Assistance in Tax Matters.

The stated purpose of the European Commission's DAC8 is to 'provide tax administrations with information to identify taxpayers who are actively using new means of exchange, notably crypto-assets and e-money, in order to curb tax fraud and evasion'. It is consistent with the recently approved OECD CARF and its CRS.[81] On 8 December 2022, the European Commission proposed a text amending Directive 2011/16/EU on administrative cooperation in the field of taxation. This update expands on the reporting and exchange of information between tax authorities within the EU to cover income or revenue generated by users residing in the EU while operating with crypto assets.[82] Specifically, this update would improve the ability of Member States to counter tax fraud, evasion, and avoidance by requiring all RCASPs to report transactions of clients residing in the EU and would include both domestic and cross-border transactions.[83] Financial institutions are required to report on e-money and central bank digital currencies. The DAC8 is set to be implemented by 2023 across all EU Member States.

7 CONCLUSION

This chapter has shown that crypto assets can be used in a very wide range of transactions as they become increasingly integrated into the world economy. Their characteristics of typically having little market activity, extreme volatility, and pseudonymity has the potential to create considerable difficulties in applying and auditing transfer pricing. This chapter has highlighted a range of taxable events that can arise over the 'life cycle' of a crypto asset and explained how transfer pricing issues might arise in each of those events. Finally, this chapter discussed the recent 'crypto winter' and explained that it creates a considerable incentive for non-arm's length prices to make losses deductible for tax purposes. There are also issues with tax administrations and enforcement of crypto assets that several international initiatives are currently attempting to address. The success of those initiatives given the inherent pseudonymity of crypto assets is still not known.

80. CARF (*supra* n. 10), Introduction at [26].
81. https://ec.europa.eu/commission/presscorner/detail/en/qanda_22_7517 Q1, para. 4.
82. https://ec.europa.eu/commission/presscorner/detail/en/qanda_22_7517 Q1, para. 2.
83. https://ec.europa.eu/commission/presscorner/detail/en/qanda_22_7517 Q3.

Index